DEMOCRATIC FAILURE

NOMOS

LXIII

NOMOS

Harvard University Press
I *Authority* 1958, reissued in 1982 by Greenwood Press

The Liberal Arts Press
II *Community* 1959
III *Responsibility* 1960

Atherton Press
IV *Liberty* 1962
V *The Public Interest* 1962
VI *Justice* 1963, reissued in 1974
VII *Rational Decision* 1964
VIII *Revolution* 1966
IX *Equality* 1967
X *Representation* 1968
XI *Voluntary Associations* 1969
XII *Political and Legal Obligation* 1970
XIII *Privacy* 1971

Aldine-Atherton Press
XIV *Coercion* 1972

Lieber-Atherton Press
XV *The Limits of Law* 1974
XVI *Participation in Politics* 1975

New York University Press
XVII *Human Nature in Politics* 1977
XVIII *Due Process* 1977
XIX *Anarchism* 1978
XX *Constitutionalism* 1979
XXI *Compromise in Ethics, Law, and Politics* 1979
XXII *Property* 1980
XXIII *Human Rights* 1981
XXIV *Ethics, Economics, and the Law* 1982
XXV *Liberal Democracy* 1983

NOMOS LXIII
Yearbook of the American Society for Political and Legal Philosophy

DEMOCRATIC FAILURE

Edited by
Melissa Schwartzberg and Daniel Viehoff

NEW YORK UNIVERSITY PRESS • *New York*

NEW YORK UNIVERSITY PRESS
New York
www.nyupress.org

References to Internet websites (URLs) were accurate at the time of writing.
Neither the author nor New York University Press is responsible for URLs that may
have expired or changed since the manuscript was prepared.

Library of Congress Cataloging-in-Publication Data
Names: Schwartzberg, Melissa, 1975- editor. | Viehoff, Daniel, editor. | American
Society for Political and Legal Philosophy. Annual Meeting (2018 : Boston, Mass.)
Title: Democratic failure / edited by Melissa Schwartzberg and Daniel Viehoff.
Description: New York : New York University Press, [2020] | Series: Nomos ; LXIII |
Includes bibliographical references and index.
Identifiers: LCCN 2020015055 (print) | LCCN 2020015056 (ebook) |
ISBN 9781479804788 (cloth) | ISBN 9781479804795 (ebook) |
ISBN 9781479804801 (ebook)
Subjects: LCSH: Democracy—Philosophy. | Representative government and
representation.
Classification: LCC JC423 .D441744 2020 (print) | LCC JC423 (ebook) |
DDC 321.8—dc23
LC record available at https://lccn.loc.gov/2020015055
LC ebook record available at https://lccn.loc.gov/2020015056

New York University Press books are printed on acid-free paper, and their binding
materials are chosen for strength and durability. We strive to use environmentally
responsible suppliers and materials to the greatest extent possible in publishing
our books.

Manufactured in the United States of America

10 9 8 7 6 5 4 3 2 1

CONTENTS

PART III. FAILURES OF KNOWLEDGE

PREFACE

MELISSA SCHWARTZBERG AND DANIEL VIEHOFF

This volume of NOMOS—the sixty-third in the series—emerged from papers and commentaries given at the annual meeting of the American Society for Political and Legal Philosophy (ASPLP). This meeting marked the first in the Society's modern history not linked to an annual conference of one of the three contributing disciplines—philosophy, political science, and law—and took place at the ASPLP's new institutional home, Boston University School of Law, on September 28, 2018. Our topic, "Democratic Failure," was selected by the Society's membership.

As always, the ASPLP conference consisted of panels featuring a principal paper from one of the contributing disciplines, and then commentaries from the other two disciplines. The first paper, "Representation Failure," was given by Jane Mansbridge, who presented via Skype from Sweden while awaiting the ceremony awarding her the 2018 Johan Skytte Prize in Political Science. Yasmin Dawood (law) and Michael Fuerstein (philosophy) served as commentators. The second panel featured a principal paper from philosophy, Derrick Darby's "Du Bois's Defense of Democracy." Commentaries were provided by Turkuler Isiksel (political science) and Mark Tushnet (law). The third panel, featuring a principal paper from the field of law, addressed "Democracy as Failure," by Aziz Z. Huq, with commentaries by Alexander Kirshner (political science) and Gerald Postema (philosophy). The current volume includes revised papers from all of the conference participants, as well as a paper solicited from Christian Salas, Frances McCall Rosenbluth, and Ian Shapiro. We are grateful to all of these authors for their excellent contributions.

Thanks also to Arina Cocoru and Sam Boren Reast of New York University for their valuable assistance during the editorial and production phases of this volume.

We wish to thank the editors and production team at New York University Press, particularly Ilene Kalish, Alexia Traganas, and Sonia Tsuruoka. On behalf of the ASPLP, we express our gratitude to the Press for its ongoing support both for the series and for the tradition of interdisciplinary scholarship that it represents. The ASPLP is also grateful to Brown University, Duke University, New York University, and Stanford University for subventions in support of this and future NOMOS volumes.

Finally, we thank former editor Jack Knight and the members of the ASPLP council—President Stephen Macedo, Vice Presidents Derrick Darby and Yasmin Dawood, at-large members Michael Blake and Ekow Yankah, Immediate Past President and Secretary-Treasurer James Fleming, as well as former Vice President Michele Moody-Adams, former at-large members David Estlund and Deborah Hellman, and former Secretary-Treasurer Andrew Valls—for their support and advice.

CONTRIBUTORS

Derrick Darby
Henry Rutgers Professor of Philosophy, Rutgers University

Yasmin Dawood
Canada Research Chair in Democracy, Constitutionalism, and Electoral Law and Associate Professor of Law and Political Science, University of Toronto

Michael Fuerstein
Associate Professor of Philosophy, St. Olaf College

Aziz Z. Huq
Frank and Bernice J. Greenberg Professor of Law, University of Chicago

Turkuler Isiksel
James P. Shenton Associate Professor of the Core Curriculum, Columbia University

Alexander S. Kirshner
Associate Professor of Political Science, Duke University

Jane Mansbridge
Charles F. Adams Professor of Political Leadership and Democratic Values, Harvard Kennedy School

Gerald J. Postema
Professor Emeritus of Philosophy, University of North Carolina

Frances McCall Rosenbluth
Damon Wells Professor of Political Science, Yale University

Christian Salas
Economist, Bates White

Melissa Schwartzberg
Silver Professor of Politics, New York University

Ian Shapiro
Sterling Professor of Political Science, Yale University

Mark Tushnet
William Nelson Cromwell Professor of Law, Harvard University

Daniel Viehoff
Assistant Professor of Philosophy, New York University

INTRODUCTION

MELISSA SCHWARTZBERG AND DANIEL VIEHOFF

We regularly hear that democracy is in crisis, at risk of failure, although our Cassandras evince little agreement concerning the harbingers of doom. At moments of turmoil and of relative calm alike, scholars worry whether democracy can ever fulfill the promise of its ideals, or if failure is endemic—while others doubt that democracy may be sufficiently resilient against threats, whether internal or external.

Two articles from the *New York Times*, one from each of the previous two centuries, highlight the perennial quality of these debates. In March 1861, on the cusp of the American Civil War, the *Times* published an article asking, "Is Democracy a Failure?"[1] The piece began as follows:

> Among the many voices raised in Europe over the disaster of secession, amid the groans of sorrow, cries of indignation and tones of sympathy which reach us from many lands beyond the sea, there is one neither loud nor mocking, but which, like the endless monotone in the poet's description of the uproar in hell, is more tormenting than all the other sounds combined. We mean that complacent "We told you so" of the friends of the old order of things—of the men who have always predicted the downfall of the Republic—not from any knowledge of us, but from the arbitrary assumption that Democracy is a false principle, and that, therefore, every Republic must be a failure.

The answer from the *Times* was that it is too soon to tell whether the experiment had failed, because the United States had so far been merely an "aggregate of confederated States," featuring "contemptible provincialisms," governed by the parochial concerns of states and local communities. Only on the brink of bloody war could the United States determine its capacity for the radical change that would make the confederation into a republic.

Decades later, on October 23, 1927, the *Times* published an article describing a debate between historian Will Durant and philosopher Bertrand Russell on the question, "Is Democracy a Failure"— Durant for the affirmative, Russell for the negative.[2] Durant claimed that although democracy ostensibly entailed government by the people, any "tyro" or "sophomore" knows that to be false. If it were instead rule by the "best," by men of "ability and integrity," it might still be justified. Alas, Durant suggested, only those who "follow the machine" can be elected and remain in office, and this machine has acquired its power as economic liberty, equality, and fraternity have disappeared.

Russell, on the other hand, argued that we should evaluate democracy by reference to the distribution of welfare it generated, noting that in comparison it has performed quite well, and that alternatives have not been rule by the "wise." Rather, "government by the best" would necessarily be the "5 percent," who lack the incentive to invest in public education; and only the power that the electoral sanction confers upon the masses prevents those governing from cruelty. Finally, Russell argued:

> There is a third reason which I think in the present state of the European world is very visible and obvious, and that is democracy makes a more stable form of government and more easy to put up bulwarks against civil war and strife than any other form of government. In undemocratic countries you get insurrections, revolutions, all sort of changes of government by violent means, and the only way I know of to prevent a change of government by violent means is to have a rule that the majority shall have the lawmaking power, because then if you do have an appeal to force the victory would go to the constituted authorities.

Present-day democratic theorists again confront such fundamental questions about democracy's merit, especially when compared to rule by experts (or what contemporary political philosophers refer to as "epistocracy") and democracy's resilience in the face of both internal and external challenges. The authors in this volume ask whether the critics of democracy—the "tormenters"—are right that democracy is ineluctably doomed, or whether the ability to hold power to account will save it from collapse. They ask about democracy in comparative perspective—are some failures specific to democracy, or do they occur in any regime? Can democratic representation serve "epistemic" aims—will it empower the wise among us, or facilitate the aggregation of citizens' knowledge for the common welfare, or will representation be subject to capture by populists or agents bent on undermining democratic institutions? Finally, what types of democratic institutions— representation or directly democratic institutions, strong or weak parties, judicial review or parliamentary supremacy—best protect against the risk of democratic autophagy, that democracy will consume itself through democratic means?

The first section of the volume examines whether the history and normative foundations of democracy suggest that failure is inescapable. In "Democracy as Failure," Aziz Huq argues that, since antiquity, democracy has always courted failure. Its birth logic contains violence, its institutionalization derives from rotten compromises, its authority cannot be fully justified, and its outcomes are unstable. Democracy, understood as a regime in which the exercise of political power is shaped by the participation of adult citizens, will never meet its aspirations; some of these deficiencies may lead to collapse, but others may yield beneficial results. As such, the preoccupation of pundits and scholars about democratic failure is likely to be otiose at best, alarmist at worse.

In his response, "Failing Democracy," Gerald Postema explores a distinct set of "modalities" of failure. He argues that not all of the disappointments produced by democratic decision-making are properly construed as failures and suggests that we need to distinguish between "intransitive" and "transitive" failing, i.e., between "failed democracy" and a given agent's "failing democracy." Postema shares with Huq the view that—at least in some cases, if not inevitably—democratic institutions may be "deformed," their responsiveness to the popular will becoming populist, or their dependence on members' common trust and belonging turned into hatred. But democratic failure may also derive from participants' unwillingness to hold other agents accountable for defying democratic norms and values.

As suggested by his title—"Why No Good, Very Bad, Elitist Democracy Is an Achievement, Not a Failure"—Alexander Kirshner poses to Huq the question of comparative evaluation: to wit, whether the failures Huq identifies are distinctive to democracies or whether they also bedevil nondemocracies. For instance, Kirshner suggests that the sort of "boundary problems" that trouble Huq—i.e., how the boundaries of democratic decision-making can be fixed without prior appeal to the democratic question of eligibility, courting the risk of arbitrariness—are not specific to the justification of democracies but to any polity. More generally, it may be that democracies fail to live up to ideals such as equal political agency, but it may also be the case that non-ideal democracies remain superior to their non-democratic alternatives, that their failures remain comparative successes.

The second section of the volume zeroes in on the concept of representation as a source of failure. In "Representation Failure," Jane Mansbridge argues that failures of democratic autonomy—of giving law to oneself—are endemic to contemporary representative systems. Though representation and majority rule presuppose that not everyone who is obliged to obey a norm will have themselves voted in favor of it, Mansbridge suggests that we might hold on to autonomy as a democratic ideal and seek to refine our institutions and practices to realize it more closely. In particular, Mansbridge holds that ongoing recursive and reciprocal communication between constituents and representatives, and between administrators and stakeholders, would improve citizens' autonomy; although instruments of direct democracy might supplement representative institutions, properly designed representative systems might themselves be capable of realizing—if in the form of "shards, threads, and intimations"—the ideal of autonomy.

Yasmin Dawood responds to Mansbridge in "Democratic Theory and Democratic Failure: A Contextual Approach." Like Postema, Dawood defends a dual approach to the democratic failure, and, like Kirshner, argues for the importance of comparative evaluation. But she provides a different model, distinguishing between democratic failure writ small and writ large. The failure of democracy to live up to ideals constitutes deficiencies of democracy writ small; the task of democratic theory is to establish a "ceiling," which constitutes a standard for evaluating the practice of democracy. On the other hand, the role of democratic theory with respect to democratic failure writ large—the collapse of democracy into authoritarian or hybrid regimes—is to identify a floor, a baseline below which a regime cannot or should not venture if it is to remain democratic. Through contextual analysis, the theorist can diagnose the conditions and consequences of shifting practices to identify the potential for failures (and successes) writ both small and large.

In his chapter, "Democratic Representatives as Epistemic Intermediaries," Michael Fuerstein argues that representation may help us to remedy two key epistemic problems—that citizens will be ignored and that they will be ignorant—issues to which the authors in the third part of the volume will return. Fuerstein argues that representatives are best characterized as "epistemic intermediaries," who help to integrate knowledge both between policy experts and non-experts, on the one hand, and among diverse non-experts, on the other. Clarifying these two epistemic problems helps to shed light on the classic distinction between representations as "trustees," who form independent judgments about their constituents' interests, and as "delegates," who promote the interests of their constituents as conceptualized and articulated by the constituents themselves. The choice between trustees and delegates may depend upon the epistemic circumstances in which representatives and constituents find themselves and might vary depending on the domain and context. The value of representation rests in part in its ability to incorporate a variety of relevant perspectives into decision-making: The institutions that Mansbridge identifies as especially promising (e-townhalls and deliberative polling) for fostering autonomy may indeed facilitate mutual engagement in a way that not only would not exist in a non-democracy but would also not be achievable under direct democracy.

Christian Salas, Frances McCall Rosenbluth, and Ian Shapiro demonstrate the value of the contextual and comparative analysis recommended by Dawood in their chapter, "Political Parties and Public Policy," in which they argue that the solution to failures of representation, and of democracy more generally, cannot lie with weakening parties. Rather, democratic success depends upon political competition among strong parties for the political middle; when two parties compete for votes, they must offer alternative policies that benefit most voters. The fragmentation of parties, particularly on the left, reduces spending on public goods in favor of redistributive transfers favoring insider groups. Moreover, efforts to democratize parties by weakening party discipline, and through open lists and primaries, also have harmful consequences: Hierarchical parties produce democratic accountability through rendering leaders' power conditional upon backbenchers' support for strategic moderation. Tempting though it may be to remedy democratic failure with institutions that appear more responsive to individual voters' preferences, strong parties must play the central role in identifying and defending the broad interests of the community as a whole.

The third section of the volume, "Failures of Knowledge," considers the challenge to democracy posed by "epistemic" problems. Derrick Darby's chapter, "Du Bois's Defense of Democracy," turns to W. E. B. Du Bois's *Darkwater: Voices from Within the Veil* to address the problem of widespread ignorance. Drawing on Du Bois, Darby argues that we must resist the temptation of epistocracy—limiting the franchise to those deemed "competent"—to remedy democratic failures. Darby holds that a key pretext for excluding those of marginalized classes, races, or gender from political rule has been their ostensible ignorance. But those who seek to exclude the "ignorant" wrongly believe that they possess superior knowledge across domains, including of the interests and the injuries of the allegedly ignorant. All persons are "sage souls"; each possesses knowledge that others do not. Saving democracy from failure requires inclusivity: Universal suffrage enables those deemed ignorant to contribute to the project of securing justice for all citizens.

Turkuler Isiksel takes up Darby's discussion of the pretextual argument in her response, "Pretextual Politics and Democratic Inclusion," suggesting that Du Bois's willingness to take seriously the voter ignorance objection to enfranchisement ensnares him in a "charade." By treating those who would restrict suffrage to the competent as if their arguments are sincere, Du Bois enables them to pretend that their efforts to do so are not merely pretexts for excluding people of color from power, a trap into which contemporary theorists and politicians alike tend to fall. Moreover, Isiksel argues that what makes disenfranchisement objectionable is not primarily its epistemic costs, or the instrumental benefits that the ballot might have in improving people's conditions or in reducing the likelihood of grave injustice. Rather, disenfranchisement is simply a grave injustice, a moral wrong. To focus on Du Bois as primarily a democratic theorist fails to capture the global orientation of his political thought in countering white supremacy.

In the final chapter, "Democratic Remedies If Ignorance Threatens Democracy," Mark Tushnet invokes Du Bois's concept of "sage souls" in support of the view that elites who are knowledgeable about some politically relevant matters remain ignorant of others. Drawing a connection between Du Bois and Dewey, Tushnet proposes that such elite ignorance explains why democracy withstands epistocratic challenges. Tushnet emphasizes the value of "shopfloor knowledge," knowledge held by ordinary people as opposed to elites, in contributing to the iterative process of democratic experimentalism. Finally, Tushnet suggests that removing barriers to knowledge acquisition, such as poverty, must be a crucial remedy: Although voters might rationally choose to delegate a policy choice to someone with more information, the key barriers to acquiring knowledge—to participating in democratic learning—must drop.

NOTES

1. "Is Democracy a Failure?" *New York Times*, March 14, 1861, p. 4.

2. "Two Philosophers Debate Democracy; A Failure, Durant Contends, Because Politicians, Not the People, Rule. Russell Defends System; It Promotes Happiness, Progress and Intelligence, British Scientist Declares," *New York Times*, October 23, 1927, p. 12.

PART I

MUST DEMOCRACY FAIL?

1

DEMOCRACY AS FAILURE

AZIZ Z. HUQ

I can't go on. I'll go on.

—Samuel Beckett, *The Unnamable* (1953)

The theory and the practice of democracy alike are entangled with the prospect of failure. This is so in the sense that a failure of one kind or another is almost always present at democracy's inception. Further, different kinds of shortfalls dog its implementation. No escape is found in theory, which precipitates internal contradictions that can only be resolved by compromising important democratic values. Worse, out of localized failure comes wholesale breakdown. A stable democratic equilibrium proves elusive because of the tendency of discrete lapses to catalyze wider, systemic disruption. At the same time, the very pervasiveness of local failure obscures the tipping point at which systemic change occurs. Social coordination in defense of democracy is therefore very difficult and its failure correspondingly more likely.

This thicket of intimate entanglements has implications for both the proper description and normative analysis of democracy. At a minimum, the nexus of democracy and failure elucidates the difficulty of dichotomizing democracies into the healthy and the ailing. It illuminates the sound design of democratic institutions by gesturing toward resources usefully deployed to mitigate the costs of inevitable failure. Finally, it casts light on the public psychology best adapted to persisting democracy. These epistemic, psychological, and institutional projects have not been identified, or extensively discussed, in recent political philosophy. The latter tends to focus on social choice questions, deliberative democracy, or contorted accommodations with Rawlsian political liberalism.[1] But to grasp the proximity of democracy's entanglements with failure is to temper the aspiration for popular self-government as a steady-state equilibrium. It is to open new questions about the appropriate political psychology for a sound democracy. It means limning new questions about democracy's optimal institutional specification. It is, for these reasons, a worthwhile enterprise for political philosophy.

In developing these claims, I use the terms "democracy" and "failure" in the following senses. By *failure*, I mean simply a falling short of an aspiration or goal that is inherent in a specific enterprise. Consider, by way of example, what it means to fail as a parent. I fail if I expose my child to avoidable yet disabling injury. I also fail her, though, if I needlessly lose my temper at her trivial mischief. This second sort of failure is not in isolation fatal, but it can have grave effects over time. This is a capacious understanding of failure: It takes as a counterfactual an idealized well-functioning and inclusive democracy, one that enfolds the best of the manifold flawed polities we can observe in the world. I adopt this definition in part because of the possibility that small dysfunctions can, over time, aggregate to systemic threats. Hence, in the parenting context, a broken leg may heal, but the cumulative effect of my repeated failures to maintain my composure may, in the fullness of time, inflict great harm on my daughter's psyche and well-being. In other words, big things can have small beginnings.

I define a *democracy* for present purposes as a set of institutions through which all the adult citizenry of a nation routinely and effectively shapes how political power is exercised.[2] Although relatively thin, this definition still incorporates a certain clutch of normative commitments. It entails a certain kind of inclusion of all the polity; a linkage between that whole people and political power (i.e., not control by a minority); and a commitment to maintaining the system of popular control. My definition is, however, mechanistically catholic. It allows for elections, direct democracy, and sortition. Deliberation is not required.[3] No one mechanism has a monopoly on the democracy label.[4] More important than any procedural entailment is the system-level possibility of public views materially influencing how state power is deployed. A litmus test for democracy is hence the presence of substantial uncertainty, before new leaders or new policies are selected, about who those leaders are or what those policies will be.[5] Alternatively, one might ask whether the modal adult citizen has the possibility of participating in the choice of who exercises political power.[6]

These institutional preconditions pertain directly to a democracy's claim to legitimacy qua democracy. In the absence of uncertainty over elective choice, and in the absence of some relationship between electors and those elected, there is no plausible argument that a government has a moral argument for compliance on the ground that it is a democracy. Although the actual sociological predicates of state legitimacy and legal compliance likely vary across polities, I think it is fair to say that in observable democratic systems, participants generally believe, to some degree, that citizens have an obligation of compliance with law, even some law with which they disagree, simply because they are participants in a democracy. Moreover, the rule of law necessary for democratic endurance requires officials and judges to have a specific disposition of respect and acceptance toward the law. Continued electoral competition requires incumbents to hold a certain attitude of restraint toward their opponents. Being a member of the loyal opposition remains its own ethics of patience and restraint. Mere "legalism"—the position that ethical obligations are exhausted by rule-following alone[7]—is singularly unpropitious as a psychology of democracy. Unlike chess or Go, therefore, democracy is a game that rests on normative choices and that requires normative commitments from its participants. The plausibility of these normative demands turns on how well basic democratic institutions work. Hence, the manner in which democracy's necessary mechanisms are vulnerable to failure has implications for the strength of a state's moral claim to legitimacy, and perhaps the strength of its sociological legitimacy.

The argument of this chapter has two strands. One aims to tightly hitch the idea of democracy—which typically has a positive valence—with the prospect of failure—usually glossed as negative. Despite incompatible evaluative tilts, I will suggest that democracy cannot be understood except in light of its likely and certain failures, both theoretical and practical. A second strand of the argument then links failure writ small to failure writ large.

The thought that democracy itself is a kind of failure is not new. A long tradition of political thought, starting in Book VIII of Plato's *Republic*, condemns democracy as flawed in its inception and practice.[8] The republican thought of the Florentine republics, as John Pocock famously showed, also recognized an especially rich array of "theoretical reasons" for self-government's failure.[9] One can thus imagine an "anatomy of anti-democracy," akin to the genealogies of anti-liberalism carved by Isaiah Berlin and Stephen Holmes, one that carries Plato's theme forward to Hobbes and Schmitt, and thence to anarchists, contemporary libertarians, and critical theorists.[10] That's not my aim here, although the republican intuition that self-government coexists with its incipient failure ties in with my analysis. Equally, I am not concerned with limning an alternative to democracy. I accept as true Churchill's familiar dictum that democracy is the least bad option available.[11]

Further, I concede that "democracy" as an ideal type does not exist. There are only actual, existing democracies that are congeries of imperfectly formed, variably managed institutions and political formations. None are as good as they could be, but only some are fairly denominated as failing. Indeed, it is useful to think about democracy in terms of those actual, existing institutions as a means to develop from the ground up an understanding of how democracy is constrained by its own normative and pragmatic commitments. It is a way of surfacing what a Marxian would call democracy's "internal contradictions," the seeds of its inevitable crises. This inductive approach is different from the posture adopted by other prominent theorists who offer instead "a model for institutions to mirror."[12] My approach thus stands in a revived tradition of non-ideal theory, or political realism, although I hope to avoid having the gravitational pull of brute facts push me into any "uncritical defense" of the status quo.[13] Although not all of the tensions I highlight can be avoided, almost all can be managed to some extent though institutional design, legal checks, or shared normative commitments among political elites.

FOUR SPECIES OF DEMOCRATIC FAILURE

There are four margins along which democracy, in very different senses, fails. Mapping these four salients, each of which stretches out into a no-man's land of ambiguously justified government arrangements, is a way to grasp the complex intimacy of democracy and failure.

Democracy's Violent Midwife

Democracy began among Greek city-states, in the sixth century BCE, and was in rude health until at least the fourth century BCE. More than two thousand years later, in the late eighteenth century, it was taken up on both sides of the Atlantic after monarchy had, in different ways, been repudiated.[14] Only in the late twentieth century did it become globally hegemonic—not coincidentally as one of the two early Atlantic adopters assumed a mantle of global stewardship. Both the first and the second historical eras of democracy, therefore, punctuated a very different status quo with its own entitlements and beneficiaries. The fact of violence (and what would under other circumstances be denominated a crime), and the attendant unsettling of an institutional status quo, generate a first set of constraints and contradictions. These limit democracy and to some degree orient it toward failure.

The origin of Athenian democracy is conventionally located in Cleisthenes's reforms of 508–07 BCE. Herodotus portrayed these as a ploy to consolidate power against aristocratic rivals in the wake of a Spartan occupation.[15] But democratic reforms were only feasible "in the aftermath of two oligarchic coups d'états and a devastating military defeat,"[16] that is, as one equilibrium in a longer series of nonlinear avulsions in governmental form. Without crisis and defeat, it is not clear Athenian democracy would have emerged. Moreover, Athenians themselves "chose" to look back on a distinct "founding, authorizing moment": the public murder of Hipparchus by Harmodius and Aristogeiten some six years earlier.[17] So even if Paul Cartledge is correct that the murderers did not act on any political passion, and even if the Peisistratid tyranny with which Hipparchus was associated did not come to an end until Sparta invaded, it is still quite telling that the self-perception of the world's first democracy hinged on the commission of a crime. It was a widely shared recognition that an act of violence was needed to separate democracy from a prior epoch.[18]

Two millennia later, both the American and French revolutions also pivoted on violent acts. In one, the thrum of Jefferson's distinctive cadences could not hide the bloody and martial quality of America's entrance on the world stage.[19] In the other, a no-less-eloquent guillotine blade bisected the monarch's sublunary body, setting in motion both international and domestic paroxysms.[20] Even if revolutionary events were initially set into motion on the belief that a revised ancien régime could be restored, purged of the despotic tendencies or fiscal depredations,[21] the fact of violence demarcated two regimes. It thereby raised stakes for reluctant revolutionaries, closing off doors to retreat or reconciliation. Even seemingly incrementalist pathways to democracy, such as Britain's, were entwined with violence. The enactment of the Great Reform Act of 1832 in the United Kingdom, a landmark of democratic reform, was prompted by the so-called Swing riots of 1830–31.[22] Democratic reform would be taken up again in 1867 in large part because of the continued, sometimes violent, militancy of the Chartist movement, which in turn had emerged from the perceived betrayal of the working classes in the 1832 legislation.[23]

The connection between violence and democratic origin is not universal. Not every democracy's birth is marked by violence; in other cases, the violence that does occur is not a repudiation of the former dispensation. Decolonization in South Asia and Africa, for example, was often characterized by violence directed at other members of a nascent polity rather than at a former regime. India's partition is an example of a democratic origin where violence occurred but was not aimed at repudiating the former colonial regime, and, indeed, ended up inscribing religious and regional distinctions that were in some measure a function of the imperial imagination.

When democracy is demarcated with extralegal violence—as is often, if not inevitably, the case—it generates distinctive theoretical and practical difficulties. Democracy as a going concern depends on a stable set of institutions constituted by and operating under law. Shorn of a commitment to the rule of law, democratic institutions cannot operate in an orderly and effective fashion. When democracy has violent origins, by contrast, it will have encoded in its historical DNA the legitimacy of extralegal appeals against established institutions. The possibility of ultra vires force in service of a better state hence becomes salient and unavoidably available as a destabilizing rhetorical move and practical possibility. Violence invites more, potentially unraveling, violence. At the very least, it creates the rhetorical platform to justify and legitimate a repudiation of the state's putative monopoly on force.

In the French case, the initial criminal act could not be contained, but spilled over into iterative violent purges of the body politic. And in the newly independent United States, too, violence persisted to a degree that embarrasses the dominant, hagiographic historiography of the Founding. The roughly one in five former colonists who supported the Crown were harassed by their neighbors—sometimes tarred and feathered—dispossessed of their lands, and in some cases formally banished; some 60,000 ultimately left the new nation.[24] Aligned, although not identical to, violence is the possibility of extralegal constitutional change. The first American constitution (the Articles of Confederation) was then unlawfully abandoned for a second (now canonical) version. "Illegality," as Bruce Ackerman has written, "was a leitmotif at the Convention from first to last."[25] That did not breed violence (although it entrenched and enabled the violence of slavery). But the subsequent success of American democracy, such as it is, rests on an impressive historical erasure of its own origins. That erasure in turn might be one cause of the nearly pathological reverence for the Constitution's drafters today.

The violent origins of democracy, more generally, signal to supporters of the old regime that their presence in the new polity is at the sufferance of newly enfranchised majorities. The split marked by extralegal violence can lead to profoundly anti-democratic civil violence and demographic purges. Democracy established by violence thus in practice often proximately depends not just on persuasion, but also on violent purgatives, for its endurance. The same problem, it should be noted, arises even in the absence of a founding crime. After the collapse of the Soviet Union, several of its former satellite states across Eastern Europe enacted lustration measures targeting tens of thousands of former state officials and employees.

Yet at the same time, democracy as a going concern depends on the apolitical rule of law in which losers are not hounded from home, ordinary lives, or country. A democracy must be able to manage public disagreements about policy and governmental performance through a predictable and stable set of institutional arrangements. Democracy won't persist unless honest politicians—note the adjectival caveat!—know that they won't be locked up for imagined offenses; unless they know that in opposition they will be able to campaign and criticize; and unless they know that the subsequent round of elections will not be engineered to ensure a repeat performance of their defeat.[26] That is, they depend on the state's legitimate monopoly on force. A democracy that begins in crime has already betrayed its fragile commitment to the rule of law. It has thus created conditions in which it is more than reasonable for those out of power to legitimately wonder whether the legal commitments upon which a democracy rests will be kept in subsequent periods.

Democracy as Ugly Compromise

Whether constructed on a crime or not, a new democratic order will of practical necessity be designed to limit the power of duly formulated majorities to achieve what would otherwise be legitimate policy ends. Constraints on the exercise of democratic choice, which are often baked into a new constitutional text and enforced by an unelected judiciary, do not bite on all possible democratic coalitions uniformly. Rather, it is more likely that a democratic constitution—understood either in terms of a formal text or a set of unwritten but consolidated arrangements such as Britain's or Israel's—will constrain asymmetrically some of those who wanted for political authority under a prior regime. Where those compromises undermine the essential institutional elements of a democracy, the latter's plausible claim to legitimacy starts to corrode.

As I have already noted, democracies are normally fashioned in conditions that do not favor the sort of ideal constitutional design envisaged by deliberative democracy's advocates. Commonly accompanied by violence, the end of an ancien régime will likely be characterized by political turmoil as new factions jockey for pivotal powers within the new institutional dispensation. Even if violence against former rulers does not erupt, violence as a by-product of contestation over civil power often proves endemic. Civil strife undermines the possibility that new institutions of state either will be designed through democratic processes or will instantiate democratic ideals in operation. Not only are the ordinary processes of democracy consultation and debate hindered. Civil strife also intensifies internal schisms that ordinarily could be navigated through legislatures, constituent assemblies, and like collective bodies.[27] Where bargains are struck, they are as likely to reflect exhaustion as political principle. An ethics of institutional creation under such conditions is best framed as *Hippocratic* in quality—striving, as physicians do, to avoid the creation of any new harms rather than the creation of the best imaginable form of government.[28]

Even if a democracy is not crafted under conditions of crisis, it is likely to be circumscribed by endogenous constraints. Incremental processes of democratization through legislation are often best understood as concessions by powerful groups (such as a monarchy or a landholding class) to cede just enough authority in the form of a permanent democratic institution so as to dissipate the threat of more serious violent uprisings.[29] A leading political economy of this dynamic underscores the redistributive character of new democratic arrangements. But their formal model does not imply that incremental democratization will lead to a level playing field. To the contrary, a subsequent extension of this model suggests that once democratic arrangements are in place, political elites will renege and use their material resources as a way to capture a disproportionate share of de jure political power—thus curtailing the inevitable redistributive implications of a broader franchise.[30] Recent empirical work, moreover, suggests that powerful elites tend to succeed in entrenching their preferences in new constitutional norms beyond revanchist democratic tides.[31]

Under the modal conditions of its creation, therefore, democratic arrangements will be negotiated with some factions or social groups exercising disproportionate influence as a result of their ability to threaten new civil strife. Historically, propertied factions tended to have this upper hand. This fact has escaped no one. During the Putney debates of 1647, Cromwell's son-in-law Henry Ireton cautioned the Levellers that universal male suffrage would "come to destroy property thus. You may have such men chosen or at least the major part of them, as have no local or permanent interest. Why might these men not vote against all property?" To

Ireton, this seemed an obvious and dangerous fallacy since, by definition, the aim of "government is to preserve property."[32] Many since Ireton have concurred. James Madison, for example, defined the iniquity of faction in distributional terms. He warned in Federalist 10 that democracies "have ever been found incompatible with personal security or the rights of property."[33] The US Constitution was designed to avoid this incompatibility, and not necessarily to promote a democracy in which, as Sir Thomas Rainsborough said at Putney, elective institutions acknowledge that "the poorest he hath a life to live . . . as the greatest he."[34]

The history of democratic institutional design, accordingly, has been a history of partial blockages and circumventing countermeasures intended to stymie *sub silentio* the inevitable redistributive effects of an enlarged franchise. This is just as true when a democratic order emerges through a series of incremental reforms as when it arises through a single, convulsive change: The constraints I identify attend efforts at constitutional amendment as much as those aimed at constitutional creation.[35] A range of measures can achieve this end without evincing any obvious infidelity to democratic principles. These range from limitations on eligibility for elected office, voter qualifications, or—Madison's solution—the use of a large geographic unit to dilute the power of redistribution-minded majority.[36] Indeed, it is striking that the prospect of asymmetrically constrained democratic power has become so embedded and accepted that two of its principal instruments—representation and judicial review—have come to be considered natural, even inevitable, elements of a well-run democracy.[37] As Bernard Manin reminds us, in the late eighteenth century a "government organized along representative lines was seen as differing radically from democracy, whereas today it passes for a form thereof."[38] In its original, parliamentary form—prior to the emergence of mass-based parties—representation would ensure that only those "who inspired the trust of their constituents as a result of their local connections, their social prominence, or by the deference they provoked" obtained elective office.[39] By selecting for social rank, representation would defuse redistributive sentiment. The depth of democracy's defeat by the political practicalities of its origin is nowhere better exemplified than in the bare fact that so many assume that representation is integral—rather than anathema—to democracy.

The second device commonly used to constrain democracy, and yet often painted as "representation reinforcement," is a high court tasked with the resolution of constitutional questions.[40] As described by Ran Hirschl, the role of a judiciary in a new democracy is instead one of "hegemonic preservation." This means giving judges the constitutionally defined role of protecting rights to property, as well as other market-preserving entitlements, as a way to forestall democratic majorities' ability to redistribute resources.[41] This "insurance" against too much democracy provides a hard constraint to democratic rule while it simultaneously generates a patina of legality for a new state.[42] The posture of the early US Supreme Court with respect to slavery, and the Indian Supreme Court with respect to land redistribution, provide striking examples of this thesis.

Particularly in the United States, but also elsewhere, there is a persistent notion that courts not only should but indeed will be a mechanism for protecting democracy in practice. This is a serious error. The independence of the judicial power is not correlated to the judicial commitment to democratic consolidation or expansion. In the United States, the Supreme Court under Chief Justice Earl Warren is commonly celebrated for decisions on race, electoral reform, and criminal justice. The Warren Court is taken as proof of the connection between judicial independence and an expansive, substantive commitment to democratic rule. But the Warren Court's role in the American polity is aberrational rather than representative.

For much of American history, the most important effect of judicial review on democratic norms was the maintenance of racial exclusions via decisions upholding fugitive slave laws, the right to move slaves across jurisdictional lines, and the legal subordination of "free" blacks in the form of separate but equal. After the Civil War, it enabled the dismantling of Reconstruction and embraced only vaguely disguised racial circumscription of the franchise.[43] Until the mid-twentieth century, civil society formations such as unions and minority religious groups obtained little or no shelter from the courts. The Court today has declined to limit partisan gerrymandering or rein in dark campaign money at the same time that it has embraced racially disproportionate restraints on the franchise, such as voter identification requirements and election roll purges. As the twenty-first century unfolds, it seems likely that once again the Court's approaches to campaign finance, redistricting, commercial speech, the right to unionize, and the discrimination against disfavored racial minorities will in the aggregate narrow, rather than expand, democratic space. Outside the United States, courts have generally fared ill as defenders of electoral choice in the recent wave of democratic backsliding.[44] In short, judicial independence has in practice worked better as a hedge against property dispossession than democratic dispossession.

There is nothing structural about the manner in which the US Supreme Court is selected, or the array of canonical textual and precedential sources at its ready disposal, that conduces to a pro-democracy role. Judges are appointed by dominant political coalitions. These have an incentive to use appointments as a device to entrench themselves against electoral competition. The context in which the vast majority of the constitutional text was first adopted was not properly democratic. And, as noted, the commitment of key drafters to democratic practice was in fact quite precarious. It should thus be no surprise that the Court has in the long run done more to damage than to aid democracy.

A different argument to the effect that the structural conditions of democratic origins impede democracy would start not from the power of domestic interest groups, but would instead look at the supranational and international institutions such as the (now defunct) Bretton Woods system, the World Trade Organization, the European Union, and the web of bilateral and multilateral treaties as a network designed to encase and constrain domestic (usually democratic) governments' freedom of policy choice. According to an illuminating recent history of neoliberal thought, these comprised "an extra-economic enforcer for the world economy in the twentieth century" that has emerged as wealth's conventional safeguards of representation and franchise restrictions have withered in efficacy.[45] More generally, international competition fosters conditions that thwart certain democratic impulses. Hence, analysts working in a Marxian tradition observe that the mobility of industrial and financial capital creates a "reservation profit" that works as a floor below which capital flight occurs.[46]

Material indicia of the success of democracy-limiting strategies abound. Among the most important are the persistence of slavery or its functional analogs as a feature of societies commonly denominated as democratic, and enduring the various ideological justifications for the systematic marginalization and subordination of women. Consider the first of these as an example (although a parallel narrative could be offered about gender-based exclusions). One estimate suggests that between twenty and thirty percent of the Athenian population in the late fourth century BCE were enslaved.[47] Of the eighty-four clauses of the 1787 US Constitution, six directly concern slavery, and another four had substantial implications for the peculiar institution that were recognized and debated at the Philadelphia Convention.[48] Provisions tying the presence of slavery to the size of a state's congressional delegation, and thence to its influence in the Electoral College, shaped the early Republic's politics, ensuring that slaveholders dominated both the antebellum White House and Supreme Court.[49]

Until the late twentieth century, moreover, the southeast of the United States subsisted in a state of "subnational authoritarianism," in which one-party rule was ensured through the electoral abnegation of the African American population. That population, in turn, was again the lynchpin of a profitable agrarian economy that faltered only with the introduction of mechanization at the beginning of the twentieth century. A similar point could be made about the exclusion of women from the franchise until 1919, a measure that reflected widely accepted social norms of domestic authoritarianism. As in the Athenian case, these facts are strikingly neglected in conventional talk of American democratic history. The failure in common parlance to recognize that racial and gender exclusions are fatal to the very label "democracy"—as I think they are—is telling evidence that we as a society still fail to take seriously the experience and interests of excluded groups, primarily African Americans, who labored under the authoritarian hand of Jim Crow. It is an epistemic failure that continues to catch our common tongue in culpable neglect.

The failures of democracy that flow from the initial demand for compromise, in short, are a dominant feature of the landscape even in putative paragons of democracy, such as the United States. A plausible prediction based on the common circumstances of democratic creation is that democracy's advent typically will be accompanied by the persistent subordination and exclusion of subaltern populations. At the same time, devices such as representation and judicial review will work to curb the most ambitious redistributive agendas within the demos. To be clear, it is not that democracy as a social form is somehow to *blame* for social stratification or economic inequality. It is rather that the conditions under which democracy is likely to emerge are conditions that tend to wed democracy to stratification and inequality as the price of initial adoption, and thus constrain the scope for the operation of democratic principles. The resulting absence of procedural equality might not be a problem in and of itself,[50] but in extremis it may have implications for the felt legitimacy of democratic orders.

There is one final way in which what happens at a democracy's inception is necessarily insufficient to ensure its sound functioning. It is easy to conceptualize democracy as being adopted, or rejected, as a package, at a single moment of time. This is commonly how the US Founding is imagined, for instance. But there are necessary elements of a democracy that cannot be adopted or embraced at a Founding moment. In particular, any choice of democratic form requires the possibility of rotation out of office. Even on the minimalist account I have stipulated, democracy is not compatible with an absence of uncertainty as to who will occupy key public offices moving forward. But the possibility of rotation in public office requires trust among officeholders at the crucial moment when power is transferred. And trust is commonly not created *ex nihilo*, or overnight. Trust must instead be learned; it is a habit and as such can be acquired only through repetition and experience.[51] But at least the first (and perhaps the second) time power must change hands, an immense amount of trust is needed—a trust that cannot be predicated on past precedent, but that must often be spun from the gossamer of a constitution's paper promises. In at least one regard, therefore, a democracy will necessarily be wanting at the moment of its creation—and thus susceptible to failure—because it will want for the crucial element of trust that can be constructed only over time.

The possibility that these failures will overwhelm the operation of democracy's three essential institutional elements, and hence vitiate its claim to legitimate authority, is unavoidable and pervasive. There is also a potential interaction here with the first democracy/failure nexus: The perception that democratic procedures are stacked in favor of elites may itself provoke a belief that extra-legal violence is warranted as a means to alter unjust distributions. The first and second species of democratic failure described here, in short, can mutually reinforce each other in damaging ways.

Democracy as Theoretical Aporia

The practice of democracy cannot be disentangled from certain theoretical commitments. As noted earlier, democracy is not a game, like chess or Go, that is defined by a closed set of rules enabling and inviting complex, strategic choices. Rather, a wide range of different institutional arrangements can be imagined from the basic conceptual building blocks of popular choice, ex ante uncertainty, and institutional continuity. There is no guarantee that choices can be made between various potential arrangements without difficult sacrifices. It is also possible that a normative question implicit in the design of democracy will have no stable or satisfying answer. In these cases, it is plausible to talk of "failure" as a necessary, and not merely contingent, feature of its instantiation.

This point requires some elaboration. We can usefully begin with a canonical formulation of democratic institutions in political thought supplied by Jean-Jacques Rousseau. The social contract that Rousseau specifies is intended to reconcile two aims. It "defends and protects" the "person and goods" of each member, even as it ensures that each "obeys only himself and remains as free as before."[52] This tension between individual rationality and the collective good, Rousseau suggests (rightly, I think), is implicit in democracy. It must be confronted because democracy is among those forms of government subject to a "basic legitimation demand," whereby "something must be said . . . in the mode of justifying explanation or legitimation."[53] Rousseau's solution is to place all persons and powers "under the supreme direction of the general will," with "each member as an indivisible part of the whole."[54] The relation of private to general wills in Rousseau's account is the crux of his mediation between the two aims of social control. As such, it has generated considerable interpretive division, including debate about whether Rousseau was indeed "drawn to democracy" in more than superficial rhetoric.[55]

What is relevant here is less whether it is accurate to characterize Rousseau's solution as democratic and more whether he was able to identify any convincing justification for the potential member of a polity concerned about the private-/general-will trade-off. A broad array of sensitive and careful scholars of Rousseau suggest not only that he failed to identify such a justifying reconciliation, but that his work can be glossed as an ironic repudiation of the very possibility of such a settlement. Hence, Bernard Williams denied the possibility of "theoretical" resolutions to the competing moral demands of democracy and instead suggested that "Rousseau was right to impose impossible conditions."[56] Judith Shklar suggests that his analyses are utopian and as such "stand as reproaches to actuality."[57] In a rather less charitable register, Sir Isaiah Berlin complains that "Rousseau mysteriously passes from the notion of a group of individuals in voluntary free relations with each other . . . to the notion of submission of something which is myself, and yet greater than myself."[58] That is, the twin normative impulses that animate a seminal account of legitimate democratic rule are standardly viewed as irreconcilable. Worse, Rousseau's effort at rapprochement arguably catalyzed a new and volatile ideological amalgam in the shape of the general will. Even if some duller, sublunary justification for democratic rule can be offered, as Williams intimated, it will fail to navigate the theoretical impasse. It will leave a normative shortfall, and theoretical aporia, as its residue.

Rousseau's account of the social contract points toward a second obdurate theoretical tension at the heart of the democratic project. He observes that a social contract must bind a defined group of members and as such requires some account of demographic boundaries. According to him, the people are defined as such because they are "already bound by some union of origin, interest, or convention," even if they have not yet "borne the true yoke of laws."[59] Setting aside the question whether these prerequisites are ever plausibly satisfied—Rousseau says they are, in Corsica—it is instead worth underscoring that no electoral, sortition-based, or representational procedure can get off the ground without an account of boundaries. A tension arises between theoretical predicates of democracy in practice because there is no good answer to the boundary problem, and the ways in which it is in practice solved generally lack a sound footing in theory or empirical fact, even if its psychological pull is almost irresistible. So Frederick Whelan's complaint in these pages that democracy's boundary problem is "insoluble within the framework of democratic theory" still echoes today.[60]

Whelan's conclusion resonates because the boundary problem's theoretical settlements are impractical, while the solutions observed in practice are hard to justify on any normatively attractive basis. To begin with, it is a familiar observation that democratic procedures cannot resolve the initial scope of a democratic policy, leaving what some call a "paradox internal to democracies."[61] But if Rousseau's intuition about the moral directives animating the scope and formation of a democracy are to serve as a guide, a democratic polity should at a minimum encompass all those whose "person" or "goods" are materially affected by a polity's decisions. This raises both practical and theoretical difficulties. Many democratic decisions are characterized by negative externalities, although their vector and scale will vary tremendously from case to case.[62] It is hard in practice to see how the demographic scope of a democracy can be recalibrated for every decision a polity must take, depending on whether there are large or small spillover costs. At the same time, a polity defined to account for all negative spillovers would plainly exceed the criteria of "origin, interest, or convention" that Rousseau imposed. Rather, embracing the logical entailment of Rousseau's commitment would seem to require that all those affected, and perhaps even all those potentially affected, by a polity's decisions should by rights have a share in that polity's decision. The resulting "all affected interests" principle, as Robert Goodin has demonstrated, conduces quickly to a global definition of the polity.[63] But such a definition raises serious questions of "performative" feasibility as to whether procedures exist, or can be imagined, for the aggregation, weighing, and enactment of preferences within the polity.[64] Corsica and the globe, that is, present implementation problems of such different magnitudes that it is reasonable to think that the design of democracy for the latter is simply a distinct problem from the design of democracy for the former.

Resisting the impulse toward globalism, David Miller has suggested ways to "radically weaken the force" of an all affected interests principle. Miller's strategy is in part to show that the principle can be implemented only at the cost of compromising other morally relevant considerations, since as the equality of individual interests. In part, it is to contend that the principle simply lacks force. On this latter score, he makes three points. First, he has suggested that the range of issues a democracy can address be constrained by ruling out ex ante decisions with large negative spillovers. Second, he suggests that a polity's spillovers will vary in magnitude, such that only some need be counted (although this point is pressed into service of a different argument). Third, he suggests that the all affected interests principle only applies to *government* decisions, and then only if someone has "no escape" from their negative effects.[65] If these points are correct, the all affected interests principle can be honored without serious damage to other normative compulsions.

I am not convinced, however, that Miller has identified ways in which the boundary problem can be plausibly mitigated; rather, I think he shows why its resolution necessitates trade-offs between the various moral predicates of democracy. Consider his first point. Although Miller is correct that democratic procedures might place out of bounds decisions with large negative spillovers, the suggestion faces high practical hurdles. Contra Miller's recommendation, I am aware of no democratic constitution that creates systematic zones of autonomy for noncitizens instead of citizens. To the contrary, it is more common for citizens to benefit from immunities from state action than noncitizens, even when the latter are permanent residents within the polity. It is, moreover, hard to imagine a plausible set of democratic preferences that would conduce to the arrangement Miller suggests—at least without some substantial constraint of what democratic preferences can be realized.

Miller's second basis for weakening the all affected interests principle—that some effects are trivial—seems to me again practically difficult to implement. Many state policies affect discrete tranches of nonresidents in predictable yet trenchant ways: Consider a state's decision to extend a domestic subsidy for a valued local crop or good (which is the economic equivalent of imposing a tariff); its decision to bar some kind of family-based migration; or its decision to support (or to not support) the development of a new pharmaceutical that will mitigate a globally prevalent disease. All these decisions seem comfortably within the range of plausible democratic discretion, yet all bear heavily on discrete yet distinct groups dispersed variously around the world, perhaps in ex ante unpredictable ways. As these examples suggest, his "no escape" limitation is of more theoretical than practical interest.

To see this more concretely, consider his suggestion that migrants are not "coerced" by border controls because they can opt to settle in other countries.[66] This might at one time have fit the European context, where (at least until recently) multiple options for migrants existed. But it poorly describes the plight of asylum seekers at the southern border of the United States. In any case, Miller does not attend to the dynamic effect of his proposal—which again can now be glimpsed in the growing pan-European resistance to accepting migrants—of interlocking barriers to entry for migrants that leave, in the aggregate, no humane, bearable option. Even accepting Miller's points, therefore, I think that considerable charge remains in the moral dilemmas of the boundary problem.

The insolubility of the boundary problem means that there is always an open question as to composition of the polity, and the nature of the bonds uniting its members—and this openness increases the risk of democratic failure. In practice, the boundary problem is putatively solved by an appeal to "some union of origin, interest, or convention." But as Joseph Schumpeter observed, this imposes no tractable constraint on the definition of democratic boundaries, such that a "race-conscious" or an "anti-feminist" nation presents no concerns of democratic legitimacy.[67] Indeed, the many nations that define citizenships partially in terms of the jus sanguinis principle—including putatively liberal states such as France and Germany—and the long persistence of gender-discriminatory rules for derivative citizenship in US law, suggest that Schumpeter's solution is not outlandish, even as an account of practice in supposedly liberal polities. The Schumpeterian solution to the boundary problem is also consistent with practices of subnational authoritarianism—whereby racial or religious groups within the geographic scope of the polity are excluded from the franchise, and thereby subject to some form of permanent and deep social stratification—that otherwise would seem inconsistent with democratic commitments. That is, an answer to the boundary problem that sounds in "origin, interest, or convention" almost necessarily conduces to certain local failures of democratic practice.

At the same time, as an empirical matter, biological or cultural grounds for democratic self-definition, found with dismaying regularity in contemporary political discourse, are unfaithful to historical fact and sociological realities. Race or ethnicity, to the extent they are even stable, coherent categories,[68] are not reliable proxies for criminality or expected economic contribution.[69] As Samuel Scheffler has observed, efforts to define the polity in terms of culture necessarily ignore or deny the fact that "culture and cultures are always in flux, and that individuals normally relate to cultures through the acknowledgement of multiple affiliations and activities."[70] With the possible exception of polities that rely on skill-based criteria for immigration, such as Canada, the use of "origin, interest, or convention" in contemporary national self-definition in current practice yields no morally compelling answer to democracy's boundary problem.

I will sketch quickly a third theoretical concern, although as an empirical matter, I think its force is substantially less than the two I have aired already. Pace Rousseau's image of the general will as "always right" and as a justification for the extinguishing of all "partial society," there will always be disagreement, always a dose of Madisonian faction, in a democratic society.[71] The theoretical challenge that this creates is the familiar difficulty of aggregating a collective's interests in the face of Arrovian cycling. I am not sure this is a great challenge, despite the hand-wringing it generates among public choice scholars. For one thing, in practice democratic bodies prove remarkably adept at managing instability and reaching durable social choices.[72] For another, the identification of a decision protocol wholly immune from potential cycling may not be critical to democratic decision-making. Collective decisions can be legitimate provided they are "accompanied by a justification for its choice in terms of the other alternatives that could have been chosen and the principle that guided the choice."[73] The social choice challenge to democracy, in short, is less substantial than it first appears.

To summarize, I have focused on the way that questions implicit in the *theory* of democracy—Rousseau's challenge, the boundary problem, and Arrovian cycling—create insuperable problems for the *practice* of democracy. In my view, it is the first two—and not the cycling problem—that present the most intractable challenges because they tend to generate local failures of democracy, such as subnational authoritarianism or illiberal or even racist migration regimes. Their potential dissolving effect on democratic orders, however, goes beyond these local lapses: As the following section details, the intractability of these problems also creates a space for political leaders and movements who oppose democracy as a going concern. These deficiencies of theory, that is, can spawn practical failure in ways that I take up now.

Democracy as Its Own Gravedigger

I have so far delineated a series of practical and theoretical challenges that a democratic polity cannot wholly avoid. I have suggested that these difficulties are irresolvable without slighting valuable democratic goals. This implies that democracy falls short—it has retail failures—at its origin and in its operation, and in its translation from theory to practice. All of the limitations on democracy adumbrated thus far, however, have a local character: They impugn one discrete dimension or feature of democracy's operation.

My final argument about the entanglement of democracy and failure builds on these local failures but goes beyond them to posit a causal connection between local failures of democracy and its global, systemic breakdown. Democracy, through its local failings, generates the psychological, institutional, and political conditions in which the whole system of popular choice breaks down. Democracy's failures, as a result, are important not only because of their immediate effects (although those can certainly be significant), but also because of their dynamic consequences for systemic stability. Democracy, I thus contend, can become its own gravedigger.

To motivate this possibility, it is useful to start by reflecting on the ordinary operation of an elective democracy. In most elections for national leaders, voters must choose between one or more candidates. Outside a handful of exceptional cases, just less than 50 percent of them will be immediately disappointed by the result. In the 2018 Turkish elections, for example, Recep Tayyip Erdoğan won just under 53 percent of the national vote, despite the fact that he declared a state of emergency, purged the military and civilian bureaucracies, and inveigled overwhelmingly positive coverage from state and private media. Once in office, moreover, a leader is very likely to disappoint some, perhaps even all, of her supporters. Not all their interests will be pursued with equal vigor; some of their hopes will inevitably be dashed. Few of those who voted against her may be inclined to see her performance as a success. All of this means that in the ordinary case, many of the participants of an electoral democracy—perhaps most—will experience an acute sense of disappointment, even dismay. Yet those participants are expected, again and again, to find time in their hectic work and family lives to inform themselves of the substance of a democratic choice, and then to take the time and effort—some say irrationally—to express that choice.[74] As a social practice with material costs at the individual level, that is, democracy is not obviously self-sustaining.

It is not just the pure act of democratic selection that demands effort while supplying scant psychological payoff. It is not at all clear that the policies or candidates chosen by a democracy will be successful. As contemporary experience with climate change, pandemic illness, and economic inequality show, democracies are not always good at recognizing serious threats; they are often tardy in responding to them. And, having worked up a response, a democracy may infer that it has leeway to respond haphazardly to a crisis—inviting an even more acute crisis down the road. In David Runciman's account, "failure leads to success, success leads to failure," and all "moments of truth for democracy are an illusion."[75] The difficulty of institutionalized learning on the part of elected bodies (as opposed to civil services) seems to me of greater practical importance than the sempiternal debate about whether a democratic collective will make a wiser decision than an individual acting alone.[76] At the level of policy, therefore, members of the voting public will often have good reason for dissatisfaction with the democratic system.

Discontent and dismay toward both the personnel and the practical effects of democracy can take different forms. One possibility is that participants will engage in what Pierre Rosanvallon calls "counter-democratic" measures of surveillance, denunciation, and oversight.[77] Alternatively, and perhaps more likely, they can lapse into a general apathy and disengagement from democratic processes brought on by a sense that not only are their views and actions causally irrelevant, but that ensconced leaders will typically home in on unjustified, and even immoral, policies. When a democracy maintains authoritarian enclaves— the American South until the 1960s, the female gender until the 1920s on both sides of the Atlantic—emotional commitments to democracy are also likely to be overall thinner; to the extent that enfranchised members of the system have a commitment in that system, it may be inextricably connected to the maintenance of their own dominance. And obviously, those subject to authoritarian practices are unlikely to have much faith in their polity's democratic claims.

But this sort of general malaise in the face of democratic choice, and the concomitant absence of any deep commitment to democracy as a going concern, presents a systemic threat to democratic endurance. Since the 1930s, it has been abundantly clear that both political elites and voting publics can bring to power candidates and movements that are systemically opposed to the maintenance of democratic practice.[78] Although local discontents with democratic performance are not the only cause of a more general democratic failure, it seems very likely that the growth of such discontent makes it easier for an anti-system candidate or party to seize power and then dismantle democratic competition from within. In the 1990s, Peter Mair offered precisely this diagnosis to explain the initial rise of anti-systemic populist parties and candidates in Europe.[79] Twenty years later, the patterns that Mair identified of low voter turnout, high voter turnover, declining political party membership, and public disengagement from politics have engendered a wave of populist chancers across Europe, including Silvio Berlusconi, Marine Le Pen, Geert Wilders, Beppo Grillo, and Norbert Hofer.[80]

A different kind of dysfunction can unfold in the legislative policy domain. Consider in this regard an argument associated with the public choice theorist Mancur Olsen:[81] Democracy operates in time. Legislation produced at one point in time will persist, unless a sunset clause has been included. Policies and institutions created by democratic processes, moreover, often prove more difficult to dissolve than to create: Once created, policies create pools of beneficiaries that will fight to maintain a legislative status quo. Separation of powers systems, and even bicameralism in the absence of separated powers, creates multiple veto gates, hence favoring a politics of such resistance.[82] Over time, a sort of legislative calcification occurs: As more and more law is added to the statute books—with each law being difficult to undo—the burden of successive exercises of democratic choice drains surplus state capacity to address new needs or previously excluded populations. Weighed down by the accumulating baggage of electoral promises, a democracy over time becomes increasingly incapable of responding to new challenges, or indeed, of even adapting to slowly shifting circumstances. The arrow of legislative time, in this fashion, generates a congealing of policy commitments that ultimately proves disabling.

A final dynamic operates through the causal channel of political structures, rather than policies or voting practices. The nineteenth-century English constitutional commentator Walter Bagehot offered a justification for Victorian monarchy that has a bearing on the stability of democratic rule today. According to Bagehot, a democracy will of necessity have complex institutional arrangements as a means of accounting for the plurality of interests to be represented. (He might have added here that complexity flows significantly from the hegemonic preservation strategies of existing elites and property holders documented above.) The opacity of the ensuing arrangements, however, undermines public understanding and confidence in government. In Bagehot's view, therefore, a simpler and less democratic governmental form such as monarchy was necessarily more stable—and more publicly satisfying—than a more complex one, such as democracy. Looking to the US Constitution, Bagehot condemned its want of any "ready, deciding power," a dearth that left it incapable of effectual response to the problems of post–Civil War Reconstruction.[83] In this way, Bagehot thought, the very institutional design decisions intended to ensure the Constitution's ratification and survival paradoxically led to its downfall.

Not all of these arguments about the dynamic effect of retail democratic failure on the risk of system failure should be given equal weight. Their force is an empirical, not a theoretical, matter. At least as applied to the United States, I think Olsen's and Bagehot's arguments have only limited force. I am not sure, though, whether those arguments would have a more potent charge in different national contexts. Moreover, exogenous social and economic forces—in particular the perception of rapid cultural change or economic transformations that undermine the possibility of individual betterment—also contribute to systemic crises of democracy.[84] With all those caveats, I nonetheless think there is some reason for concern that democracy's various failures, even if initially local in scope, can over time have destabilizing systemic implications. In a sense, this is simply a modern proof of Plato's dictum that democracy has inherent to it the tendency to degrade into tyranny (although refashioned on empirical rather than metaphysical grounds).[85] All show in different ways the possibility that democracy can be its own gravedigger.

These three dynamics, moreover, interact with the theoretical failures that I have sketched in the previous section. Recall that we have no satisfying account of how private wills are fully identified with the general will, and we lack a solution to the boundary problem. This means that democracy abides alongside a persisting uncertainty on matters key to its core claims to legitimacy. As a result, the average participant in a democracy will never receive a robust or even a clear statement of some basic terms of legitimation. However dimly aware they are of the ensuing theoretical gap, they are vulnerable to appeals that exploit their regime's want of robust normative foundations. As a result, they may well be vulnerable to political appeals that hinge on what Isaiah Berlin once called the "evil . . . mythology of the real self."[86] Appeals to ethnic or religious templates of nationhood can be invoked as justifications for suppressing political opposition or disallowing the associational life that leads in time to political opposition. Rousseau's deeply misleading idea of a general will can be conjured to justify measures that suppress channels for contesting and revising democratic judgments.

That this theoretical concern has some practical heft is made clear by the fact that the very fallacy Berlin decried turns out to be characteristic of the contemporary anti-democratic populist wave. In an influential recent treatment, Jan-Werner Müller has defined populism as a political strategy based on a "moralistic imagination of politics" as a Manichean confrontation between a morally purified "people" and a corrupt and irremediable "elite."[87] Populism so defined can be observed as a hegemonic political formation in Latin America (on the left), Europe, the United States, Israel, and India (on the right). A central conceptual element of populism across these cases is the rhetorical elision of pluralism, which flows seamlessly rather often into a dismantling of institutional checks on state power and a suppression of divergent opinions and associations.[88] Populism as such need not always prove an antechamber to autocracy.[89] But it is a species of hegemony that easily and quickly bleeds into a domination inconsistent with democratic persistence.[90]

LIVING WITH DEMOCRATIC FAILURE

I have tried up to this point simply to capture a loosely affiliated array of connections between the project of democracy and the prospect of its failure. To an extent that is not recognized in the political philosophy work on democracy, I have argued, failure is not a risk for the democracy project. It is a certainty. Both at its inception and in operation, as well as in theory, democracy predictably and unavoidably falls short in many discrete ways. Given its origins and the circumstances of its ongoing operation, several distinct kinds of failure will be observed in a democratic system. The difficulty of avoiding these failures, at a bare minimum, suggests a need to consider democracy through the lens of realist rather than ideal theory: The latter runs the risk of specifying criteria of success that simply cannot be reached under any plausible set of circumstances. An ideal theory lens, moreover, misses an important dynamic: Retail disappointments can generate both a public psychology and a set of policy outcomes that set the stage for more systemic breakdowns of democratic order. Theoretical failures open the door to the political appeals of populists lacking a firm commitment to democracy. This is not to say that the ordinary operation of democracy *alone* conduces to failure; it is rather to suggest that this risk abides even in its otherwise mundane daily functioning.

All this should not, however, be taken as grounds for abandoning the ambition to maintain democracy as a going concern. Rather, cognizance of the pervasiveness of failure can provide a stimulus to fresh lines of theoretical inquiry and practical activity. I set forth below practical lessons and theoretical entailments that might be drawn from the observation of pervasive and at times concatenating democratic failure. These conclusions fall into three loose categories. First, there is a relatively simple descriptive point about the identification problem raised by the risk of systemic democratic failure. Second, a suite of lessons can be drawn about particular elements of a public psychology well fitted to democracy given the predictable frailties of democracy's theoretical justifications. Finally, I consider implications of the pervasiveness of democratic failure for key elements of constitutional design in a democracy.

The Identification Problem of Systemic Democratic Failure

If failure is embedded right at the origin of democracy, and if the project of implementing democracy immediately confronts hard theoretical and practical limits, and if those hard limits can cascade over time into a more systemic kind of failure, then it is far from clear that any simple, crisp line can be drawn identifying *the* juncture at which democracy as a going concern has been compromised beyond repair. It is always possible to point to some way in which democracy has failed. Many of those failures are, moreover, absolute so far as the affected group is concerned. Subnational authoritarianism is an obvious example. Moreover, there are no clear guidelines for predicting when a given cluster of democratic failures will snowball into a more systemic breakdown. As a result, even as it will almost always be possible to identify *some* failure, it will also be difficult to know whether there is *enough* failure to imperil the structural persistence of democratic competition.

This theoretical concern, which is immanent in the analysis so far, resonates with recent empirical work on how democracies founder. In the past half century, the modality of democracy failure has changed. Whereas once the modal form of democratic failure was the military coup or the emergency declaration, now democracies fail by inches. They are corroded from within by anti-systemic incumbents who employ constitutional and legal authorities to undermine the institutional, legal, and social predicates for meaningful forms of democratic contestation.[91] Democratic failures now occur as incremental processes, separated into small parts each of which may be superficially legal, with system-level effects emerging only gradually over time.

The theoretical analysis of democracy as failure worked through here suggests that this epistemic problem is even more acute than previously intimated. It also suggests that the problem generalizes beyond those cases in which an anti-systemic candidate or party tries to unravel democratic competition. In the absence of a complete and sudden disruption in democracy's functioning, taking the temperature of democratic health will *always* present a considerable challenge. Consider again the crude litmus tests for democratic health that I proffered at the outset of this chapter: the existence of ex ante uncertainty about a selection procedure's outcome. The analysis so far proposes why various efforts to delineate "bright lines" beyond which a democracy cannot tread without inviting a systemic collapse encounter such difficulties.[92] In a context of pervasive democratic failure, isolating ex ante the critical step change will often be well-nigh impossible.

Although the limited scope of my project here does not permit an extended inquiry into a substitute for bright lines, two potential alternatives merit notice. First, it is possible that rather than looking for discrete step changes to the quality of democracy, it is more worthwhile to look for the direction of change. Democracy should be imagined as a system-level characteristic, akin perhaps to individual health, and gauged as such. We should focus on whether its general state is improving or declining. Second, efforts to classify leaders and parties in terms of their commitment to democracy as a system may be a better investment than the search for an elusive bright line marking democratic failure. Although such classifications are likely contentious, I suspect they are no less controversial than judgments about the quality of democracy at large.

Democratic Failure and Errors of Political Psychology

Other distinctive lessons can be drawn from the mapping of democracy's failures about how democracy can be misconceived. I label these errors of "public psychology" because they are ways in which public, political discourse—rather than academic debate—goes awry. Of course, there is no reason to anticipate that scholars would be immune from such mistakes; indeed, to the extent scholars become Gramscian organic intellectuals for anti-systemic populist movements, there is every reason to think that they will indulge and even revel in misapprehensions.

First, the relation of democracy's theoretical difficulties to the risk of populist and anti-systemic destabilization explains the peril of what William Galston calls "anti-pluralism."[93] Democracy's persistence is at risk, that is, when its leaders substitute what Arendt called "the factual plurality of a nation or a people" with "the image of one supernatural body driven by one superhuman, irresistible 'general will.'"[94] Arendt here is repudiating Rousseau's account of the social contract. I think she is also repudiating the Hobbesian account of a contract between individuals that gives rise to the delegation of sovereign power to a singular levitation unbound by residual contractual bounds to a people. Further, I take her thought to be inconsistent with the premise, common to both Rousseau and Hobbes—and recently emphasized by Richard Tuck in his revisionist account of Hobbes as a proto-democrat in *De Cive*—that "the people have no existence separate from the sovereign" and that the sovereign relates to its constituent members solely as "individuals."[95] All these positions, Arendt suggests, are ersatz substitutes for "the lost sanction of religion" that once legitimated state-building projects.[96] Of course, the appeal of such legitimating bromides runs deep. And it may well be, at the end of the day, that the force of these corrosive denials of pluralism can be extirpated from the public vocabulary of politics only by a thoroughgoing attack upon, and repudiation of, the standard account of sovereignty.

Second, it follows from a pluralist orientation that the policy outputs of a democratic process ought to be viewed with some caution. The project of democracy, that is, also requires that one bear in mind constantly the contingency and partiality of any claim of representation or judgment. Whatever the epistemic merits of democracy as a theoretical matter, there is practical hazard in the presupposition that a democracy's outputs are *eo ipso* correct as a factual or moral matter. Perhaps they are more likely to be correct in some sense than, say, decisions by a single ruler or a narrow clique, but that comparative advantage does not entitle democratic outputs to any conclusive moral weight.[97] Indeed, it ought to be a truism by now that democratic decisions are often wrong on the facts and flawed on normative grounds. Even if their finality must be conceded on pragmatic grounds, therefore, their moral heft should be strictly construed.

Third, a related cognitive error concerns the possibility of a final, definitive response to democracy's boundary problem. For, if it is a mistake to conjure some unitary popular sovereignty, it is also problematic, and equally inconsistent with democracy as a political project, to assume that the polity has well-defined boundaries. That claim is not just empirically unsound—although one should not underestimate the profound and tendentious fallaciousness tendered by way of sovereignty talk—it is also a theoretical error. The boundaries of the polity are not settled once and for all but are always up for renegotiation. The denial of such fluidity is another sort of betrayal of the idea of democracy.

The history of repudiated franchise boundaries is a warning against confidence that the final outer perimeter of enfranchisement has been reached. Many generations' sturdy beliefs in the good sense of excluding the poor, women, or racial minorities from the voting booth now seem errant and apparent follies. The so-called Great Reform Act of 1832, for example, excluded the working classes, who took to the streets as the Chartist movement to demand a democratic voice. America's Constitution, of course, endorsed and enabled the exclusion of women and African Americans—lacunae corrected only in 1919 and the 1960s respectively. For the great part of American history, those exclusions seemed both obvious and necessary. There is no reason to think that we are not making kindred errors today. Indeed, the earlier noted tendency to gloss linguistically over the moral failings of the past by talking of democracy as an American trait dating back to the eighteenth century suggests that we remain prone to such errors. Our own beliefs about the mandatory reach of the franchise—as well as our beliefs about the necessity and strength of migration controls—should be more contingently, more modestly calibrated in light of that history, and in light of the constant possibility that our own secure normative coordinates will be disproved by fresh moral insight, or by technological and social transformation.

Institutional Responses to Democratic Failure

An agenda for democracy-minded reform of constitutional and legal institutions would be both expansive and necessarily tailored to the particular facts of the polity in question.[98] The prevalence of local democratic failure, and its dynamic interaction with systemic collapses, suggests a need for general prescriptions, though, that apply across heterogeneous national contexts. Without being exhaustive—a task that would require consideration, inter alia, of whether representative elections should be abandoned in favor of sortition; whether migration policy requires first-order rethinking; and whether democratic capitalism is truly an oxymoron at a moment of neoliberal triumph—I draw two generally applicable institutional responses to democratic failure both from the above analysis and also my own prior work on the constitutional design of democratic orders.

First, a sound democracy should have a way of identifying and learning from its mistakes and of correcting its shortfalls. Especially where a democratic failure leads to excision or exclusion from collective decision-making, mechanism design presents serious challenges. The population designated as salient for democratic ends always has an interest in patrolling entry to the polity because new members necessarily dilute and diminish the voice of some extant faction. Franchise expansion is therefore most likely when common cause can be fashioned between democratic "insiders" and those excluded from the polity. These alliances will almost always face opposition. One way to anticipate and facilitate inclusionary alliances is through the careful design of a constitutional amendment rule. In contemporary constitutional practice, a wide variety of such rules can be observed, ranging from the exceedingly obdurate to a near identity between legislative and constitutional changes.[99] Moreover, amendment rules can be de facto or de jure variegated, such that different kinds of amendments must overcome varying procedural hurdles.[100] An amendment regime could usefully accommodate the need for corrective expansions to the franchise by allowing them to be passed by a less onerous rule than the mine-run of constitutional changes. It would thus anticipate, and discount, inevitable endogenous opposition to such alternations motivated by a fear of diluted voice.

Second, I have suggested that theoretical weaknesses pertaining to the basic terms of democratic legitimacy open the door to populist and anti-systemic leaders. These leaders will, as Ginsburg and I show elsewhere, endeavor to shut down the possibility conditions for further democratic contestation. As a result, any democratic constitution should address precisely and clearly the question of whether and how misconduct by elected leaders can be sanctioned. (This sounds self-evident but notice that the US Constitution fails this simple test.) Different jurisdictions rely on a range of procedures, including votes of no confidence, impeachment, anti-corruption commissions, and criminal prosecutions. I have argued that illegality is often threaded into democracy's origin, and also that the stable operation of a democracy depends on compliance with the rule of law. There is often the template of original legal defiance, as a result, to tempt a Jefferson into the Louisiana Purchase, a Lincoln into the suspension of habeas corpus, or a Truman into the seizure of the nation's steel mills. There is always the possibility, that is, that illegality will succeed, and thereafter be embraced as the law of the land. Indeed, this may well be a good characterization of how historical practice in the United States is folded into constitutional law.[101] The allure of illegality—which is a species of moral hazard—set aside the necessity of legality for durable democratic persistence, creates an obvious tension that ought to be recognized and managed. At a minimum, such recognition implies the wisdom of institutions that mitigate the moral hazard of redemptive illegalities. It seems singularly unwise to relegate that task to democratic majorities. After all, those majorities have already by assumption made an erroneous choice of leaders. Instead, a fulsome recognition of democratic failure presses toward the need for politically independent institutions, rooted in bureaucratic norms, for the investigation of high-level criminality and malfeasance—institutions that even supposedly advanced democracies such as the United States singularly lack.[102]

CONCLUSION

The central claim of this chapter is that democratic practice involves plural failures of different but concatenated kinds. Recognition of that fact, and a better understanding of the specific manifestations of local failure as well as their causal relation to systemic breakdowns, is missing from political philosophy writing on democracy. It is also, perhaps to more substantial consequence, absent from the practice of institutional design and public understandings within democracy. I believe it is an unpleasant thing to acknowledge that the lodestar of modern political life is doomed to fall short, time and again, for varying and inevitable causes. Yet that recognition can profitably be integrated into an ethics of democracy, one that is considerably more humble, cautious, and provisional than the triumphalism that has characterized recent writing on the matter.

NOTES

Thanks to the participants in the ASPLP conference held at Boston University School of Law in September 2018 and a session of the Chicago Center for Democracy in April 2018 for useful challenges and comments. Particular thanks to Jerry Postema and Alex Kirschner for their extended commentaries on this chapter at ASPLP. Michael Albertus, Cliff Ando, Tom Ginsburg, Andreas Glaesser, Sue Stokes, Daniel Viehoff, and Jim Wilson also provided very useful feedback. All failures are mine.

1. See, for example, the coverage of David Estlund, "Democratic Theory," in Frank Jackson and Michael Smith, eds., *Oxford Handbook of Contemporary Philosophy* (Oxford: Oxford University Press, 2005), 208–30.

2. For a minimalist definition of democracy, see Thomas Christiano, "Freedom, Consensus, and Equality in Collective Decision-Making," *Ethics* 101 (1990), 151.

3. The absence of deliberation in ancient Athens is argued by Daniela Cammack, "Deliberation in Ancient Greek Assemblies," *Classical Philology* (forthcoming).

4. Philippe C. Schmitter and Terry Lynn Karl, "What Democracy Is . . . and Is Not," *Journal of Democracy* 23 (1991): 75–88.

5. Mike Alvarez, José Antonio Cheibub, Fernando Limongi, and Adam Przeworski, "Classifying Political Regimes," *Studies in Comparative International Development* 31 (1996): 3–36.

6. Tom Ginsburg and Aziz Huq, *How to Lose a Constitutional Democracy* (Chicago: University of Chicago Press, 2018).

7. Judith Shklar, *Legalisms: Law, Morals, and Political Trials* (Cambridge, MA: Harvard University Press, 1986), 2.

8. Plato, *The Republic* (London: Penguin Books, 2003), 290–94.

9. J.G.A. Pocock, *The Machiavellian Moment: Florentine Political Thought and the Atlantic Republican Tradition* (Princeton, NJ: Princeton University Press, 2016), 75–76.

10. For examples, see Jason Brennan, *Against Democracy* (Princeton, NJ: Princeton University Press, 2016); Slavoj Žižek, *The Year of Dreaming Dangerously* (New York: Verso Books, 2012).

11. I have often heard from academic colleagues an argument to the effect that one should prefer to be born and raised in contemporary China rather than contemporary India, given their respective growth rates. The claim is offered as proof of democracy's dispensability. Setting aside the irony of academics advocating the destruction of the very institutions of free exchange that enable them, the comparison seems to be so obviously an example of selecting on the desired outcome—ignoring the many periods of Chinese history and contemporary examples of autocracy that lacked economic growth—that it borders on the frivolous.

12. Joshua Cohen, "Deliberation and Democratic Legitimacy," in Alan Hamlin and Philip Pettit, eds., *The Good Polity* (New York: Blackwell, 1989), 17, 22.

13. Laura Valentini, "Ideal v. Non-ideal Theory: A Conceptual Map," *Philosophical Compass* 7 (2012): 654–64, 659.

14. John Dunn, *Setting the People Free: The Story of Democracy* (London: Atlantic Books, 2005), 13–21.

15. Ibid., 34; Herodotus, *The Histories* (trans. Robin Waterfield) (Oxford: Oxford University Press, 2008), V: 66–67, 69.

16. Josiah Ober, *Demopolis: Democracy Before Liberalism in Theory and Practice* (Cambridge: Cambridge University Press, 2017), 31.

17. Paul Cartledge, *Democracy* (Oxford: Oxford University Press, 2016), 58–59.

18. In similar terms, David Armitage underscores the Roman perception of a "right relationship between civil war and civilization." David Armitage, *Civil Wars: A History in Ideas* (New York: Vintage, 2017), 35.

19. David Armitage, *The Declaration of Independence: A Global History* (Cambridge, MA: Harvard University Press, 2007), 28.

20. R. R. Palmer, *Twelve Who Ruled: The Year of Terror in the French Revolution* (Princeton, NJ: Princeton University Press, 2013), 23–25.

21. Hannah Arendt, *On Revolution* (London: Penguin Books, 2006), 34.

22. Rioting occurred in or near constituencies that elected crucial pro-reform politicians in 1831. Toke S. Aidt and Raphaël Franck, "Democratization under the Threat of Revolution: Evidence from the Great Reform Act of 1832," *Econometrica* 83:2 (2015): 505–47.

23. Malcolm Chase, *Chartism: A New History* (Manchester: University of Manchester Press, 2007).

24. Maya Jasanoff, *Liberty's Exiles: American Loyalists in the Revolutionary World* (New York: Knopf, 2011).

25. Bruce Ackerman, *We the People 2: Transformations* (Cambridge, MA: Belknap Press, 1998), 49.

26. For an argument to this effect in refutation of Hobbes's argument for a single sovereign, see Jean Hampton, "Democracy and the Rule of Law," *Nomos* 36 (1994): 13–44. For an argument based on observed practices, see Aziz Huq and Tom Ginsburg, "How to Lose Your Constitutional Democracy," *UCLA Law Review* 65:1 (2018): 78–169.

27. Jon Elster has made a similar argument about constitution making more generally. Jon Elster, "Constitution-making and Violence," *Journal of Legal Analysis* 4:1 (2012): 7–39.

28. Aziz Z. Huq, "Hippocratic Constitutional Design," in Tom Ginsburg and Aziz Z. Huq, eds., *Assessing Constitutional Performance* (New York: Cambridge University Press, 2016).

29. Daron Acemoglu and James A. Robinson, "Why Did the West Extend the Franchise? Democracy, Inequality, and Growth in Historical Perspective," *Quarterly Journal of Economics* 115:4 (2000): 1167–99.

30. Daron Acemoglu and James A. Robinson, "Persistence of Power, Elites, and Institutions," *American Economic Review* 98:1 (2008): 267–93.

31. Michael Albertus and Victor Menaldo, "Gaming Democracy: Elite Dominance During Transition and the Prospects for Redistribution," *British Journal of Political Science* 44 (2014): 575–603.

32. Andrew Sharp, ed., *The English Levellers* (Cambridge: Cambridge University Press, 1998), 113–14.

33. James Madison, "Federalist No. 10," in Isaac Kramnick, ed., *The Federalist Papers* (New York: Penguin Books, 1987).

34. Quoted in Keith Thomas, "The Levellers and the Franchise," in *The Interregnum* (London: Palgrave, 1972), 55–72.

35. Aziz Z. Huq, "The Function of Article V," *University of Pennsylvania Law Review* 162 (2013): 1165–1236.

36. Adam Przeworski, *Why Bother with Elections?* (London: Polity, 2018), 30–39.

37. In contrast, the model of the mixed constitution first described by Polybius hinges on the existence of a harmonious balance. Polybius, *The Rise of the Roman Empire* (London: Penguin Books, 1979), 317.

38. Bernard Manin, *The Principles of Representative Government* (Cambridge: Cambridge University Press, 1997), 4.

39. Ibid., 202.

40. This was offered as a normative claim in John Hart Ely, *Democracy and Distrust: A Theory of Judicial Review* (Cambridge, MA: Harvard University Press, 1980).

41. Ran Hirschl, *Towards Juristocracy: The Origins and Consequences of the New Constitutionalism* (Cambridge, MA: Harvard University Press, 2009).

42. The idea of judicial review as insurance is developed in Tom Ginsburg, *Judicial Review in New Democracies: Constitutional Courts in Asian Cases* (Cambridge: Cambridge University Press, 2003).

43. See *Williams v. Mississippi*, 170 U.S. 213 (1898).

44. Aziz Z. Huq, "Democratic Erosion and the Courts: Comparative Perspectives," *NYU Law Review Online* 92 (2018): 21–31.

45. Quinn Slobodian, *Globalists: The End of Empire and the Birth of Neoliberalism* (Cambridge, MA: Harvard University Press, 2018), 23.

46. Wolfgang Streeck, *Buying Time: The Delayed Crisis of Democratic Capitalism* (New York: Verso Books, 2014), 74–75.

47. Ellen Meiksins Wood, *Democracy against Capitalism: Renewing Historical Materialism* (New York: Verso Books, 2016), 185.

48. David Waldstreicher, *Slavery's Constitution: From Revolution to Ratification* (New York: Hill and Wang, 2009), 3.

49. Shlomo Slonim, "The Electoral College at Philadelphia: The Evolution of an Ad Hoc Congress for the Selection of a President," *Journal of American History* 73:1 (1986): 35–58.

50. Charles R. Beitz, "Procedural Equality in Democratic Theory: A Preliminary Examination," *Nomos* 25 (1983): 69–91.

51. Adam Przeworski, "Acquiring the Habit of Changing Governments through Elections," *Comparative Political Studies* 48:1 (2015): 101–29.

52. Jean-Jacques Rousseau, "On the Social Contract," in John T. Scott, ed., *The Major Political Writings of Jean-Jacques Rousseau* (Chicago: University of Chicago Press, 2012), 172.

53. This idea is developed in Bernard Williams, *In the Beginning Was the Deed* (Princeton, NJ: Princeton University Press, 2005), 4–5.

54. Rousseau, "On the Social Contract," 176.

55. Robert Wokler, *Rousseau* (Oxford: Oxford University Press, 1995), 71. For a less positive view, see Richard Fralin, *Rousseau and Representation* (New York: Columbia University Press, 1978).

56. Williams, *In the Beginning Was the Deed*, 16–17.

57. Judith Shklar, *Men and Citizens: A Study in Rousseau's Social Theory* (Cambridge: Cambridge University Press, 1986), xiii.

58. Isaiah Berlin, *Freedom and Its Betrayal* (Princeton, NJ: Princeton University Press, 2014), 48.

59. Rousseau, "On the Social Contract," 199.

60. Frederick G. Whelan, "Prologue: Democratic Theory and the Boundary Problem," *Nomos* 25 (1983): 13, 16.

61. Seyla Benhabib, *Another Cosmopolitanism* (Oxford: Oxford University Press, 2006), 35.

62. Arash Abizadeh, "On the Demos and Its Kin: Nationalism, Democracy, and the Boundary Problem," *American Political Science Review* 106:4 (2012): 867–82.

63. Robert E. Goodin, "Enfranchising All Affected Interests, and Its Alternatives," *Philosophy & Public Affairs* 35:1 (2007): 40–68.

64. Compare Christian List and Mathias Koenig-Archibugi, "Can There Be a Global Demos? An Agency-Based Approach," *Philosophy & Public Affairs* 38:1 (2010): 76–110.

65. David Miller, "Democracy's Domain," *Philosophy &Ppublic Affairs* 37:3 (2009): 201, 214–18.

66. Ibid., 218–22; David Miller, "Why Immigration Controls Are Not Coercive: A Reply to Arash Abizadeh," *Political Theory* 38:1 (2010): 111–20.

67. Joseph Schumpeter, *Capitalism, Socialism and Democracy* (New York: Harper, 1950), 244–45.

68. Both race and gender have become increasingly fluid, albeit in expected ways. Rogers Brubaker, *Trans: Race and Gender in an Age of Unsettled Identities* (Princeton, NJ: Princeton University Press, 2016).

69. There are many arguments for why race, ethnicity, and religion provide questionable grounds for resolving the boundary problem, and I do not presume to exhaustively consider them here. Suffice to say that I view all such resolutions as unavoidably suspect even if omnipresent.

70. Samuel Scheffler, "Immigration and the Significance of Culture," *Philosophy & Public Affairs* 35, no. 2 (2007): 93, 105–6.

71. Rousseau, "On the Social Contract," 182–83; Madison, *Federalist 10*.

72. This empirical point is developed at length in Gerry Mackie, *Democracy Defended* (Cambridge: Cambridge University Press, 2003).

73. John W. Patty and Elizabeth Maggie Penn, *Social Choice and Legitimacy: The Possibilities of Impossibility* (Cambridge: Cambridge University Press, 2014), 194.

74. For concerns in this vein, see Przeworski, *Why Bother with Elections?*, at 1–2.

75. David Runciman, *The Confidence Trap: A History of Democracy in Crisis from World War I to the Present* (Princeton, NJ: Princeton University Press, 2013), 33–35.

76. Indeed, improving the epistemic competence and rationing of voters can have both good and bad effects on institutional performance in a democracy. Scott Ashworth and Ethan Bueno De Mesquita, "Is Voter Competence Good for Voters?: Information, Rationality, and Democratic Performance," *American Political Science Review* 108:3 (2014), 565–87.

77. Pierre Rosanvallon, *Counter-Democracy: Politics in an Age of Distrust* (Cambridge: Cambridge University Press, 2008), 33–74.

78. Ginsburg and Huq, *How to Save a Constitutional Democracy*.

79. Peter Mair, *Ruling the Void: The Hollowing of Western Democracy* (London: Verso, 2013), 2–7, 22–44.

80. David Van Reybrouck, *Against Elections* (New York: Seven Stories Press, 2016), 15–18.

81. Mancur Olson, *The Rise and Fall of Nations: Economic Growth, Stagflation and Social Rigidities* (New Haven, CT: Yale University Press, 1982).

82. Paul Pierson, "When Effect Becomes Cause: Policy Feedback and Political Change," *World Politics* 45, no. 4 (1993): 595–628.

83. Walter Bagehot, *The English Constitution* (Oxford: Oxford University Press, 2001), 38, 159. The problem is developed in these terms in Margaret Canovan, "Populism for Political Theorists?," *Journal of Political Ideologies* 9:3 (2004): 241–52.

84. For an exploration of different explanations for democratic failure, see Tom Ginsburg and Aziz Huq, "Defining and Tracking the Trajectory of Liberal Constitutional Democracy," in Mark Graber et al., eds., *Constitutional Democracy in Crisis?* (Oxford: Oxford University Press, 2018).

85. Plato, *The Republic*, 290.

86. Berlin, *Freedom and Its Betrayal*, 51.

87. Jan-Werner Müller, *What Is Populism?* (Philadelphia: University of Pennsylvania Press, 2016): 19–20.

88. Aziz Z. Huq, "The People against the Constitution," *Michigan Law Review* 116 (2018): 1123–44.

89. For an acute analysis of the resurgence of the UK's Conservative Party in these terms, see Stuart Hall, "The Great Moving Right Show," *Marxism Today* 23:1 (1979): 14–20.

90. Ranajit Guha, *Domination without Hegemony* (Cambridge, MA: Harvard University Press, 1977).

91. This position is developed in Ginsburg and Huq, *How to Save a Constitutional Democracy*.

92. An example is the Bright Line Watch Project, which is housed at Dartmouth and Yale Universities, and can be reviewed at http://brightlinewatch.org/.

93. William A. Galston, *Anti-Pluralism: The Populist Threat to Liberal Democracy* (New Haven, CT: Yale University Press, 2018).

94. Arendt, *On Revolution*, 50.

95. Richard Tuck, *The Sleeping Sovereign: The Invention of Modern Democracy* (Cambridge: Cambridge University Press, 2015), 104–5.

96. Arendt, *On Revolution*, 152.

97. The best recent defense of democracy's epistemic merits is explicitly comparative in character. Hélène Landemore, *Democratic Reason: Politics, Collective Intelligence, and the Rule of the Many* (Princeton, NJ: Princeton University Press, 2012).

98. For an attempt to provide general prescriptions for both new and established democracies, see Ginsburg and Huq, *How to Save a Constitutional Democracy.*

99. There are different ways to measure constitutional rigidity. Astrid Lorenz, "How to Measure Constitutional Rigidity: Four Concepts and Two Alternatives," *Journal of Theoretical Politics* 17:3 (2005): 339–61.

100. Huq, "The Function of Article V."

101. Frederick Schauer, "The Political Risks (If Any) of Breaking the Law," *Journal of Legal Analysis* 4:1 (2012): 83–101.

102. For an extended analysis of the trade-offs entailed by the design of such institutions, see Aziz Z. Huq, "Legal and Political Checks on Apex Criminality," *UCLA Law Review* 68 (2018): 1506–30.

2

FAILING DEMOCRACY

GERALD J. POSTEMA

"Liberal democracy has enjoyed much better days," wrote Cass Sunstein in a 2018 contribution to *The New York Review of Books*.[1] Political observers—journalists, political scientists, legal and political theorists, and even novelists—announce with varying degrees of alarm the rise of authoritarianism in formerly democratic states.[2] Hungary, Poland, Turkey, the Philippines, and Venezuela are on the top of the list, but a rising chorus of voices worries about developments in the United States as well.[3] Many observers agree that, while the pace of change may vary among democracies, such change is typically slow and incremental rather than dramatic and revolutionary, a matter of retrogression or backsliding rather than rapid authoritarian reversion or large-scale democratic breakdown.[4] Moreover, many agree that the problem is not that liberal democracies have failed to take effective action to stem this tide but that democracies themselves *are failing*. They see "constitutional rot," corrosion from within, and slow, insidious, imperceptible degradation of democratic institutions and traditions.[5] Sunstein notes that some find chilling parallels to the rise of Nazism in Germany. A German philologist reflecting on that period observed that the people of Germany could no more see it "developing from day to day than a farmer in his field sees the corn growing. One day it is over his head."[6]

These observations are alarming, and the evidence offered to substantiate them is worrisome. Schumpeter warned that, while you cannot fool all the people all of the time, you can fool enough of the people enough of the time to do permanent damage.[7] We should be concerned not only with the collapse of democracies—especially our own—but also with permanent damage that is done to them. However, for several reasons, it is often difficult to determine when this occurs. First, democracy-threatening changes are often made through regular legal or political channels; changes to fundamental democratic institutions and underlying constitutional norms are often publicly represented as consistent with law and interpreted as making democratic improvements.[8] Second, in recent decades attacks on democratic institutions rarely take the form of clear frontal assaults; rather, informal norms and conventions essential to the operation of a democratic constitution and democratic polity decay from within.[9] Informal norms that are essential to the effective operation of a constitutional democracy do not have hard edges. They are subject to change as the practice in which they are embedded changes. In the heat of politics, it is not easy to distinguish violations from repudiations, repudiations from challenges, challenges aimed at removal from challenges aimed at improvement. Finally, alarming challenges may occasion a response, but that response may signal the operation of a relatively healthy, if not perfect, democracy rather than a democracy in decline.

I do not mean to make light of the warnings of democratic decline, deterioration, and rot, but only to highlight the difficulty of real-time assessments of the health of a given democracy. These difficulties are serious indicators of an imperfect democracy under threat. However, Aziz Huq argues in his important chapter that the difficulty is even greater than I have indicated, because failures of democracies have deeper and more persistent sources.[10] Democracy and failure, he argues, are born together and travel through political history together; failure is endemic to democracy, it is not a risk but a certainty, predictable and unavoidable.[11] Because democracies tend to fail by inches, and there is already a close relation between democracy and failure, it is especially difficult for observers—and, I should think, responsible officials and citizens—to detect systemic breakdown.[12]

Huq's analysis rests on large empirical and historical claims, but I will leave to others to assess the truth or plausibility of these claims. I propose in this chapter to seek to better understand them. I welcome Huq's identification of "species" of failure and I find his examples intriguing, but I fear that they may obscure modalities of failure to which democracies are vulnerable and the extent to which those failures are endemic to democracies in our non-ideal world. I propose to explore these modalities of potential failure. Thus, what follows is not a critique of themes at the center of Huq's chapter but a series of reflections prompted by those themes.

The following conclusions will emerge from my analysis: (a) that while there are a number of ways in which democracies are weak and vulnerable and fall short of our aspirations, these either are not endemic or are not properly regarded as failures; (b) that some disappointments are properly regarded as failures and endemic, rooted in the very nature of concretely realized democracies, but that efforts to safeguard against such failures or repair damage caused by them are possible; (c) that we must distinguish between intransitive and transitive failing, i.e., between *failed democracies* and some individual or collective agent's *failing democracy*. I hope to underwrite the suggestion that some of the defects of democracies highlighted by Huq are ultimately a matter of transitive failure, our failure to do our (official or citizen) parts in maintaining the health of our democracy. We need not wait for a clear signal of the failure of our democracy to meet our responsibilities as democratic citizens. Failure to do so fails our democracy and each other.

DEMOCRACY

Key to understanding the modalities of democratic failure is a working understanding of democracy. Commonly, political and legal theorists work with thin understandings of democracy, usually defining it in terms of some major institution or limited set of institutions, or a particular decision rule or procedure, for example, majority rule. Huq proposes a relatively minimal understanding in this vein; however, he focuses not on a decision procedure but on the regular mode of operation of democratic institutions. "Democracy" for his purposes selects "a set of institutions through which the adult citizenry of a nation effectively shapes how political power is exercised."[13] This understanding intentionally does not specify the mechanisms by which those who are vested with political power are chosen; rather, we have a democracy in view to the extent that there is substantial uncertainty before leaders are selected who they will be and what policies they will pursue when in power. The normative commitments of this understanding are minimal, but significant;[14] they involve broad inclusion in electoral activity and popular control of government by the whole population. Elsewhere Huq elaborates somewhat his minimal understanding. He recognizes three "pillars" of democracy— elections, freedoms of speech, press, and association, and the rule of law.[15] Huq has his own reasons for preferring his relatively minimal understanding, which I will not challenge; rather, I will sketch here a somewhat more robust understanding of democracy that, I hope, will enable an illuminating exploration of the modalities of democratic failure.

Elements of an Understanding of Democracy

The understanding I have in mind has several key features. First, "democracy" as I propose to understand it refers to a species of what Aristotle called *politeia* or *constitution*, in a wide sense. Democratic *politeia* defines a *mode of governance*, a set of institutions by which power is constituted, exercised, and constrained. It also refers to a certain kind of *polity*, an order of the public or common part of a community and an ethos widely practiced by its members. These two dimensions of the democratic *politeia* are intricately interwoven.

Second, mechanisms for holding elected officials accountable to the law and to democratic ideals are vital to democratic structures of governance. Democracy depends crucially on the rule of law, on providing protection and recourse against the arbitrary exercise of power. Democracy requires that officials exercise power only through law, that elected officials be held accountable to the law and to norms of democracy. Accountability is a key component of democracy, and of its essential infrastructure, the rule of law.[16] The mechanisms of accountability must include devices enabling "horizontal accountability"—mutually constraining institutions within government—and "vertical accountability"—formal and informal arrangements by which a democratic public constrains the day-to-day exercise of power by public officials.

Third, democratic institutions are designed explicitly or purposed implicitly to serve certain values or principles. We can understand democracy and its modalities of failure only if we understand the values that its institutions are meant to serve. Although the key values served, and their proper interpretation, are contestable, self-governance and basic political equality—the standing of each as one another's equal—will very likely figure among the deepest of them. Yet, as Huq reminds us, we must understand democracy not merely as an abstract ideal, but rather, as a historically realized structure, a set of values or ideals given concrete existence and vitality in a specific, historical polity and its concrete institutions and practices. The possibly contested ideals are not just ideals *for* the polity in question, but values and commitments *of* that polity. Thus, arguments about a polity's democracy always take place in medias res—in the midst of an historical realization of democratic ideals. Such contestation takes the form of articulating and defending claims about what members ("we") are committed to by *this* (*our*) *politeia*, its founding, and its subsequent history. This contestation, if morally serious, will acknowledge that the realization of democracy is imperfect and its foundational values can be compromised in various ways.

Fourth, the realized constitution of a democratic polity includes far more than the institutions of governance formally articulated in its legal constitution. Recent legal theorists have argued that, in the United States at least, the *written* or *visible* Constitution draws on a deeper, informal *unwritten* or *invisible* constitution for its meaning and force.[17] This informal matrix includes unwritten principles of interpretation of the written text, structurally fundamental judicial precedents (so-called super precedents), historical "gloss," broad principles like "Ours is a government of laws, not of men," and slightly less abstract principles like "*nemo judex in causa sua.*" But, equally important for the functioning of our *politeia* are more specific conventions for behavior of the president, members of Congress, administrative officials, and courts, especially conventions regarding their relationships and relative independence.[18] Informal norms are essential to the operation of the Constitution in the United States. Some may actually fix, or help to fix, the precise meaning of formal provisions of the written Constitution, but typically they determine the textually unarticulated boundaries of appropriate or required behavior within the four corners of the text. Such norms typically supplement the text, and in some cases, may even qualify it.

Informal constitutional norms and conventions operate at varying levels of generality. Many of the conventions that make up the unwritten constitution of a democratic polity are conventions respecting the conduct of officials, often those of specific government departments. Some are relatively concrete rules—for example, the rule that the president must put investments in a blind trust, that the president must respect the independence of the Justice Department, and that public officials must, inasmuch as it is feasible, tell the truth in public. Other standards are more general, expressing or manifesting commitment to general values of democracy; among these are norms of mutual respect, mutual self-restraint, forbearance, and tolerance.[19] The more general norms govern relations of officials across many or all departments of government and some govern proper democratic conduct in the polity as a whole.

Formal and informal constitutional norms and institutions are interdependent in important ways. The broad principles and formally articulated rules orient activity within the constitutional domain and give it purpose, while specific conventions indicate the concrete manner in which to honor publicly the principles in quotidian activities and interactions among officials, and between officials and members of the public. Formal constitutional institutions can do the work for which they are designed only when complemented by compatible informal practices. Likewise, constitutional conventions operate in the environment of, and take their focus and meaning from, the network of formal constitutional norms and values they purport to serve. This interaction is dynamic. Changes in one can prompt or retard changes in the other. When the relationship between formal and informal institutions is broadly functional, constitutional conventions and informal norms turn parchment and promise into practice. They give relatively indeterminate constitutional provisions more determinate shape, defining and refining powers left discretionary, and orient their exercise. Serving a democratic constitution, constitutional conventions often work to realize democratic values over the medium and long term, softening stark majoritarian elements

of the formal institutions and giving minorities a stake in the ongoing success of the democratic process. In service of rule-of-law values, they provide mechanisms for holding accountable those who
exercise power.

However, this ideally symbiotic relationship can be distorted.
The informal environment may be hostile to the formal constitution and its fundamental aims. Because the formal constitution is
more salient to the public, it is possible for substantial changes of
the informal background to occur that move the constitution as
a whole in a non-democratic direction, while the visible constitution remains unchanged. Democratic constitutional forms can be
"hollowed out," converted into non-democratic or significantly
less democratic modes of governance.[20] In addition, long-standing
norms can effectively limit who can participate actively in the
political domain, thereby compromising fundamental democratic
values.

Realized Democracy as a Form of Normative Practice

As we explore modalities of democratic failure, we must keep in
mind a feature of realized democracies that has been implicit in
our discussion thus far: A realized democracy is a complex normative practice or network of normative practices.[21] As we have seen,
constitutional norms are not only standards *for* a given polity, but
also norms *of* that polity. Conventions are observable in the norm-
responsive conduct and attitudes of members, and their standing,
content, and force derive in part from their embedding in a normative practice. Norm-responsive conduct is public in the sense
that it is oriented to other members of the community. The con-
vergence of norm-responsive conduct in a given community is not
accidental. Members comply not for their own part only, as a matter of personal policy; rather, they see their conduct as something
done by, with, and with respect to members of their community.

These norms and conventions arise from conduct that is part
of the normative practice rather than from some kind of formal
enactment. What is done as a recognized part of the practice is
open to assessment according to standards of competent performance. Thus, what conduct amounts to—that is, what is done—is
a function of how it is taken up by others, how they understand it,

and how they respond to it. Participants in a normative practice undertake commitments to judge performances (as apt or correct, mistaken or wrong), to act according to those judgments, to challenge their conduct and that of others, and to recognize appeals to these judgments in vindication of their own or other members' conduct. These commitments involve taking responsibility for their own actions and judgments and recognizing the standing of others to hold them to this responsibility. The practical meaning of the conduct, the status of the performance, and the status of the standard by which the performance is judged are determined by how representations of the conduct and the standard figure in practical deliberation of members of the practice community, i.e., how they fit into a network of reasons and modes of accountability. The key to understanding the conditions of existence, the content, and the force of conventions, then, lies in part in recognizing the role they play in the network of practical deliberation and accountability in which members participate.

Conventions claim normative force, that is, they claim to offer reasons for action. They not only identify eligible conduct; they mark the conduct as *to be done*. Sound conventions may be "arbitrary" in the limited sense that they could have been otherwise, but they are not by that fact alone pointless. Their normative force also depends on the values they purport to serve and the effectiveness of their service to those values. They may be, and those who follow them may acknowledge them to be, suboptimal. Other conceivable norms might better serve these values or serve more compelling values, if they were established. Yet, conventions have the distinct virtue of existence; conduct, deliberation, and accountability are oriented to and by them. They may remain in place and still have normative force if no better arrangement is available to focus interactions that serve their underlying value. This is because conventions are practice-dependent; the grounds for conforming to them essentially include the fact that they are widely practiced. A convention may be suboptimal and retain its (perhaps limited) normative force, but it may also lack or lose that force, if it serves an unsupportable value or fails effectively to serve a supportable one. The convention may be practiced in a community but lack genuine normative force.

If the above is correct, then determining the existence, content, and normative force of a constitutional convention or practiced democratic norm is a complex, inescapably normative and discursive matter. Conforming conduct is an important part, but, as we have seen, the norm-relative meaning of the conduct depends on uptake, and uptake is a matter of the role that the conduct plays in the relevant network of reasons and accountability. So, whether a convention has a place in that network is settled by *argument*. Such arguments will involve assessments of compliance, proper and competent responses to apparently convention-relevant conduct, and the relations the alleged convention may bear to other conventions.

Constitutional conventions and norms get their force, in part, from the role they play in informal constitutional practice and its networks of practical deliberation and accountability, and that practice, in turn, is influenced by the broader constitutional norms and values—democratic values and rule-of-law standards—we expect formal constitutional institutions to serve. At the same time, the norms are maintained not simply by strict compliance, but rather by active assessment of norm-responsive conduct by members of the polity, the agents themselves, and participants affected by it or observing it. Active accountability holding, rather than rigid compliance, is the lifeblood of practiced democratic conventions and norms. Such norms emerge, change, gain strength, or wither depending on the manner and extent of the response of participants to conduct that conforms or falls short of them.

Thus, the nature of the challenge represented by prima facie deviations from a democratic convention or informal norm will depend on several things: (1) the seriousness with which participants take responsibility for their practice; (2) the extent to which others are engaging in the deviant conduct; (3) the nature and plausibility to other participants of the claims deviators make in defense of their conduct; and (4) the reasons and values to which participants appeal when holding deviators accountable. If we understand democratic conventions and informal norms as nodes in networks of interaction, practical deliberation, and accountability, then we must admit that change, and hence the unraveling, of conventions is not something that *just happens* to the conventions (and indirectly to members of the community they govern). It is something participants in the practice *do* (through their action or inaction), something for which they bear responsibility. We will return to this thought near the end of our exploration of the modalities of democratic failure.

MODALITIES OF DEMOCRATIC FAILURE

Professor Huq proposes to understand "failure" of democracy for his purposes not merely as some unwelcome feature or consequence of the regular working of democracies. Rather, it must involve, he insists, falling short of a goal or aspiration that is in some sense internal to democracy.[22] In addition, the term captures movement of a practice away from the ideal. Failure is a matter of "retrogression," backsliding, degeneration, or decomposition. Huq singles out four species of failure for special attention. These are, to my eye, not kinds of failure, but rather different occasions for failure. I will not spell out Huq's species of failure; rather, I will attempt to explore various modalities of failure and locate those that his species seem to exemplify.

Second Best. We might explain the first such modality in familiar Rawlsian terms.[23] When we wish to achieve a range of just or otherwise politically desirable outcomes, we might seek to define a procedure that, by its natural mode of operating in conditions that are likely to obtain, generates the desired outcomes. If we design a procedure that guarantees such results, we achieve *perfect procedural justice*. More likely, however, we will feel we have succeeded even if proper working of the procedure produces desired results with a probability that is relatively high but falls short of certainty. If we devise a procedure that significantly better than feasible alternatives, we might regard ourselves as having achieved *imperfect procedural justice*. If perfect procedural justice is our target, but the best we can hope to devise is a procedure that promises something short of perfection, we might regard our imperfectly just procedure as second best.

Imperfect procedures can disappoint because sometimes they do not produce desired outcomes. For example, a procedurally just criminal trial may result in conviction of an innocent defendant. Moreover, disappointment is endemic to the imperfect procedure we have devised. Yet, to regard as a *failure* endemic to it seems to misunderstand what the designer of the procedure sought to create. Perfection was not a feasible target. Of course, when the imperfect procedure yields unwelcome results, we may not ignore the moral claim that its victims can make on us. Presented with compelling evidence of the conviction of an innocent person, we may not merely stick with the conviction in the face of this evidence; rather, we must exonerate and compensate the victim.

Democracy is a mode of governance, and citizens look to government to deliver—to provide in good measure peace, security, and material well-being. It can do so only imperfectly, of course. Disappointment is inevitable, but such disappointment is not evidence of *failure*. If democracies' shortfalls are matters of achieving only some analogue of imperfect procedural justice, it would be a mistake of understanding to regard these imperfections as endemic failures. Yet, acknowledging this should not prevent us from doing what is necessary and possible to repair our deficient democratic practices and find ways to lighten the burdens of their victims. This disappointment may be unavoidable, but the procedure may be operating as effectively as we have reason to expect. Such disappointment is not sufficient reason to abandon trust in the procedure, or to motivate disillusionment regarding its operation.

Justice and Democracy in Pluralist Polities. However, inadequate delivery of material goods of governance may have deeper roots in democracy. We live in a morally complex world. Compelling values—peace and justice; privacy, liberty, and security—often pull in different practical directions. In a world of many different values, it should be no surprise that democracy realized in a particular polity may seek to serve different and potentially conflicting values. Democracies committed to constraining the exercise of ruling power by law put major obstacles in the way of efficient execution of the "will of the people." These constraints can cause disappointment, even great frustration, among its citizens, but, again, it would be a mistake to regard them as evidence of that democracy's *failure*. The failure lies in the popular understanding of the nature and commitments of the polity's democracy.[24]

There is, however, a deeper source of tension within democracy, a tension at the heart of democracies in modern polities. Pluralism characterizes our social world, not just the multiplicity of values but also diversity of not unreasonable perspectives on matters of social and political justice, and on moral value more generally. As Rawls reminded us (and Madison long before him), reasoned discussion may lead people with conflicting understandings to some degree of agreement, but it can also drive them further apart.[25] Diversity of normative perspectives is among the most salient, serious, and potentially perilous circumstances of modern politics. Its significance for democracy goes beyond its being the prevailing milieu of modern polities: It is a key element of the (or at least a) central aim of democracy. Democracy is the core of the polity's public constitution; members of the polity are deeply committed to justice, but they recognize that reasonable fellow members may be committed just as deeply to views of justice that diverge fundamentally from theirs.[26] The tension within democracy is not limited to the conflict between individual well-being and the common or collective good. No less problematically, it involves conflict between the pursuit of justice and the demands of democratic fairness, mutual respect, and equality. Morally responsible people, seeking to realize in their community what they take to be justice, must come to recognize that they are unable (justly) to achieve it on their own and that they must enlist their fellow members in the project.

They are unable to achieve justice on their own for at least two reasons.[27] The first reason is epistemic. Responsible citizens are better able to understand their own ideals of justice, and can effectively seek realization of their ideals, when they gain insights from engagement and reasoned discourse with representatives of divergent views and ideals. "Under conditions of human existence, we cannot know what [the ideal of justice and its realization] would be—unless we disagree about it," writes Gerald Gaus.[28] People with different perspectives use different tools or heuristics to think about realizing political ideals; they see their common reality in sharply different ways. Studies of collective intelligence reveal that aggregate results of explorations from diverse perspectives are likely to be far more accurate than individual efforts.[29] Although there is no guarantee of consensus, responsible persons deeply committed to realization of justice as they see it have a strong, epistemic interest in enlisting help from diverse perspectives.

An intrinsic, moral reason supplements this instrumental, epistemic reason for seeking a common framework of public deliberation. A fundamental principle of equality requires that we seek to define and construct a public constitution in which the diverse perspectives on justice of fellow members can be uttered, heard, registered, respected, and in some way incorporated into the structure of our pluralist polity. Democracy must incorporate these voices, not because the polity can better approximate ideal justice, but because its fundamental commitment to constituting a community of equals demands it. Justice is not just an outcome ideal. The concerns and values that lie at the heart of justice as an ideal of social ordering also make demands on the processes by which we construct and realize that ordering.[30] It is not possible faithfully to respect fundamental equality of all members of our polity while enacting unilaterally one of the competing conceptions of justice. Only in the name of a scheme that speaks for the whole community, an "omnilateral will," as Kant put it, can one justly make moral demands on another.[31] Put more simply, mutual respect requires that members of a democratic polity accord each other an equal and substantial role in determining the social and political order. Unilateral determinations of the social order are by that fact alone unjust.

Democracy, so understood, represents a kind of willing and morally reasonable compromise, a practice and process by which those who are committed to competing perspectives on justice and its realization work together to achieve a workable, responsible, justice-oriented public world in which they can participate on a basis of mutual respect. The specific institutionalized form of the democratic mode of governance of a given polity represents a second working compromise of ideals of democracy. It is important to keep in mind, however, that members' commitment to democracy does not require that they abandon their substantive ideals of justice in the face of recalcitrant diversity. Rather, they must seek to find room in the public domain for deep commitments to these ideals and to efforts to realize them.

However, this ordinary operation of democracy creates the likelihood of persistent disappointment and frustration. This is because democracies are likely to produce arrangements that any given number of members may judge to fall short of justice, not merely because of temporary defects in execution or contingent defects of design, but because it is impossible for deeply conflicting perspectives on justice to be served simultaneously. Disappointments of this kind may be endemic but it is not reasonable to regard them as evidence of *failure* of democracy. To look only to democracy's outcome-justice deliverables is to fail to keep in view the fundamental aims and values of democracy.

That said, however, we must recognize that democracy, just by virtue of its nature and fundamental aims, is susceptible to a deep and systematic weakness. Flourishing democracy requires a kind of moral skill or capacity of those participating responsibly in it, namely, the capacity simultaneously to hold commitments that are frequently in conflict. Democratic citizens must deal with several sets of such competing commitments; I will mention only two. First, democratic citizens must acknowledge and honor their own most important particular attachments and associative obligations, and the identity they provide them, and respect similar attachments of others, on the one hand, while engaging wholeheartedly in the broader civic fellowship of the polity and embracing the identity it offers. Second, democratic citizens must be able simultaneously to preserve a deep commitment to their ideals of substantive justice—revisable, of course, in the light of new insights gained from others, including those with perspectives widely divergent from their own—while respecting the values of democracy, and the individuals and polity that it serves, however imperfectly. It requires citizens to hold dear certain principles of substantive justice alongside a commitment to their fellow citizens and the democratic practice that binds them together, recognizing that doing so may compromise or delay realization of substantive justice as they see it.

The familiarity of this kind of skill should not obscure the difficulty of exercising it or, indeed, the difficulty of acquiring it. Each generation must teach this skill to the next. Democracy is always vulnerable to those who have not learned this skill or who reject it as naïve or weak. It is vulnerable to those who see compromise of their cherished ideals as nothing but betrayal, to those who see any defeat as a failure of democracy to deliver justice, to those who see opponents as enemies and their opposition as existential threats, and to those who ignore or deny the diversity of perspectives on justice evident in their polity and insist that justice (as they see it, or for their kind) be done. There are, as we have seen, strong epistemic and moral reasons for adhering to the results of properly executed democratic processes, but for some people these reasons are not compelling. For them, it is usually better to get it *right* than to get it *together.*

Democracies always face the challenge posed by anti-democratic forces and elements within the polity. Moreover, while democracies are vulnerable to those whose commitment to its fundamental aims is weak, it is especially vulnerable to those among the uncommitted who recognize the strategic political value of exploiting the constitutional and legal forms of democratic practice. I will return presently to the problem they pose for democracy.

Failures in the Realization of Democratic Ideals. Democracy, as we have proposed to understand it, is a (incompletely) realized ideal embedded within a network of normative practices. It is vulnerable to defects and deficiencies due to features essential to them. One such feature stands out: Democracies are historically and socially situated; they emerge, flourish, evolve, and sometimes die in particular material, social, and economic circumstances that change over time. The values any given democratic polity seeks to realize are inevitably shaped by its practice as it lives in and interacts with its social and economic environment. Aziz Huq calls attention to three forms of what he views as democratic failure that, I believe, depend on the historically situated nature of democracies. I will reflect on two of them.

First, Huq calls attention to the fact that democracies typically are born of circumstances characterized by significant inequalities of social and especially economic power.[32] These inequalities bend the institutions of democratic governance, even those that appear egalitarian or have strong redistributive potential, toward the interests of established centers of power. Moreover, this tendency persists even when the centers of social and economic power shift. This is an inevitable consequence of the fact that democracies are realized normative practices and do their work in a broader context of social, economic, and material arrangements. Democratic practices inevitably fall short of the ideals they profess. This kind of falling short, we can agree with Huq, is as predictable as it is discouraging. The failure is not a mere accident of history but may be endemic to the nature of realized democracy.

Yet the audacity of democracy is that its most ardent defenders regard these inevitable inequalities not as fate or fatal, but as obstacles to more nearly perfect realization of its values, as challenges to be addressed. While fatalism about this fact may be tempting, democrats resist it, in the hope that it is possible, perhaps with enormous effort, for democratic practices to work with some degree of effectiveness to live up to their promise.

Second, Huq highlights what appears to be a practical paradox faced by all democratic polities. Democracies seem to be forced into a kind of bootstrapping endeavor: Conditions of successful operation of democratic practices depend upon effective democratic practices already being in place.[33] Huq singles out institutional, and especially interpersonal, trust as a primary condition of successful democracies. Democratic constitutions, we have seen, can function only when certain norms of democratic conduct, and concrete conventions by which their abstract demands are rendered determinate, are widely practiced. Interpersonal trust is made visible, enacted, and reinforced through general adherence to these conventions and norms. They give trust a concrete and more particular face. At the same time, trust gives life and meaning to these norms and conventions.

This condition, we can agree, is intrinsic to realized democratic practices, but the bootstrapping endeavors involved are not especially doomed to failure.[34] Trust involves a readiness to rely on another party, submitting something of value to the care of the other party. Trust typically has an interactive dimension.[35] One entrusts something of value to another hoping to trigger trust-fulfilling behavior on the part of the other party. Trust can be *proleptic*. One may not fully trust another and yet one's entrusting something of value to that person may *communicate* trust, by virtue of the public meaning of such conduct. Thus, trust can start small and grow. Entrusting can trigger trust-responsive conduct that then encourages further trust on the part of the original party, the party trusted, and others who observe the interaction. There is no guarantee that this kind of exchange will have large trust-initiating and trust-warranting consequences, of course, but also there is no deep conceptual or practical paradox in what might otherwise look like naïve bootstrapping.

We can draw two lessons from this very limited exploration of the foundations of democratic practice in interpersonal and civic trust. The first is a lesson for those who think about institutional design. Those designing democratic institutions must take care to reinforce trust-enhancing dimensions of interaction within and between institutions of government. They must also take care to avoid crowding out the kind of motivations—especially, concern for the public good, and personal investment in the success of the democratic process—that are the lifeblood of democratic practices and institutions. The second lesson is for participants in democratic practices. The conduct of participants can have a profound impact on the vitality and viability of the practices. In non-intimate contexts, conduct has meaning as trust-expressing or trust-responsive in virtue of publicly recognized patterns of such conduct, patterns congealed in recognized conventions and norms. Conduct that takes place in the context of democratic practices takes its trust-relevant meaning from the norms and conventions of that practice. Thus, conduct complying with those norms, or holding others accountable to them, or conduct taken in defiance of them, can bring about or endorse changes in the norms, but it also can strengthen or undermine the trust that underwrites them. Political actors, especially public officials, must always be mindful of how their conduct might promote, preserve, or undermine their democratic practice.

Characteristic Deformations of Democratic Practices. I propose to explore one more modality of failure, one that, I believe, comes closest to Huq's notion of failure endemic to democracy, although it is not "certain" or "unavoidable." Sometimes valuable practices become distorted by factors or forces deeply rooted in the nature of the practices, features that in other circumstances are important to the recognized value of the practice. We are likely to view them not merely as incidental defects, but as perversions of the practice, as *deformations characteristic* of the practice, because they are intimately tied to the nature of the practice, or to features at its core.[36] In such cases the harms, wrongs, or evils are in some important part due to features of the practices that are otherwise valued and are among the reasons people participate in them and regard themselves as bound by their terms. Because the deformations are rooted deeply in the nature of the practices, the practices are not merely vulnerable to them, they are generally prone to them.

A few examples of the idea of characteristic deformations will bring the notion closer to home. Valued character traits, for example, may be vulnerable to characteristic deformations. Piety, for example, is vulnerable to self-righteousness. Integrity seeks coherence of principle and practice, of profession and action, but it is vulnerable to self-deception and the temptation to rewrite one's past to fit one's current self-conception. Nietzsche wrote, "'I have done that,' says my memory. 'I cannot have done that,' says my pride, and remains inexorable. Eventually—memory yields."[37] Perhaps the lesson we can draw from Nietzsche's observation is that the virtue of integrity that we prize does not merely seek coherence of principle and practice over time, but rather moderates the effort to achieve that coherence with a willingness to take responsibility for one's actions and a robust capacity for regret and making amends. That is to say, integrity is a complex virtue that incorporates elements that work together to safeguard against the deformations to which its core element is vulnerable.

As piety and integrity are vulnerable to characteristic deformations, so too is democratic practice. Populism is one such deformation. It seeks unfettered expression of popular will and is impatient with institutions that constrain that will, especially rule-of-law institutions that seek to protect against the arbitrary exercise of power. It is also impatient with or denies the pluralism of modern social life and narrows the scope of the empowered people to a unitary subset of people "like us."

A related deformation arises from the understandable, indeed, valuable need members of a democracy feel for a secure sense of belonging. They feel an intense need for a common identity shared with fellow members that can engender a sense of solidarity and trust, and that is expressed in loyalty and a willingness to sacrifice for each other. Yet communities that realize these values are prone to demand unquestioned conformity and to regard criticism of community practices as evidence of disloyalty. Moreover, the trust and solidarity extended to fellow members are often denied to non-members, replaced with suspicion and mistrust. These reactions can be exacerbated by members' desire to associate only with fellow members and hence to cut themselves off from the experience of the good will and potential cooperation available from those regarded as outside the boundaries of the community. Solidarity based on common identity can be distorted by mistrust, prejudice and, at the extreme, hatred.

The notion of characteristic deformations of a practice offers some insight into another of Huq's species of democratic failure: the persistent problem of boundaries. The commitments to each other characteristic of a democratic polity, the special responsibilities members owe to each other, naturally focus attention on "we" rather than "me." Yet "we" is exclusive, as well as inclusive; it presupposes division and distinction. Especially in times of threat—but alas not only then—this important dimension of communal life can yield distortions. Prompted by suspicion and mistrust, members may pour collective energy into erecting and protecting towering barriers to admission to membership and treat strangers in their midst as pariahs, strangers to whose moral claims they are indifferent. Among the most discouraging conclusions of Levitsky and Ziblatt's book is the claim that the norms sustaining democracy in the United States were born in racial exclusion and for much of its history "rested to a considerable degree, on racial exclusion . . . As long as the political community was restricted largely to whites, Democrats and Republicans have much in common."[38] Current struggles in the United States and elsewhere over immigration reveal democratic distortions preventing appreciation of moral arguments of many immigrant people for the extension of membership to them. Core, valued features of community like trust, solidarity, loyalty, mutual commitment, and a sense of common identity can be distorted into xenophobia, communal self-absorption, and blindness to the moral claims and moral standing of others.

Boundaries seem essential to democratic polities. It is reasonable to believe that only within a bounded community are the mutual commitments foundational to a democracy possible. The idea of a global "moral community" is, *for this purpose,* merely notional. Yet, the decisions we make as a bounded democratic community can have profound effects on the lives, interests, and well-being of people beyond the borders of our community. We owe some of our moral obligations, perhaps our most stringent obligations, to persons regardless of their membership status. A characteristic deformation of democratic community is indifference to such effects and obligations because of the very features we most value about democratic communities. If a democracy is to preserve its moral claim on our allegiance, we must make efforts to protect against our democratic community from this characteristic deformation.[39] The difficulty of the task, of course, should be lost on no one who pays any attention to contemporary problems of migration facing democracies in Western Europe, North America, Australasia, and elsewhere. The stability and perhaps even the long-term viability of these democracies depends on willingness of their governments and populations responsibly to address this problem. I do not believe failure of such efforts is guaranteed, but neither is success.

Another characteristic deformation of democratic practice deserves mention. The potential for this deformation arises from features of democratic practice we identified earlier, namely, the necessity of formal articulation of the principles and procedures of democratic order, and the interdependency of the formal institutions of democracy and the informal infrastructure that gives them vitality and determinacy. We noted that populist and quasi-authoritarian governments can "undermine constitutionalism . . . with often striking attention to the forms of law."[40] They preserve the forms of democratic practice, but transform the underlying informal practice, thereby hollowing out the legal, constitutional forms.[41] This makes it especially difficult to challenge the changes on strictly legal grounds. Democratic backsliding may be "invisible to purely legal assessment."[42] While this kind of deformation of democracy is not inevitable, it is due to features deep in its nature, in particular, the multilayered character of its practice and interdependence between formal and informal layers. It is vulnerable to attacks from within that hollow out its visible shell and turn it into a tool for ready use by anti-democratic forces.

Speaking of this development in contemporary Poland, Marcin Matczak argues that protection against such deformation lies in the hands of the judiciary. He argues that judges must be willing to look beyond bright lines of legal rules to the effects of such facially legal and constitutional moves on democratic processes and deeper principles of democracy and the rule of law.[43] Rigid judicial adherence to bright-line legal rules, in the name of the rule of law, disserves the constitution and the democracy it seeks to order.

Adam Ferguson understood the dynamic of this deformation. He wrote,

> If forms of proceeding, written statutes, or other constituents of law, cease to be enforced by the very spirit from which they arose; they serve only to cover, not to restrain, the iniquities of power: they are possibly respected even by the corrupt magistrate, when they favour his purpose; but they are contemned or evaded, when they stand in his way.

He suggested a form of protection against it different from Matczak's.

> The influence of laws, where they have any real effect in the preservation of liberty, is not any magic power descending from shelves that are loaded with books, but is, in reality, the influence of men resolved to be free; of men, who, having adjusted in writing the terms on which they are to live with the state, and with their fellow-subjects, are determined, by their vigilance and spirit, to make these terms be observed.[44]

Responsibility for the healthy functioning of constitutional democracy, Ferguson argues, falls squarely on its participants, the official ruling elites, in the first instance, but also on citizen democrats, "men resolved to be free." These reflections on the hollowing-out deformation characteristic of democracy alert us to the essential role in democracy of informal norms and conventions that give democratic values concrete content. Ferguson brings this insight home, implicating individual and communal responsibility for maintaining those norms and conventions. A democratic constitution, without vigilant citizens and officials committed to democratic practices, is mere parchment. Democratic institutions without democratic citizens are soulless machines.

FAILING DEMOCRACY

This prompts a shift in our attention from the intransitive to transitive mode, from modalities of democratic failure to ways in which we can fail democracy. Aziz Huq worries that modes of failure endemic to democracy obscure for participants in democratic practices the point at which change becomes deterioration and deterioration leads to collapse. This uncertainty, he thinks, makes mobilization for resistance difficult.[45] However, Ferguson's insight, and our earlier reflections on the nature of democratic practice, suggest that clarity on this matter, however important from an observer's perspective, should not paralyze participants in democratic practices.

Constitutional norms are always in flux. They change, decay, and die, but they can survive violations, because their viability and normative force depend on more than compliance. Also vital is the critical engagement of participants in the practice in understanding, interpreting, and applying the norms; so too is their willingness to hold violators accountable for their deviations. Norms change through a combination of altered expectations of compliance and changed understandings of the norms' content or scope, or of the values that they are meant to serve. Violations are cause for concern, but they alone do not weaken or destroy such norms. Whether they undermine norms depends on their reception and the critical response to them.

Thus, a key responsibility of participants in normative practices serving worthy values is to hold fellow participants accountable to the norms and conventions of the practice. A fundamental demand of practices committed to democracy and the rule of law is the mutual responsibility to hold those entrusted with political power accountable to the formal and informal norms and conventions of democratic practice. Well before clear signs of democratic deterioration emerge, responsible participants in democratic practices seek publicly to determine whether realized democratic norms are honored, defied, or challenged, and if challenged, whether the direction of change is truly in the spirit of democracy and the rule of law.

All realized democracies familiar to history fall short of the ideal; most democracies need reform. It is difficult to determine in real time when changes amount to welcome reform of imperfect democratic practices. Moreover, not every change that appears to be an improvement moves the practice toward its ideal; neither does every apparent movement away from the ideal actually cause a weakening of the practice.[46] Yet, participants in democratic practices need not, indeed must not, suppress their demand for an accounting for violations of practiced democratic norms. Regular maintenance of democratic norms requires active, critical assessment of the conduct of ruling officials in light of those norms and the conventions that make their demands concrete. The vigilance that Ferguson called for is not an extraordinary response to constitutional emergency. Calling publicly to account those who exercise political power is not a crisis-mode activity for democratic officials and citizens; rather, it is ordinary, quotidian democratic activity. Commitment to mutual accountability holding is a core component of democratic normative practice.

Yet, fidelity to democratic institutions and values—faithful participation in democratic practices—involves critical engagement, not uncritical submission or merely reflexive sanctioning of perceived violations. Existing norms often fall short of effectively realizing democratic values. Aware of this shortfall, citizens may be inclined to cheer rather than oppose breaches of constitutional norms, especially when the violations are public and unapologetic. Those who cheer defiant repudiations of constitutional norms may do so because they oppose democratic or rule-of-law constraints on the exercise of political power, or because the norms seek to empower a diverse citizenry on an equal basis. Others may cheer violations because they sense an opportunity to achieve partisan political goals, even at the cost of hollowed out democratic institutions. In both cases, support for norm breaking is motivated by a rejection of democratic and rule-of-law values, rather than fidelity to them. However, those who are committed to faithful participation in democratic practices may reasonably see such public challenges as creating opportunities for renegotiating imperfect constitutional norms. Fidelity demands of them a subtle understanding of democratic practice.

The normative force of constitutional practices has three related sources: the importance of the values they are meant to realize, the effectiveness of their performance of that task, and reasonable expectations of mutual compliance with the norms. The former considerations give fidelity its critical edge, while the latter lends it a conservative dimension. Faithful participants must give due consideration to all three concerns when they assess practice-relevant conduct. They must also recognize that constitutional norms hunt in packs. They work because they work together; or they fail because they work against each other. In some respects, this gives them tensile strength, but challenges to one such norm can also reverberate throughout the system, causing unexpected and potentially unwelcome adjustments.[47] Reform-minded challenge to constitutional norms that fails to give serious attention to replacing them with revised norms can open the door to practices poisonous to democracy.

However, faithful critical engagement is likely to face a serious tactical problem. How should participants respond to defiance of constitutional norms they regard as binding and important, and, more generally, how should they respond to pressures to change or replace existing norms where there is significant disagreement about the shape of background democratic values and the best way to realize them?[48] The stakes are likely to be high, because constitutional norms shape democratic processes by which important policies are determined. In addition, often the very norms that constrain political activity in the name of democratic values are under fire. The temptation for faithful participants to play what Mark Tushnet calls "constitutional hardball"[49] may be strong, and even stronger for citizens with weak commitment to democratic values. Because constitutional norms are effective and binding only if participants can reasonably expect a degree of mutual compliance, it is likely that "taking the high road" will not be a compelling tactic.

No clear algorithm is available to guide this decision, but the following considerations must shape deliberations of participants in democratic practices. Fidelity to underlying democratic values—commitment to the role of democracy in constituting and nurturing a community of equals—must be the guiding star. This requires resisting short-term partisan gains when they threaten to weaken democratic institutions. Tit-for-tat "hardball" responses may in some cases increase the costs of violations of constitutional norms for opponents enough to encourage their future compliance, but retaliation unjustifiably risks further erosion of democratic norms.

Retaliation can also further weaken public trust in the willingness of governmental institutions and officials to live up to democratic values. Embattled opponents must also keep in mind the interdependence of constitutional norms. The most effective democracy-sustaining response to opposition hardball may be to work to strengthen supporting norms that are not explicitly under attack.

Yet we must recognize that certain broad features of a polity can undermine the point and effectiveness of critical engagement in democratic practices. Respected media and effective organizations of civil society sustain the public domain in which such engagement can thrive. However, media can be compromised, co-opted for strictly partisan purposes and the public domain can be fragmented, its segments mutually alienated.[50] Where there is no common body of facts, alleged facts exist only as partisan products, and there may be no common space for fruitful interaction; discursive engagement across partisan divides may prove impossible. Hyper-polarization of the polity that is reflected and reinforced by like polarization in the wider society exacerbates this condition. In communities where disagreements on matters of policy and principle are crosscutting such that adversaries on one issue find themselves allies on another, it is possible for parties to engage each other, even when disagreements on some issues go very deep. However, in polarized societies, groups tightly align themselves along multiple dimensions and the perceived need to maintain tribal loyalty obscures or overwhelms the potential for serious engagement on any one issue.[51] This feeds the perception, poisonous to democracy, that any political loss is unrecoverable, any challenge represents an existential threat, and every adversary is a mortal enemy. Democratic engagement requires that parties believe that losers can return to fight another day. But in such straightened conditions, there appears to be no long term; in the eyes of such combatants, loss in the near term is fatal to the group and every value it holds sacred.

These three conditions reinforce each other. They are increasingly evident in several modern, established democracies and they pose enormous obstacles to vital critical engagement in democratic practices. Yet, they are remediable. Thus, another important task of committed democrats, alongside holding officials accountable to valuable constitutional norms, is seeking ways to reverse trends of hyper-polarization and corruption of the informational environment of the public domain.

A liberal democratic polity comprises a complex system of institutions and practices. Its design should include devices to restore its equilibrium when external or internal shocks disturb it. Although perfection of our realized democratic practices may never be within our grasp, resilience is, and resilience is the product of responsible democratic citizenship. If democracy in our time and in our own nation seems to be failing, among the questions we must ask are whether and how we may be failing it, and what we can do to strengthen it.

Notes

1. Cass R. Sunstein, "It Can Happen Here," *New York Review of Books*, June 28, 2018 issue.

2. For example, Patrick Kingsley, "Taking an Ax to Democracy as Europe Fidgets," *New York Times*, February 11, 2018, A1, A10; David Frum, "How to Build an Autocracy," *The Atlantic*, March 2017; Wojciech Sadurski, "How Democracy Dies (in Poland): A Case Study in Anti-Constitutional Populist Backsliding" (January 17, 2018). Sydney Law School Research Paper No. 18/01. Available at http://ssrn.com; Marcin Matczak, "Poland's Constitutional Crisis: Facts and Interpretations," The Foundation for Law, Justice, and Society (2018), www.fljs.org/; Wojciech Sadurski, *Poland's Constitutional Breakdown* (Oxford: Oxford University Press, 2019); Steven Levitsky and Daniel Ziblatt, *How Democracies Die* (New York: Crown, 2018); various contributors to *Can It Happen Here? Authoritarianism in America*, Cass R. Sunstein, ed. (New York: Dey St., 2018); Mark A. Graber, Sanford Levinson, and Mark Tushnet, eds., *Constitutional Democracy in Crisis?* (New York: Oxford University Press, 2018); David Runciman, *How Democracy Ends* (New York: Basic Books, 2018); and Philip Roth, *The Plot Against America* (New York: Houghton Mifflin, 2004). Some dissenting voices can be heard, e.g., Norm Eison, "Depressed About the Future of Democracy? Study History," *New York Times*, September 29, 2018; Daniel Treisman, "Is Democracy in Danger? A Quick Look at the Data," www.danieltreisman.org/. Treisman argues that "the current rate of democratic backsliding is not historically unusual" and the likelihood of breakdown in the United States is "extremely low," although he concedes that there is a rise in undemocratic public attitudes and erosion of democratic norms.

3. Tom Ginsburg and Aziz Z. Huq, *How to Save a Constitutional Democracy* (Chicago: University of Chicago Press, 2018); Yascha Mounk, *The People*

vs. Democracy: Why Our Freedom Is in Danger and How to Save It (Cambridge, MA: Harvard University Press, 2018); William A. Galston, *Anti-Pluralism: The Populist Threat to Liberal Democracy* (New Haven, CT: Yale University Press, 2018); Runciman, *How Democracy Ends.*

4. Aziz Z. Huq and Tom Ginsburg, "How to Lose Your Constitutional Democracy," 65 *UCLA Law Review* 78 (2018): 68–169; Ellen Lust and David Waldner, "Unwelcome Change: Understanding, Evaluating, and Extending Theories of Democratic Backsliding," USAID 2015, https://pdf.usaid.gov/; Nancy Bermeo, "On Democratic Backsliding," *Journal of Democracy* 27 (2016): 5–19.

5. Jack M. Balkin, "Constitutional Rot," in Sunstein, *Can It Happen Here?*, 19–36; Noah Feldman, "On 'It Can't Happen Here,'" in Sunstein, *Can It Happen Here?*, 158.

6. In "It Can Happen Here," Sunstein quotes this passage from Milton Mayer, *They Thought They Were Free: The Germans, 1933–45* (Chicago: University of Chicago Press, 1955, 2017).

7. Joseph A. Schumpeter, *Capitalism, Socialism and Democracy* (New York: Harper & Row, 1950), 264; quoted in Stephen Holmes, "How Democracies Perish," in Sunstein, *Can It Happen Here?*, 396.

8. Sadurski, "How Democracy Dies," 5–6; Bermeo, "On Democratic Backsliding," 15; Ozan O. Varol, "Stealth Authoritarianism," *Iowa Law Review* 100 (2015): 1684; Matczak, "Poland's Constitutional Crisis," 2–5.

9. Gabor Atilla Toth, "The Authoritarian's New Clothes," The Foundation for Law, Justice, and Society (2018), www.fljs.org/; David Landau, "Abusive Constitutionalism," *UC Davis Law Review* 47 (2013), 189–260.

10. Aziz Z. Huq, "Democracy as Failure," in this volume.

11. Ibid.

12. Ibid.

13. Ibid.

14. Ibid.

15. Ginsburg and Huq, *How to Save a Constitutional Democracy*, 9–15.

16. See Guillermo O'Donnell, "Delegative Democracy," *Journal of Democracy* 5 (1994), 55–60, and Lust and Waldner, "Unwelcome Change," 3, 11. I argue that mutual accountability lies at the core of the rule of law in "Law's Rule: Reflexivity, Mutual Accountability and the Rule of Law," in Xiaobo Zhai and Michael Quinn, eds., *Bentham's Theory of Law and Public Opinion* (Cambridge: Cambridge University Press, 2014), 7–39, and "Fidelity in Law's Commonwealth," in Dennis Klimchuk, ed., *Private Law and the Rule of Law* (Oxford: Oxford University Press, 2014), 17–40.

17. See, for example, Akhil Reed Amar, *America's Unwritten Constitution* (New York: Basic Books, 2013); Laurence H. Tribe, *The Invisible Constitution* (Oxford: Oxford University Press, 2008).

18. Keith E Whittington, "The Status of Unwritten Constitutional Conventions in the United States," *University of Illinois Law Review* 2013 (2013) 1847–70; Daphna Renan, "Presidential Norms and Article II," *Harvard Law Review* 131 (2018), 2189–2282; Adrian Vermeule, "Conventions of Agency Independence," *Columbia Law Review* 113 (2013) 1163–1238; Tara Leigh Grove, "The Origins and Fragility of Judicial Independence," *Vanderbilt Law Review* 71 (2018) 465–545; Adrian Vermeule, "Conventions in Court," Harvard Public Law Working Paper 13-46, http://dx.doi.org/10.2139/ssrn.2354491.

19. Levitsky and Ziblatt, *How Democracies Die*, 8–9, 102–12, 137–38; Sadurski, "How Democracy Dies," 7.

20. Sadurski, "How Democracy Dies," 5–6; Toth, "The Authoritarian's New Clothes."

21. I have elaborated upon the notion of a normative practice in "Custom, Normative Practice and the Law," *Duke Law Journal* 62 (2012), 707–38.

22. Huq, "Democracy as Failure," in this volume.

23. John Rawls, *A Theory of Justice*, 2nd ed. (Cambridge, MA: Belknap Press, 1999), 74–75.

24. Of course, the frustration may stem not from a misunderstanding of democracy, but from a rejection of some of its central values. I will address this problem presently.

25. John Rawls, *Political Liberalism*, expanded edition (New York: Columbia University Press, 2005), xxvi, 4.

26. I speak here of justice as shorthand for the wide variety of values and principles that might be thought to define a decent and properly ordered society.

27. This sketch of the aims of the democratic constitution broadly construed is common to many political theorists. My thoughts here reflect to some extent the argument of Gerald Gaus in his *The Tyranny of the Ideal* (Princeton, NJ: Princeton University Press, 2016).

28. Ibid., xix.

29. Ibid., 93–98.

30. See Gerald J. Postema, "Integrity in Workclothes," *Iowa Law Review* 82 (1997) 840–43.

31. Immanuel Kant, *The Metaphysics of Morals*, Academy edition 6: 263, 306–7, 312ff. in Immanuel Kant, *Practical Philosophy*, Mary Gregor, tr. and ed. (Cambridge: Cambridge University Press, 1996), 415.

32. Discussion in this and subsequent paragraphs refers to Huq, "Democracy as Failure," in this volume.

33. Ibid., 9.

34. For a general discussion of interpersonal and civic trust, see Gerald J. Postema, "Trust, Distrust, and the Rule of Law," in Paul B. Miller and

Matthew Harding, eds., *Fiduciaries and Trust: Ethics, Politics, Economics and Law* (Cambridge: Cambridge University Press, 2019).

35. Philip Pettit, "The Cunning of Trust," *Philosophy and Public Affairs* 24 (1995): 202–25; Victoria McGeer, "Trust, Hope and Empowerment," *Australasian Journal of Philosophy* 86 (2008): 237–54; Pettit and McGeer, "The Empowering Theory of Trust," in Paul Faulkner and Thomas Simson, eds., *The Philosophy of Trust* (Oxford: Oxford University Press, 2017), 14–34.

36. Lauren Winner introduced me to this idea of the characteristic deformations of practices. See her intriguing discussion of deformations of certain religious practices in Lauren F. Winner, *The Dangers of Christian Practice* (New Haven, CT: Yale University Press, 2018).

37. Nietzsche, *Beyond Good and Evil*, W. Kaufmann, tr. (New York: Vintage Books, 1966), 80.

38. Levitsky and Ziblatt, *How Democracies Die*, 143–44.

39. For further discussion of the demands of equality on the extension of membership, see Gerald J. Postema, "Covenant Membership as a Community of Equals," in M.N.S. Sellers and Stephan Kirste, eds., *Encyclopedia of the Philosophy of Law and Social Philosophy* (Rotterdam: Springer, 2020).

40. Sadurski, "How Democracy Dies," 6, quoting an unpublished lecture by Martin Krygier.

41. Ibid., 5–6.

42. Ibid., 5.

43. Matczak, "Poland's Constitutional Crisis," 7.

44. Adam Ferguson, *An Essay on the History of Civil Society* (1767), F. Oz-Salzberger, ed. (Cambridge: Cambridge University Press, 1995), 249.

45. Huq, "Democracy as Failure"; see also Bermeo, "On Democratic Backsliding," 6, 15; Sadurski, "How Democracy Dies," 5.

46. Gaus perceptively discusses "smooth" versus "rugged" reform landscapes (Gaus, *The Tyranny of the Ideal*, 61–74). Lust and Waldner ("Unwelcome Change," 6) give examples to suggest that the improvement landscape for democracies may be rugged in Gaus's sense.

47. Kim Lane Scheppele, "The Rule of Law and the Frankenstate: Why Government Checklists Do Not Work," *Governance* 26 (2103): 559–62.

48. I am grateful to the editors of this volume for urging me to consider this problem.

49. Mark Tushnet, "Constitutional Hardball," *John Marshall Law Review* 37 (2004): 523–53. Hardball tactics involve deliberate violations of established norms of fair play for political advantage.

50. Ginsberg and Huq, *How to Save a Constitutional Democracy*, 230.

51. Jennifer Hochshild, "What's New? What's Next? Threats to the American Constitutional Order," in Mark A. Graber et al., *Constitutional Democracy in Crisis?* 96.

3

WHY NO GOOD, VERY BAD, ELITIST
DEMOCRACY IS AN ACHIEVEMENT,
NOT A FAILURE

ALEXANDER S. KIRSHNER

In the 2015–16 NBA season, the Golden State Warriors failed to win all of their games. They lost 9 of the 82 they played. In the 2017–18 English Premier League season, Manchester City failed to win all of its matches, securing just 100 of a possible 114 points available. In 1985, the Chicago Bears of the NFL failed to win all of their games, finishing the season 19–1. And the 1906 Chicago Cubs lost 36 of the 156 baseball games they played, failing to complete a perfect season. Each of these teams fell short of achievable ideals. They failed.

As the reader likely suspects, each of these failures might more reasonably be described as successes. For example, no NBA team has ever won more games in a season than the 2015–16 Warriors. No Premier League team has accumulated more points than Manchester City. And the Bears and the Cubs enjoyed similar success. These examples suggest the limitations of describing the nonfulfillment of an ideal as a failure, an approach taken by Aziz Huq in his forceful analysis of democratic failure. The problem is not semantic. There is nothing linguistically amiss with stating that the Warriors failed to achieve the ideal of an undefeated season. And I see nothing amiss with insisting that the story of democracy is the story of consistent failure to achieve democratic ideals.

My concern is with evaluation. How should these failures impact our assessment of democracy? More fundamentally, how should they affect our comparative assessment of that practice? I fear that Huq's approach may treat as disappointments what, given the relevant and realistic alternatives, might justifiably be thought of as achievements. In part this liability is generated by the fact that our ideals—a democratic society, a perfect season—are difficult to reach. In part this liability arises from the fact that the ideals in question implicate and are impacted by individuals who do not want to achieve them—all of the Warriors competitors aim for them to lose; many citizens of democracies are not committed to democratic ideals. As I hope to show, the specific sources of failure identified by Huq actually help make a case for the value of existing democracies. These sources of failure hamper democratic and non-democratic regimes alike. Their generality blocks us from using them to distinguish among political regimes. But democratic regimes provide relatively attractive mechanisms for addressing these sources of failure. The persistent possibility of losing allows us to appreciate why an almost undefeated season is an achievement. Similarly, the sources of failure identified by Huq allow us to understand the value of democracy. That, at any rate, is what I seek to demonstrate in the second section of this chapter.

Rhetorically, Aziz Huq highlights how our political institutions, perhaps necessarily, fall short of our political ideals. He rejects any tendency to equate mass democracy with the ideal of a small group coming together to discuss and deliberate about a common problem. Focusing on failure, the thought seems to be, gives us a tighter grip on the actual nature of democratic practice. And acting well as a democratic citizen, improving democracy requires recognizing failures for what they are. That seems correct. But surely systematically eschewing the bright side of democratic life carries the same analytical and motivational limitations as eschewing its failures. The question is whether we can develop a persuasive account of democracy's value that does not turn its back on those failures, an account that does not depend on a dubious analogy between existing democracies and an ideally democratic regime. The third section briefly sketches such an account. It outlines the specific value of Schumpeterian, elite democracy, the sort of political system threatened or demolished in polities like Hungary, Poland, Turkey, and Venezuela.

Before moving forward, however, it makes sense to clarify what I mean by democracy. Democratic regimes are regimes in which critically important political positions are filled by regular, rule-based, electoral competition—forms of competition in which many people can choose to participate. Moreover, the elections in question are not under the active control of a regime's ruler. Qualifying regimes are frequently termed minimal democracies by academics or simply democracies by everyone else.[1]

My definition differs from Huq's in several respects. I focus on elections, for example, and he defines democracy as a political system in which "all the adult citizenry of a nation routinely and effectively shapes how political power is exercised." For much of the ensuing discussion, these definitional differences will not be material. But our definitions differ critically with respect to who exercises power. I would treat as democratic a regime featuring competitive elections but in which only male or white citizens could vote, for instance. This allows me to consider canonical cases—like late nineteenth-century Britain and the United States as democracies. And it also allows me to confront the difficult question of whether we ought to value an electoral system that allows for the political exclusion of a large part of the population. But for Huq, in a democracy, all adult citizens exercise power. Though he claims that his work is in the "realist" tradition, his is a fairly rigorous standard. Indeed, Huq discusses many regimes—revolutionary France and pre–Voting Rights Act America, for example—that are not merely failures but not democracies at all, by his own account. Why emphasize this point? Because this is a reasonably common analytical oversight.[2] Canonical examples of democracy frequently don't meet commentators' robust definitions of the practice. Yet these commentators still use these examples to shape their arguments about democracy. Moreover, if our goal is to understand democratic failure, or the nature and value of democratic institutions more generally, we need to think carefully about what makes existing, flawed democracies valuable. An analyst of democratic failure who focuses on regimes that are not, by his own definition, democracies, may be likely—perhaps objectionably likely—to find exactly what he is looking for. In what follows, I hope to show that Huq's approach leads him to underrate systematically the value of unequal and frequently unjust democracies.

FAILING TO REACH AN IDEAL IS NOT ALWAYS REGRETTABLE

Aziz Huq identifies four sources of democratic failure—crimes in their origin, compromises of justice, failures of commitment to democratic ideals, and citizens' openness to alternative forms of government. Each of these failures falls into one or more of the following categories—they afflict both democratic and undemocratic regimes, they are unavoidable, and they are not rightly thought of as failures of democracy at all. By implication, that democracies are subject to these kinds of failure ought to have little effect on our relative evaluation of democracy. Or, like the Warriors' failure to win nine games, they should increase our estimation of the practice.

Failures Affecting Both Democracies and Non-Democracies

Each of the failures identified in Huq's chapter is as likely to impact a non-democracy as it is a democracy. These failures are not especially or intrinsically democratic. Consider the idea that democratic institutions are often established by upsetting existing institutional setups—i.e., they feature a crime in their origins. This poses a problem for democracies, Huq argues, because it inscribes illegality in their political "DNA." In turn, this inner flaw generates unattractive outcomes, undermining a societal commitment to the rule of law, fostering suspicion between regime supporters and their opponents, and complicating acceptance of political opposition. Taken together, these effects can contribute to the failure of the democracy itself.[3] And this is why we ought to treat the illegal and often violent conditions for establishing democracy as a failure.

These claims are difficult to assess. It certainly seems plausible that virtually all democracies will be established by legal and political breaks from the preceding regimes. But if that is true, it will be problematic to assume that illicit origins make democracies especially prone to violence, illegality, and widespread suspicion among political opponents. Assuming democracies have a special propensity for those maladies, perhaps that propensity arises from another feature they share. Maybe it is some more prosaic element of democratic political life—like the self-interest of political actors—that causes these disorders and would cause them even if democracies were established via procedurally impeccable processes. On the basis of the arguments provided, we have no grounds to dismiss this rival explanation. In other words, we may not possess good reasons to conclude that those outcomes are caused by those origins. And since criminal origins are an ostensible failure because of the malign outcomes they generate, we may have little reason to treat an illicit origin as a failure at all. Of course, if not all democracies have this propensity to violence and illegality, then we would actually have a reason to doubt the import of illicit origins—i.e., if all democracies have illicit origins, but not all democracies have a propensity for violence and illegality, then that propensity might arise from other sources.

My aim, however, is not to arrive at a final conclusion about the validity of this particular democratic failure. So I will simply assume that democracies are often born in illegality. And I will assume this regularly leads to the unattractive outcomes that outweigh the likely benefits of an illicit beginning (an illicit beginning might be preferable in cases where the preceding regime is undemocratic or unjust).[4] Accordingly, I will turn to a broader issue: There is little reason to believe that non-democracies are more likely than democracies to feature licit origins. If that is correct, then this failure is not a democratic failure at all, it is a failure impacting all regimes. And this is not just true of illicit origins—e.g., the boundary problem is no less of a problem for undemocratic regimes.

Why does this matter? Not because democracies will have a less "intimate" relation with failure. And not because it relieves citizens of democratic regimes from duties to stop unjust violence and gratuitous law-breaking. It matters for the same reason it matters that every NBA team lost at least nine games in 2015–16, the year the Warriors were defeated just nine times. It matters for comparative evaluation. The Warriors' losses won't make us think anyone has ever had a better season (they have not). And the failure of criminal origins should not cause us to rethink the standing of democracy relative to plausible alternatives. The mere fact that democracies suffer from a failure of this sort just doesn't have much evaluative oomph.

Huq raises a personal example that makes this point especially clear. As he notes, one fails as a parent when one needlessly loses one's temper in response to some small misbehavior. But imagine a parent who yells unjustifiably at their child just one single time. Surely, it would be better never to lose one's temper without cause. But if every parent yells at their child, then we may not view a single slip as much of a reason to think ill of that nearly perfect parent.

Unavoidable Failures

Some failures not only impact non-democracies, they are practically unavoidable. Consider the famed "boundary problem." Roughly speaking, it is often claimed that to generate decisions that are democratically legitimate and authoritative, individuals bound or affected by those decisions must have an opportunity to impact those decisions. To meet this standard, it must be determined in advance who the bound or affected will be. And this applies as well to a decision concerning who should have the opportunity to participate. Since potential participants must be selected in advance, there is no straightforward democratic means for determining who should be able to participate, for determining who "the people" should be.[5] This is one of those theoretical problems that maps neatly onto subjects of intense political debate and contestation—e.g., who should have a claim to participate, who should set political boundaries and so forth.

But if we assume the existence of the boundary problem, then we assume a fully satisfactory theoretical solution to these real-world debates may be beyond our reach. And it might still escape our grasp even under improved political conditions. As a result, few if any regimes, no matter how attractive, will successfully resolve this problem. And if almost all regimes are limited in this way, we will not be justified in shuffling our assessment of democratic regimes relative to one another or relative to autocratic regimes.

Of course, some regimes seem to manage problems of this sort better than others. We don't need a fully worked out theory of democratic boundaries to see this. I feel safe in assuming that there are weighty moral reasons not to abduct the children of individuals seeking to cross a border into a democratic polity.[6] If that assumption is plausible, it has several implications. It suggests we can elaborate standards for managing the boundary problem that some regimes might satisfy, standards that are not caught in the intricacies of the boundary problem—e.g., possible standard: Don't steal children. Moreover, if some regimes manage this problem better than others—by not separating infants from their non-citizen parents without a due assessment of the policy's justification and its alternatives, for example—then not all democracies will fall short of our standards. Finally, if we observe variation among democracies, if some democracies do a better job managing these issues than others, then we can reasonably conclude that it isn't the boundary problem that is causing regimes to fail. That conclusion makes sense. It is exceptionally unlikely that "the boundary problem" is the reason regimes like the United States and Hungary have unjustified policies concerning who can vote and who can immigrate. Suppose you identified a compelling theoretical answer to the boundary problem. And suppose that answer implied that non-citizen immigrants should vote. Do you think the US Congress as presently constituted or the Hungarian National Assembly would institute your preferred policy? A true realist would surely scoff at the possibility.

In the final paragraph of the introduction to his chapter, Huq indicates that he means to distinguish regimes that are failing from those that are not. He intends his analysis to aid our evaluation of how well those institutions are working. I have claimed that examining unavoidable failures will not impact our relative assessment of democracies. As a result, I have questioned the evaluative approach on offer. But a distinct concern may arise here. One might think that the true effect of Huq's chapter is to cast doubt on whether real-world democracies, as a general class, are likely to be legitimate and authoritative—i.e., whether the government and society will possess features of the sort necessary to generate a democratic right to rule for the government and corresponding duties for citizens to obey the laws of the polity.[7]

Yet here too the generality of the failures Huq identifies, failures that are endemic to democratic regimes, will thwart progress toward understanding the moral status of those regimes. I don't have a fully worked out theory of legitimate democratic authority ready to hand, but any such theory would fall into one of two camps: (1) theories that preclude democratic regimes that suffer from the failures Huq identifies (i.e., all democratic regimes) from being legitimately authoritative; (2) theories that do not preclude democratic regimes suffering from those failures from being legitimately authoritative.

With respect to the former, it is perfectly possible that someone might determine that no democratic regimes can be legitimately authoritative, that certain features, their illegal beginnings, for instance, preclude achieving that moral status. But even if the theory were defensible, it would seem odd to conclude that such a theory would be part of a compelling strategy for unpacking the idea of democratic failure. On the one hand, a theory of democratic authority that no democracies could satisfy would hardly, I think, be reasonably thought of as a theory of democratic authority, as an explanation of the special virtues and relationships we might think a democracy could possess. On the other hand, any democracy, even an egalitarian regime, that was not legitimately authoritative according to a theory of this sort, could hardly be deemed a failure on this basis. How can you fail at something that cannot reasonably be a goal, something you cannot achieve by definition?

Alternatively, and I believe more sensibly, one's theory of democratic authority might allow for, say, illegal beginnings and boundary problems. The idea would be that some democratic regimes with illegal beginnings or incompletely justified borders might nonetheless possess the attractive features or equitable relationships allowing for decisions and laws to be legitimately authoritative. This approach would have two further implications.

First, since all democracies will have incompletely justified borders and illegal beginnings, but only some democracies would be unauthoritative, it would be reasonable to suspect that some other features of those regimes account for their lack of legitimate authority. In other words, we have reason to doubt whether those limitations are attributable to the democratic character of that regime, since other democratic regimes don't suffer from the same limitations.

Second, democratic regimes that were legitimately authoritative despite their illegal beginnings or boundary problems would not reasonably be thought of as having failed. Regimes boasting relatively attractive practices, policies, institutions, and relationships might actually be due praise. Why? Because they have achieved relative success despite the impossibility of sidestepping the boundary problem. The nature of the failure may actually raise our estimation of the regimes in question. That is the topic I explore next.

Failures Raising Our Estimation of Democracy

Some failures have no impact on our assessment of a regime. Others can actually increase our appreciation for a polity. This claim may seem puzzling. How can a failure be a success? In fact, it isn't puzzling at all. Consider the following (fictional) example.

Imagine I often play cards with my daughter. It's possible for her to win. But I always do. Why? I am an adult and she is five years old. Still, during any hand, she might play much better than she ever has before. And that would be a success. She can succeed even if she fails to defeat me.

What is going on in this example? My daughter could have won. She didn't, but she played well. Here, the conditions of her failure—her youth and card-playing inexperience—lead us to regard a predictable failure as a success (but not a victory). In light of those conditions, we can determine in a rough way an expected baseline against which we can measure her performance. Where someone's performance exceeds relevant alternatives and expectations, we reasonably treat that effort as an achievement even if it fails to satisfy our ideals.

Bear in mind that this mode of assessment is comparative and focused on outcomes, not on my daughter's intentions or effort. There's a difference between trying hard and achieving something.[8] Our assessment depends on relevant and realistic alternatives. I am taking the term "realistic" from Huq's diagnosis of democratic failure. As I understand it, a realistic approach entails considering circumstances as they are and resisting the urge to weigh too heavily the slim possibility of realizing ideal scenarios (e.g., my daughter winning despite her youth and my outlandish card-playing skills).

Of course, Huq's "realist" approach causes him to treat democracy as a failure. But the preceding discussion suggests that a consistently realistic approach would actually lead us to make a more positive assessment of failures reached under unfavorable conditions. Accounting for unfavorable conditions should alter our expectations. We will see success even in cases where people do not achieve their ideals. The question, then, is whether the same logic carries over to the political domain. I believe it does. Here's an important example. Professor Huq notes how stable public institutions generally require compromises with groups that, out of self-interest or ideology, oppose the achievement of egalitarian institutions.[9] I use the term "requires" advisedly. It is highly unlikely those groups will embrace egalitarian self-government, and the same groups typically back up their demands with the threat of violence or political sabotage. These compromises take myriad institutional forms: representative systems that encourage the selection of wealthy elites, constitutional courts that enforce unjust constitutional bargains, federal systems that allow for subnational authoritarianism, legal commitments to international institutions that limit the possibility for egalitarian economic and political reform, and so on. As Huq rightly observes, the creation of these institutions cannot be pinned on the extant political system. Compromised institutions are created at the same time as the political system. The de facto power imbalances leading to their creation predate the political system. Nonetheless, the common, if not universal, character of these circumstances means a realist will assume that most stable political systems will fail to achieve democratic ideals.

I want to suggest the conditions limiting the democratic potential of political regimes are, from an evaluative perspective, akin to the conditions blocking my daughter from winning at cards. Acknowledging those conditions should keep us from ignoring the kind of achievement representative institutions are. On Huq's account, as I understand it, the relevant or realistic alternatives to flawed democracy are flawed autocracy or instability and violence (which will occur in cases in which political institutions do not reflect sufficiently the de facto power of contending groups).[10] We observe flawed democracies, then, when those who would benefit from egalitarian political institutions are sufficiently well organized to bargain for flawed, democratic institutions. And, assuming that we have some reason or reasons to value flawed democracies relative to the alternatives just mentioned, we will have a reason or reasons to value that achievement. In other words, it is precisely a realistic assessment of the less than ideal circumstances of their establishment that allows us to see that flawed, inegalitarian political institutions can be worthy of our admiration.

Two additional points are worth making here. First, the logic of this argument extends beyond the establishment of flawed democratic institutions. It covers their maintenance as well. Since the unfortunate and unequal circumstances common to political foundings are instantiated in democratic institutions, those circumstances will persist. It isn't the case, for example, that those opposed to democracy simply stop attempting to undermine democratic institutions once they have been created. The difficult work of defending flawed democratic institutions does not end with their establishment. This is borne out by the American experience. Consider the history of the 1965 Voting Rights Act. On some reasonable definitions, the United States only became a democracy with its passage and implementation.[11] But, regrettably, it remains the subject of political contestation, with groups at both the state and federal levels seeking to undermine the changes wrought by the policy—e.g., those groups seek to make it harder for discreet groups, like African Americans, to vote.[12] Under these conditions, it is just as significant an achievement to maintain democratic institutions as it is to establish them in the first place.

Second, treating democracy as an achievement requires no one to overlook its predictable and often blatant inadequacies. And it should not keep anyone from treating those inadequacies as reasons for action. One might be concerned that focusing scholarly attention on ideal theories of democracy makes it easier to equate existing regimes with our ideals. I suspect scholars investigating the theoretical intricacies of an ideally deliberative regime, for example, would reject that concern, insisting that their efforts highlight rather than obscure democracy's failures. Regardless, my claim is not that democratic failures should be treated as ideals, just as my view is not that we should treat my daughter's failure to defeat me as a victory. Thoroughgoing realism entails acknowledging that democracies fail to instantiate our ideals and that those non-ideal democracies are preferable to realistic alternatives. From a purely motivational perspective, a view that favors action to right a political system's failures and action to defend its achievements seems preferable to perspectives that focus narrowly on one of these avenues for democratic action.

Should Professor Huq's bracing outline of democratic failure change our opinion about transitions of democratic regimes into autocracies, about the failure of democracy? My analysis suggests not. We have little reason to reevaluate our confidence in the relative attractiveness of democratic regimes—all of the failures discussed are liable to impact non-democratic regimes and many are simply unavoidable, tout court. Moreover, some of the failures Huq described should actually increase our estimation of democratic regimes. Of course, developing my argument, I have simply assumed that something positively distinguishes unjust, unequal, unfair, diminished democratic institutions from the unjust, unequal, unfair, diminished autocracies that would be established in their stead. Is such an assumption defensible? The next section sketches an account of this sort, focusing on the kind of space democratic institutions create for political agency.

What We Lose When Democracies Fail

Autocratic regimes feature many of the institutions we associate with democracy, including elections, universal suffrage, and representative bodies.[13] Democracies are set apart from autocracies, it is often claimed, by electoral uncertainty.[14] This uncertainty generates valuable by-products like incentives for politicians to publicize corruption and to attend, in some part, to the interests of citizens.[15] The consistent generation of these by-products is what is lost, at minimum, when the unequal, unjust democracies described by Huq are undermined.

There are, however, several problems with this familiar approach to democratic failure. Since its creation in 1955, Japan's Liberal Party has been in power for fifty-eight of its sixty-three years. Japan's elections feature relatively little uncertainty. Suppose the rules of Japan's electoral system are reasonably fair and fairly enforced, should the lack of uncertainty about electoral outcomes trouble us? Should we conclude that Japan is failing as a democracy because its fair elections do not generate uncertainty? I think the answer to both questions is negative. An uncertainty-based standard just places too much emphasis on the likelihood of different forces winning office and too little on the character of a polity's political institutions. Consider another example. Suppose my colleague and I want to fill an elected, departmental position. The outcome is uncertain; either of us could win. But the outcome is only uncertain because I have offered large cash bribes to anyone who votes for me. If I did not bribe my colleagues, the outcome would be clear in advance—my colleague would win. Obviously, all else equal, there is no interesting reason to think that the more uncertain situation is the more democratic one or that the state of affairs in which I cheat is to be preferred to the state of affairs in which the outcome is clear. Electoral uncertainty is a useful empirical proxy for low barriers to entry into a political contest. But, from a normative perspective, uncertainty of electoral outcomes just isn't a good way to discriminate between regimes.

What about accountability? The possibility of an electoral loss forces political actors to be responsive to the wishes or interests of the electorate. Of course, the political systems of many democracies are corrupted by money or riven by ethnic and sectarian differences or shaped by a general lack of political interest. Taken together these features of the political landscape mean that citizens will often fail to reliably hold their representatives to account.[16] Moreover, we now know that non-democratic regimes use elections to gain information about their population and the performance of political officials. Who can run for office in an autocracy is often strictly controlled. But incumbents can be displaced. Autocracies, it is said, aim to be responsive to the people, limiting the likelihood of challenges to the ruling regime, even while shielding high-level political officials from accountability.[17] As a result of these institutional realities, autocratic regimes, like Singapore for instance, may advance their citizens' material interests at least as well as democracies.

Real democracies, as Huq observes, are unlikely to feature egalitarian institutions. As a result, formal and informal opportunities to impact the political process will not be equally distributed and this unequal distribution will not be justifiable to many of those with less influence. But we can acknowledge this and still recognize the relative value of the defining feature of real-world democracies: the rule-based, competitive procedures, like elections, allowing individuals with conflicting interests to influence matters of import. In particular, such systems provide citizens opportunities to join with others, in organizations like parties, to exert influence over outcomes that matter—these outcomes include passing legislation, blocking the creation of some unreasonable policy, affecting who is selected to make policy, shifting the views of one's fellow citizens and so on. And citizens can take advantage of these opportunities without fear of violence and legal reprisals. These flawed regimes then are distinguished by a particular orientation toward distinctive human capacities—individuals' ability to exercise agency and to do it together. They provide certain kinds of opportunities for huge numbers of citizens to exercise their agency, to use their faculties and resources to shape their shared world.[18] And that makes those institutions valuable.[19]

Critically, the exercise of agency does not require perfect political equality—the kind of equality not achieved in real-world, representative political systems. I can participate in advancing a collective enterprise of some import and think of myself as contributing to the relevant end, even if I contribute less than another participant. A classic example would be a symphony. The third cellist may play less than the first, but neither can play a symphony alone, and both can reasonably regard themselves as having played a symphony with many others. So too in politics. I can contribute to an outcome, knocking on doors, for instance, even though I have vastly less influence than an elected, political bigwig. Of course, for the vast majority of individuals, agency in a democracy will not be persistent—one will not see one's agency instantiated in all political decisions (pace Rousseau). One will inevitably be disappointed and even infuriated by some outcomes. This reflects the disagreement and inequality endemic in a polity of any size. But the mere fact that individuals will not see their agency reflected in all decisions does not mean even flawed democratic systems cannot generate meaningful opportunities for citizens to exercise their agency. Those opportunities allow citizens to justifiably recognize themselves as political agents, to justifiably see certain outcomes as products of their agency, and to engage in these activities without fear of unjustified reprisal. In other words, a system's incapacity to consistently generate laws and decisions that all (or almost all) citizens will reasonably recognize as their own, does not imply an incapacity to generate any valuable opportunities for agency—e.g., working to overturn decisions that one does not see as one's own.

By contrast, though they feature elections and offer opportunities for political action, the political systems of real-world autocracies do not share the same valuable orientation toward their citizens' agency. In non-democracies, citizens' choices are circumscribed, obviously. Seeking to advance ends inconsistent with those who control political institutions can make one liable to legal penalties and much worse. But autocratic regimes typically go well beyond merely limiting citizens' opportunities to exercise their agency. In fact, they repurpose institutions like elections to usurp citizens' capacity for agency.[20] Rather than allowing citizens to shape their political world via mass activity, the autocracies use individuals' distinctive capacity for agency against them. Elections, for example, are transformed into engines of repression.

Spelling out this idea, I'll focus on Singapore. The wealthy city-state is an ideal real-world example. First, the mechanisms it deploys to subvert citizens' agency are roughly the same as those used by other electoral autocracies like Russia. In other words, the example travels. Second, many think of it as well-run, as advancing its citizens' material well-being. By implication, when I identify the shortcomings of Singapore's political system, the wrong identified should be easy to distinguish from the instrumental shortcomings commonly associated with non-democracies.

Singapore's political system does not merely keep its citizens from challenging powerholders, blocking them from exercising their judgment and acting on it. It actually forces them to act and to act in support of the regime. It exploits their capacity for agency. Roughly speaking, Singapore's citizens have three choices during an election. They can vote for and support the candidate of the ruling party. They can vote for and support "opposition" candidates and parties, candidates and parties allowed to contest the election by the ruling party because it is in the interest of the ruling party to be opposed, but not threatened. Or citizens can refrain from voting at all. This system appears like a democratic political system, offering citizens chances to exercise their agency, by voting, organizing for their preferred candidate, writing letters to the editor, or even staying at home and refusing to vote at all. And some citizens may well identify with their choices in ways we associate with the unmanipulated exercise of agency. Non-democratic regimes use this phenomenon to build domestic and international

support. This is why they carry out the expensive processes of elections. It's why they don't merely announce an outcome in advance.
Yet, despite appearances, the elections are fundamentally manipulative, and the opportunities for agency they offer are inconsistent
with the respect due to citizens' capacity for agency.

In effect, the political systems of autocracies like Singapore
offer citizens a Hobson's choice. If a citizen supports the regime's
candidate, she obviously advances the regime's ends, illustrating
popular support for the regime. If she votes for or acts in support
of the "opposition" parties, she supports the regime's ends, lending popular legitimacy to the ruling party and undermining the
efforts of any true opposition, an opposition that might actually
threaten the position of the ruling party or group. Finally, even
those who choose to stay at home, failing to support any party,
advance the ends of the regime, allowing the regime to run up its
vote totals and signaling the demoralized state of the opposition.[21]
No matter their commitments, citizens are intentionally recruited
into making choices that inevitably advance the regime's goals.

Even after this brief explanation, I think it should be self-evident
how non-democracies use political institutions to usurp the agency
of citizens who are opposed to the regime. No matter what those
citizens do, they are compelled to advance an end they oppose.
Of course, they might resist, but doing so makes them vulnerable
to legal sanction or worse.[22] And what of citizens who support the
regime? Suppose they would support the ruling party if given the
chance. Unfortunately, they cannot do so in an unmanipulated
fashion. That chance has actually been eliminated. Sometimes my
young son will wake up on a Saturday morning and inform me
that he will not be going to daycare—"no school time," he cheerily
informs me. He is too young to know it, but daycare is not open on
Saturday. Supporters of the Singaporean regime are in a similar
position. They want to do something (support the regime/not go
to daycare), but they never had any other option (they have to support the regime/daycare isn't open on Saturday). Supporters of
the regime may feel empowered as agents, just as my son feels like
he has chosen not to go to school, but we have reason to regard
such a choice, such an exercise of agency, as less valuable than a
choice that is not so compelled. And we have reason to regard a
system designed to generate choices of this sort as less valuable

than a system that provided more space for citizens to exercise their agency. This, I believe, captures a fundamental difference between flawed, real-world democracies and flawed, real-world autocracies.

I have claimed that Singapore and a democracy are critically distinguished by their orientation toward citizens' capacity for political agency. But does my concern really just boil down to considerations of equality, not agency? To see why not, consider the following. Imagine Singapore's dominant, ruling group simply ruled and did not engage in fraudulent elections and similar popular mechanisms to usurp Singaporeans' agency. Call this imagined regime: I-Singapore. Is I-Singapore more egalitarian than the real-world Singapore—where the ruling group organizes a system of ostensibly popular politics? From the perspective of equality, from the perspective of who truly exercises political influence, the two Singapores are basically equivalent: A small group rules. But the Singapores are not equivalent tout court. The real-world rulers of Singapore employ political institutions to exploit citizens' capacity for agency; they do this to advance their ends—demonstrating their dominance and gaining valuable information about their friends and enemies. And this orientation toward citizens' agency also distinguishes real-world Singapore from real-world, inegalitarian democracies.

Are non-democracies necessarily or intrinsically manipulative of citizens' agency? Perhaps not. And it is possible to imagine that usurping citizens' agency is a novel strategy, to imagine that contemporary autocratic regimes, like Singapore, have identified a new method to demoralize their opponents and cement their support. But that would be a mistake. It is a paradigmatic, widely employed tactic of autocrats. Václav Havel's famed essay, "The Power of the Powerless," is structured around a public practice of a sort: A shopkeeper is forced to decide whether to place a sign in his window supporting the ruling Communist Party.[23] Put the sign up and the shopkeeper acquiesces to the regime and increases the pressure on his neighbors to capitulate as well. Refuse and he makes it easier for his neighbors to shun him and for the state to identify its antagonists. Inaction is not an option. In this way, Havel's essay highlights the tyrannical character of institutions whose purpose is to subdue citizens and subvert their agency.

If we were to fill out this sketch, more would need to be said about the value of agency in a competitive democracy and more would need to be done to confront potential concerns. But the main lines of argument are clear enough. Flawed, inegalitarian, unjust democratic regimes have a relatively attractive orientation toward their citizens' agency. They make space for participants to act responsibly and utilize their political capacities as they see fit. Their rivals do not. And that is what is lost just in case those flawed regimes fail.

CONCLUSION

Democratic regimes are failures. Perhaps unavoidably, they fail to meet our ideals. We should be cognizant of those failures. We ought to remedy them where we can. But if my argument has been sound, those failures give us little reason to pursue alternative forms of government. They ought not affect our relative appraisal of this regime type. Moreover, we have sound reasons to regret the demolition of democracy, to regret the transition from democracy to electoral autocracy. And our reasons for thinking that are immune to the kinds of considerations raised in Aziz Huq's deft analysis of the considerable limitations of democratic government.

NOTES

1. Adam Przeworski, "Minimalist Conception of Democracy: A Defense," in *Democracy's Value*, eds. Ian Shapiro and Casiano Hacker-Cordón (Cambridge: Cambridge University Press, 1999).

2. Steven Levitsky and Daniel Ziblatt, *How Democracies Die* (New York: Crown, 2018).

3. There is a whiff of tautology here—what leads to democracy necessarily leads to its failure.

4. Due to the exceptional circumstances of its creation, the German Basic Law famously outlines a legitimate procedure for its own demise and replacement by a new, democratic constitution—Article 146. See Ulrich Preuss, "Constitutional Powermaking for the New Polity," *Cardozo Law Review* 14, no. 651 (1992–1993): 639–60.

5. Frederick Whelan, "Prologue: Democratic Theory and the Boundary Problem," in *Nomos 25: Liberal Democracy*, eds. James R. Pennock and John W. Chapman (New York: New York University Press, 1983); Robert

Goodin, "Enfranchising All Affected Interests, and Its Alternatives," *Philosophy & Public Affairs* 35, no. 1 (2007): 40–68; Arash Abizadeh, "On the Demos and Its Kin: Nationalism, Democracy, and the Boundary Problem," *American Political Science Review* 106, no. 4 (2012): 867–82; Sarah Song, "The Boundary Problem in Democratic Theory: Why the Demos Should Be Bounded by the State," *International Theory* 4, no. 1 (2012): 39–68.

6. Caitlin Dickerson, Miriam Jordan, and Ron Nixon, "'I Want Her Back': Some Migrant Families Reunite, but Other Parents Grow Desperate," *New York Times,* July 12, 2018.

7. I am grateful to the editors for raising this possibility.

8. Trying hard itself can be an achievement if the conditions make that level of effort difficult to sustain—if, in other words, effort becomes the outcome of concern.

9. Daron Acemoglu and James Robinson, *Economic Origins of Dictatorship and Democracy* (Cambridge, UK: Cambridge University Press, 2006); Adam Przeworski, "Democracy as an Equilibrium," *Public Choice* 123, no. 3 (2005): 253–73.

10. Acemoglu and Robinson, *Economic Origins.*

11. Robert Mickey, *Paths Out of Dixie: The Democratization of Authoritarian Enclaves in America's Deep South, 1944–1972* (Princeton, NJ: Princeton University Press, 2015).

12. J. Morgan Kousser, *Colorblind Injustice: Minority Voting Rights and the Undoing of the Second Reconstruction* (Chapel Hill: University of North Carolina Press, 1999); *N.C. State Conference of the NAACP v. McCrory,* 831 F.3d 204 (4th Cir. 2016).

13. Jennifer Gandhi and Ellen Lust-Okar, "Elections under Authoritarianism," *Annual Review of Political Science* 12 (2009): 403–22; Andreas Schedler, "Electoral Authoritarianism," in *The SAGE Handbook of Comparative Politics,* eds. Todd Landman and Neil Robinson (London: SAGE Publications, 2009), 381–95.

14. Przeworski, "Minimalist Conception of Democracy."

15. Bernard Manin, Adam Przeworski, and Susan C. Stokes, *Democracy, Accountability and Representation* (Cambridge: Cambridge University Press, 1999).

16. Susan Stokes, *Mandates and Democracy: Neoliberalism by Surprise in Latin America* (New York: Cambridge University Press, 2001); Martin Gilens, "Preference Gaps and Inequality in Representation," *PS: Political Science & Politics* 42, no. 2 (2009): 335–41; Elizabeth Carlson, "Ethnic Voting and Accountability in Africa: A Choice Experiment in Uganda," *World Politics* 67, no. 2 (2015): 353–85.

17. Thomas Pepinsky, "Autocracy, Elections, and Fiscal Policy: Evidence from Malaysia," *Studies in Comparative International Development* 42,

no. 1 (2007): 136–63; Edmund Malesky and Paul Schuler, "Nodding or Needling: Analyzing Delegate Responsiveness in an Authoritarian Parliament," *American Political Science Review* 104, no. 3 (2010): 482–502; Edmund Malesky, Paul Schuler, and Anh Tran, "The Adverse Effects of Sunshine: A Field Experiment on Legislative Transparency in an Authoritarian Assembly," *American Political Science Review* 106, no. 4 (2012): 762–86.

18. Anna Stilz, "The Value of Self-Determination," in *Oxford Studies in Political Philosophy. Volume 2*, eds. David Sobel, Peter Vallentyne, and Steven Wall (Oxford: Oxford University Press, 2012).

19. By valuable I do not mean that flawed, democratic regimes are fully legitimate or authoritative—i.e., polities in which citizens are obligated to obey decisions because of the democratic nature of the procedures used to arrive at those decisions.

20. Allen W. Wood, "Coercion, Manipulation, Exploitation," in *The Free Development of Each: Studies on Freedom, Right, and Ethics in Classical German Philosophy* (Oxford: Oxford University Press, 2012), 274–303.

21. Nicholas Casey, "Venezuela Delays Presidential Vote, but Opposition Still Plans a Boycott," *New York Times*, March 1, 2018; Henri Falcón, "Why I Am Running for President of Venezuela," *New York Times*, March 16, 2018.

22. Seth Mydans, "Singapore: Damages Set in Political Case," *New York Times*, October 15, 2008.

23. Václav Havel, "The Power of the Powerless," in *The Power of the Powerless: Citizens against the State in Central-Eastern Europe*, ed. John Keane (Armonk, NY: M. E. Sharpe, 1985), 23–97.

PART II

FAILURES OF REPRESENTATION

4

REPRESENTATION FAILURE

JANE MANSBRIDGE

In the realm of aspirational ideals, failure is by definition inevitable. In democracy, an interactive cluster of such ideals, failure is multiplicatively inevitable.

Although failure to reach the aspirational goal is inevitable for each of the standards that confers democratic legitimacy on an act of coercion, our increasingly interdependent world requires a large and necessarily growing amount of legitimate coercion to survive.[1] This hard fact requires that as we strive toward the ideal we accept some "good enough" terrain on each path toward an aspirational standard. Yet we have no objective indicators telling us which spot on the path to any given ideal is good enough. That determination must vary contingently with the context, our reasons for aiming at the ideal, and the value we place on other conflicting ideals. Because democratic processes are based on a host of aspirational ideals all grounded in the near inevitability of failure, they are highly vulnerable to attack when things go wrong.

At the moment, things are going wrong in many corners of the democratic world. When trust in elected representatives plummets, governments often change unpredictably. Authoritarian versions of "democracy" are taking over in several of the newer democracies and posing threats in the United States, despite its relative democratic age. Individual political leaders increasingly claim that they represent in their persons the wants and interests of the people, because the rest of the representative system has failed them. Political actors and parties increasingly challenge the fundamental rights of liberal democracy. Reliance on referenda increases, although referenda unsupported by mediating institutions usually have deep deliberative flaws.

A moment of danger like this invites a return to first principles. An important tradition in western democracy sees giving a law to oneself as the very core of democracy. The act (not the simple state) of autonomy (auto = self, nomos = law) legitimates the coercion of the law and, arguably, makes the person who so acts a moral adult.[2] Without the philosophical trimmings, many ordinary citizens intuit the same conclusion: A law they themselves have made, ideally as a participant in a unanimous vote in a direct democracy, is the most legitimate binder of their future actions.

Failure is built into this core ideal. In a New England town meeting, where the citizens of a town form their own legislature and frequently make decisions unanimously, some citizens can sometimes be said to have given the law to themselves. But in a large polity, where representation and majority rule are necessary, the ideal of giving a law to oneself has failure in its DNA.[3] In good times, the essential failures of representation and the tensions around what is "good enough" can be taken in stride. The great majority of citizens can, rightly or wrongly, perceive even relatively bad systems as "good enough." But when sources of deep division arise – as when the economy tanks, selected groups lose visibly and severely, status losses accompany material losses, and the causes of these losses can be depicted with a human face -, then what was once thought good enough can no longer meet the demands of perceived legitimacy or bridge the underlying normative gap between the real and the ideal.

My call for a return to a first principle—giving a law to oneself—that is only rarely attainable necessitates some explanation. This chapter therefore begins with a quick foray into the contemporary ideal/non-ideal theory debate, to establish a perspective firmly on the ideal side of that debate. I argue that although giving a law to oneself fully and literally is impossible in a large-scale contemporary polity, the appropriate normative stance is to strive toward this ideal, recognizing what should be two standard caveats. First, in practice one can sometimes take only minute steps toward the ideal without compromising other valued goals. Second, in some contexts even trying to move at all directly toward an ideal will undermine the goals of the ideal itself, suggesting that one should move toward the "second best" (or plot an indirect route). Striving does not mean stupidly pushing forward on the main road when that road is beset with obstacles. The point of focusing on a first principle, I contend, is to let the ramifications of that principle penetrate deeply into our emotional and cognitive processes, allowing it to animate our invention. The goal is to try to "get it," to feel and see the human needs and aspirations behind the ideal, and to set our imaginations free to think of new and old ways to meet those needs.

Taking up this task, this chapter seeks to import the ideal of "giving a law to oneself" into the heart of both the theory and the practice of representation. This goal may seem paradoxical, because we usually cast direct democracy (giving a law to oneself in person, without representation) as the opposite of representation, defining the one by the absence of the other. But if we try to intuit the yearnings and human needs behind the ideal of giving a law to oneself, we may find ways of importing shards and intimations of that complex ideal into both our understandings of what representation should be and our practices of representation in the world. This chapter thus suggests rethinking, and by implication redesigning, representative institutions to increase the degree to which citizens may, in somewhat greater part, be said to be giving the law to themselves, with that goal interpreted not literally but through understanding its roots.

My analysis throughout aims to introduce contingency and context into decisions about when to emphasize and when to deemphasize an ideal. In some contexts, certain aspects of a democratic ideal are particularly important and thus warrant paying significant costs to approximate. In other contexts, a democratic practice comes "close enough" to an ideal to justify focusing more on other conflicting ideals or goods. In some moments and contexts, and with some practices, expanding the ways we do democracy to more closely approach its core ideals is the best way of sustaining democracy itself. In other historical moments and contexts, some attempts to expand democracy can undermine its capacity to survive. In my earlier work on small participatory democracies, I argued that trying to increase equal power beyond some feasible limits undermined the viability of the democratic enterprise itself.[4] Sustaining democracy seems particularly important today.

Assuming a goal of augmenting in representative practice both the reality and the perception among citizens that they are, in the broadest sense, giving laws to themselves, this chapter will focus on one particular means—improving the communications between constituents and their representatives.[5] The practice of representation has already taken a communicative turn. Representatives in many of the established democracies are ramping up their capacities (for better and for worse) both to influence and to learn from their constituents. Normative theory and empirical scholarship on representation need a parallel communicative turn. Without arguing that failures in communication are more important than any other failures in the realm of representation, this chapter focuses on the communicative dimension of representation in part because, although constituent-representative communication is increasingly crucial to democratic success or failure, it has been largely neglected in both the traditional and recent literature on representation. Failures in constituent-representative communication may also be somewhat remediable, perhaps even with benefits in other ideals and goods.

Along with a communicative approach, this chapter also briefly introduces a more systemic approach to thinking about representation, by including in the larger system of political representation not only legislative representation but also representation in the processes of policymaking by administrative officials and agencies and also by non-governmental ("societal") organizations. Lack of constituent-representative communication in the state administrative apparatus, and in particular the lack of explanation and justification for the many regulations we now need to govern ourselves, drives many of those subject to these regulations to despair and anger. With better communication and even involvement, those who will eventually be coerced could perhaps both help make the regulations better adapted to local conditions and come closer to seeing themselves as co-authors, at least in spirit, of the laws. So too representation in the societal sphere—through political parties, nongovernmental organizations, and the media, for example —now plays a far smaller role than it could in giving citizens productive voice, and thus some capacity to give the law to themselves, within the state's lawmaking processes.

Aspirational Ideals and the Ideal/Non-Ideal Debate

I define "aspirational" ideals as those toward which we should strive but have little or no chance of actually achieving.[6] I assume, without arguing the point here, that a large number of human ideals have this character. A moral imperative for individual agents—and, more important, for those who can affect the design of institutions—is to strive toward those ideals, all other things considered. These "other things" include other, sometimes conflicting, ideals. They include non-ideal-regarding goods. They include considerations of the "second best," in circumstances in which approximating some condition that would be good or ideal does not approximate that condition's value, and may even pull away from it.[7] Crucially, these "other things" vary by context. In the case of aspirational ideals, the statement "ought implies can" applies to striving toward the ideals, not to achieving them.[8]

In the ongoing debate regarding "ideal" and "non-ideal" theory, prompted by John Rawls's use of these words, I fall in one respect solidly in what I would call the ultra-idealist school.[9] That is, I have no problem with our setting for ourselves and striving to achieve, as much as is reasonable in any given context, ideals that in their fullness are impossible to achieve.[10] In a recent treatment of this issue on the subject of justice, David Estlund distinguishes helpfully between what he calls "proposals" and "principles." Practical proposals for actual institutions ought to be realistic; principles can be, and often are, unachievable.[11]

Estlund describes as "an oft-quoted early reference to non-ideal theory," Aristotle's comment, "the best is often unattainable, and therefore the true legislator and statesman ought to be acquainted, not only with that which is best in the abstract, but also with that which is best relative to circumstances." Estlund rejects the premise that this passage represents only non-ideal theory, pointing out that it has an ideal component as well; indeed, the ideal component is its starting point. He concludes that the passage expresses "a stereoscopic view, taking the value of understanding the unattainable best almost for granted before insisting that realistic non-ideal . . . thought is also important." Estlund's "stereoscopic" image derives from the metaphor of seeing through one eye "the way things are and have been and are becoming, and that is all," and through the other eye the ideal that can give direction.[12] In this chapter I adopt that stereoscopic view. I apply it not only to justice, the topic of almost all theorizing in this vein, but also to other ideals, in this case the ideal of giving a law to oneself.

The embrace of ideals that cannot be fully attained does not, I contend, require in any way "yearning for a world beyond politics," making "the moral prior to the political," focusing only on principles and not on institutions, forgetting that a core duty is "preventing the worst." It does not require assuming that "the motivation or capacity to act in a principled manner is pervasive among all members of a political community," that people will always deliberate rationally, or that general principles "specify right answers to practical problems." Nor does it require assuming "the total malleability of human nature," rejecting value pluralism, or ignoring conflict, power, or emotions.[13] If we distinguish between proposals and principles, I reject the claim that "principles cannot serve as standards for political life unless their implementation is feasible in the world as we know it."[14] I reject as well the idea that "taking an unattainable standard as the polestar is likely to produce, at best, the frustration of political aims, at worst, destructive distortions of politics."[15] This statement is true only if that polestar is envisioned to trump all other values.

Finally, a theory that straightforwardly admits that an ideal is impossible to achieve does not "expect too much of human beings."[16] Nor does such a theory require "full compliance."[17] On the contrary, the recognition of non-achievability provides an inherent excuse for partial compliance. Yet embracing an ideal that we know is impossible to achieve fully allows us to credit the ideal and, importantly, to investigate its underlying character while giving play to our imaginations about ways to come closer to meeting either the ideal as received from tradition, or perhaps a better conceived version of the ideal, or perhaps the ideals that we may find "behind" the ideals, the deeper ideals that animate the received ideal.[18] Such a stance toward our unachievable ideals allows them to hover around and beyond our lived experience and institutions, beckoning in worthy directions.

A COMMUNICATIVE TURN IN REPRESENTATION

Given the impossibility of direct and unanimous assent to every law, how in a large national system of political representation can citizens come closer to the ideal of giving the law to themselves? How can we change the design of representative institutions to approach that impossible goal a bit more closely? This section suggests that one feature of giving a law to oneself in a collective enterprise involves communicating one's views, being heard by other citizens and policymakers, and having what one says be adequately considered both in eventual policy and in the way that policy is expressed.[19] Reciprocal and iterative communication, or *recursive* communication, is central to this analysis. For several decades theories of legislative representation have stressed the importance of deliberation, and more recently negotiation, among the representatives.[20] But with some major exceptions,[21] democratic theorists have rarely discussed communication between the constituents and their representatives.[22]

The continuing insidious influence of the "trustee"/"delegate" distinction helps divert attention from the communicative relation between represented and representative. Possibly formulated in these terms by Heinz Eulau and colleagues in 1959,[23] this distinction derives from the two models of representation available in the eighteenth century, when recursive communication between representatives and constituents was physically almost impossible, even though the ratio of constituents to representatives was much lower then than now. Although Edmund Burke proclaimed that "it ought to be the happiness and glory of a representative to live in the strictest union, the closest correspondence, and the most unreserved communication with his constituents," in the eighteenth century neither a "trustee" nor a "delegate" was expected to communicate much with his constituents while in the capitol making law.[24] Conceptually, on the dimension of communication we have not moved significantly beyond those old models, although the technology of modern communication and transportation now makes constituent-representative contact far easier.[25] Even Nadia Urbinati's more recent "advocacy" role for representatives assumes little in the communicative dimension of the constituent-representative relation.[26]

A common theme in the major populist movements that have sprung up in Europe and the United States over the last two decades is the experience of not having been heard. In *How Democracies Die*, Steven Levitsky and Daniel Ziblatt write that the authoritarian regime in Peru in 1990 found an opening because "ordinary Peruvians" viewed the existing elites and the political establishment as "deaf to their concerns."[27] In *The Politics of Resentment*, Katherine Cramer writes of the small-town Wisconsin citizens she interviewed between 2007 and 2012 that their "animosity toward government is partly about feeling overlooked, ignored, and disrespected." As one put it, the lawmakers and others in the state capital "are just simply not listening to what the people have to say."[28] The theme is ubiquitous where populism thrives. In response, populist leaders often engage, in what Jan-Werner Müller calls "an aesthetic production of 'proximity to the people.'" Müller continues: "Victor Orbán has himself interviewed on Hungarian radio every Friday; Chávez hosted the famous show Aló Presidente, in which ordinary citizens could phone in and tell the country's leader about their worries and concerns. The country's leader would then sometimes give government members in attendance seemingly spontaneous instructions. . . . the show sometimes lasted up to six hours."[29] The production of proximity centered on listening and responding. So too "[f]or years, [Vladimir Putin] has appeared on marathon television shows to answer questions from reporters and citizens alike. Whenever a request is made for help, the government is sure to follow up with a well-reported account of a family assisted or a problem solved."[30]

Feelings of failure to be heard in the representative system have recently triggered the Pirates' Party in Europe, which rejects representation entirely, and parties like Beppe Grillo's Five Star Movement in Italy, where "the ordinary Italian can check out what is really going on through direct access to Grillo's website, provide some input online, and then also come to identify with Grillo as the only authentic representative of the Italian people. As Grillo himself explained, 'Folks, it works like this: You let me know, and I play the amplifier.'"[31]

Some citizens feel unheard because their thoughts cannot be expressed in the politics of the center:

Karlheinz Endruschat represents the Social Democrats in the struggling and ethnically mixed north of Essen, which has received disproportionate amounts of asylum seekers since 2015 compared with
the wealthier south of the city. "People care about migration, crime,
worker rights and pensions," Mr. Endruschat said. "But let's not fool
ourselves: Migration comes first." "The way the people in my district
talk about refugees, they say things for which you'd get thrown out
of the party," he said.[32]

When a populist leader "says what [the people] think," the
resulting explosion of release accounts for part of those leaders'
popularity.[33]

A second common theme in current populist rhetoric is the
experience of being disrespected. Populism includes a struggle for
recognition that arises from the perception of "social contempt."[34]
Cosmopolitan elites have contempt not only for the racism and
xenophobia of many rural and working-class citizens but also for
their presumed ignorance (French workers thinking that "Pol-
ish plumbers" will take their jobs and US workers thinking that
immigrants will take theirs, or Tea Party supporters telling their
representatives to "keep your government hands off my Medicare"[35]). That contempt, sometimes expressed in simple disregard,
can extend even to everyday culture.[36] Disregard and misunderstanding generate dismissal, with its characteristic unwillingness to
listen.

Ideally, the political representative system ought to counter,
rather than amplify, these social dynamics. Elected representatives
accountable to rural and working-class constituencies ought to
be able to communicate well with their constituents (why would
they be elected if this were not possible?) and then translate
their constituents' needs into language that representatives from
other constituencies would understand. In the aspirational ideal
of a communicative theory of representation, the representative-
constituent nexus should be a crucial node of mutual listening,
responding, listening again, asking questions, and elucidation.
At best, it should follow deliberative ideals.[37] The representative-
representative nexus should follow the same pattern. The role of
a representative as interlocutor should rest on and demonstrate
respect for the citizen. In that role the representative should be

able to hear the "things for which you'd get thrown out of the party" and communicate them both to the party and to other representatives to ensure that the representative system responded to these concerns as best it could, given normative and practical constraints. In that role the representative should also be able to explain to citizens the insights, facts, and constraints of which they are often not aware, and then to process their reactions. Such recursive communication between constituent and representative is rare in democracies today.[38]

Attentive listening and investigative questioning are more than anodyne bromides or even prescriptions for greater mutual respect. They can also produce better policy.[39] Since Mary Parker Follett first introduced the concept of "integrative" negotiation in 1925, both the theory and the empirical base of negotiation scholarship have grown increasingly sophisticated. The lesson she introduced has emerged as central: Listen for the interests behind the positions.[40] In a negotiation one's counterparts may come to the table with a position that one cannot accept, but genuinely interested questioning and close listening may reveal deeper interests that they have not fully articulated even to themselves. Inventiveness and creativity can then help uncover ways of meeting those needs that are less costly than meeting the demands originally advanced. In business these costs are usually financial. In politics, the costs may be costs in ideals. We may refuse to meet racist or xenophobic demands, for example, because our ideals make meeting such demands non-negotiable. But we may be able to find ways of responding to some of the interests behind those demands that do not require forsaking or even compromising our ideals. The parties to a negotiation may not at the outset be aware themselves of some of the interests behind the positions they are taking. Often only a repeated mutual investigation of wants and needs, introducing issues and facts that originally seemed irrelevant, can uncover some of those interests. In the aspirational ideal, representatives ought to be able to engage in this process with their constituents, then with other representatives, and then with their constituents again. In that ideal, the electoral process would select representatives for their capacities for such recursive communication.

Current representative systems incorporate major failures in representative-constituent communication. These systems generate failures in allowing constituents to be heard and taken seriously, failures in bringing constituents' insights and needs into the complex activity of making law, failures in providing the opportunity for representatives to explain the complexity of policy problems in ways the constituents can make their own, failures in creating the conditions for mutual constructive policy development, and failures, overall, to come even close to the point where citizens could rightly feel that in some small way they were giving laws to themselves, even indirectly.

Why is the act of giving the law to oneself—or some small approximation thereof—important? I have argued elsewhere that the conditions of modern interdependence, both within and among nations, create a need for many "free-use" goods—goods that, once produced, anyone can use without paying. (Toll-free roads, law and order, and common defense are the classic examples from the eighteenth century and much earlier. A stable climate, clean air, and clean water are central examples from today.) The need for free-use goods in turn creates "free-rider" (or "collective action") problems because many will not want to pay for goods that are available for free. Although some will contribute to producing the free-use goods from motives of duty or solidarity, those motives are likely to be undermined over time as citizens with weaker such motives fail to contribute. When the more public-spirited notice this failure, some will begin to feel like suckers and decrease their own contributions, "unravelling" the cooperation. Successful systems for producing free-use goods thus often rely on moral duty and solidarity as core motives but institute some coercion at the periphery to keep potential free-riders in line.[41]

The number of free-use goods we need increases steadily with increasing interdependence. In 2000, James Q. Wilson pointed out that in the 1950s, the US federal government "was limited to rather simple things—delivering mail, building highways, acquiring parks, conducting research, providing subsidies to various interests, and defending the nation." By 1991, to take only one of these functions, "we not only wanted to build more highways, we wanted to build them in ways that would aid mass transit, reduce air pollution, encourage the use of seat belts and motorcycle helmets, preserve historic sites, control erosion and outdoor advertising, use recycled rubber in making asphalt, buy iron and steel from U.S. manufacturers."[42] Wilson's conservative temperament seems to have led him implicitly to deplore this set of add-ons as wanton pandering to political activism, a source of "government overload" (a conservative phrase of the time).[43] Another reaction would be to see this list as both responding to previously unrecognized public needs for several free-use goods and recognizing the interdependence of these goods with the free-use good of a public highway system. The 1975 thesis that government overload was causing a "crisis of democracy" was correct. But Wilson's suggested response, that we should cut back on the free-use goods we ask governments to provide, was unrealistic. The conditions of highly interdependent modern life require these provisions in order to avoid important negative consequences. Constantly increasing interdependence generates a constantly increasing need for more free-use goods to regulate and facilitate that interdependence, and with each increase in the need for free-use goods the need for state coercion increases. The crisis of democracy is a crisis in finding ways to legitimate that coercion.[44]

Each democratic system today faces its own characteristic challenges in responding to the new demands of not only this ever-increasing national and international interdependence that requires ever-increasing management through state regulation, but also the increasing "post-materialist" demands of an increasingly educated citizenry and the increasing pressures in all parts of the globe from the droughts and disruption of climate change.[45]

The developing internal dynamics within various systems are also taking their toll. In the United States, extreme increases in economic inequality combined with Supreme Court interpretations preventing reform have resulted in equally extreme inequalities in the financing of political campaigns and the consequent conclusion of a substantial majority of citizens that "The rich buy elections."[46] In practice, the vast majority of US citizens are not heard, much less listened to. Controlling for the policy preferences of both the rich and interest groups, the preferences of US citizens have little to no effect on the adoption of policy.[47] At the same time, several underlying causes have produced a dramatically increased and probably long-lasting political polarization.[48] The effects of political party polarization have combined with the evolution of social media and narrowcasting, the negative rural reaction to progressive cultural changes, and the increasing tendency among post-materialist citizens to sort themselves into places of residence where others share their political views[49] to produce a polity in which voters in each party are increasingly likely to consider the other party a threat to the nation's well-being and be concerned if their children were to marry someone in that party.[50] In the veto-ridden US political system, polarization also causes debilitating inaction.

Several of these dynamics have causes specific to the United States, but other democracies have their own democracy-threatening dynamics, including widespread perceptions of political corruption that often correspond to reality,[51] the decline of political parties,[52] and an incapacity to handle current surges in refugees and immigration. In a moment when many commentators rightly worry about "How Democracies Die," "Why Our Freedom Is in Danger," the "Threat to Liberal Democracy," "The Hollowing of Western Democracy," and "Saving Democracy from Itself,"[53] the constellation of factors facing the different democracies, each with its own culture and history, differs. The overall thrust of the commentary is, however, the same: This is a moment for sustaining democracy. If enlarging democracy is an integral part of the sustaining effort, as it probably is in many instances, enlarging democracy should be doubly valued.[54] If enlarging democracy and sustaining democracy come into conflict, as they may, for example, when primaries and referenda undercut democratic effectiveness,[55] then in this historical moment significant attention should be given to sustaining democracy.

One small country has had great success in sustaining its democracy, in part by addressing the quality of representative-constituent communication in all three arenas of the representative system—legislative, administrative, and societal. In Denmark, 89 percent of the populace now say they are "very" or "fairly" satisfied with the way democracy works in their country (41% saying "very" satisfied, far higher than in any other EU country).[56] In the realm of legislative representation, the highly popular Danish "municipalization" reforms decentralized much lawmaking to the level of ninety-eight municipal regions, allowing citizens to be heard more frequently.[57] In the administrative realm, Danish agencies solicit public feedback, to the point of sending out lower-level officials with clipboards and questionnaires to ask users of services like trains about their satisfaction.[58] In the societal realm, peak associations of workers and employers give individuals a way of expressing their interests and opinions to groups they know will have a major voice in the lawmaking process.[59] Denmark's small size, relative homogeneity, and Nordic culture may make it difficult to duplicate its success elsewhere, but the larger lesson still may be that improving communication and mutual responsiveness in all arenas of the representative system could enhance both policy outcomes and the legitimacy of the democratic process.[60]

In larger countries, ongoing and recursive communication between constituents and legislative representatives has long been impossible, at least with ordinary constituents in contrast to large donors, and in a nation as large as the United States, with approximately 700,000 constituents per congressional representative. Yet even in the United States Michael Neblo and his colleagues have recently experimented with what I will call "e-townhalls" by "civic lottery," in which members of the US House of Representatives conduct one-hour conversations interactively via the Internet on important topics such as immigration or terrorism with a randomly selected group of constituents who read balanced background materials, write questions, and respond to the representatives' and other constituents' comments. The constituents, who in some cases also have the opportunity to discuss the issues among themselves before the interaction with the representative, gain in information, political interest, later activism, and satisfaction with democracy. Neblo and colleagues point out that if members of the US House of Representatives and Senate were to dedicate two hours a week, fifty-two weeks a year, to one-hour conversations on an important topic with randomly selected groups of 175 constituents (a tested and acceptable number), in six years those representatives could have interacted with one-quarter of the eligible voters in their district.[61] If such a process, now being vetted in Congress, were to become standard, most adults in the country could expect to engage in such interactive discussions at least once and possibly several times in their lifetimes. Citizens would also have friends who had recently engaged in the process and they would probably talk with one another about what happened, perhaps even preparing for what they might say if tapped (Neblo and colleagues report that participants talk about the event subsequently to an average of one and a half others[62]). Schools might prepare their students for such participation. Political groups and organizations such as unions might develop proposals for their members to put forward if a member were chosen. States and even municipalities might follow suit. If, as these institutions evolved, other institutions evolved around them for increasing the effect of citizen input, citizens might begin to feel, with some warrant, that they had come a bit closer to giving their laws to themselves.

More dramatically, we might transform the entire elected representative role so that representatives were expected to do less policymaking and more communication. Depending on the political system, the primary policymaking could be carried out by the cabinet of the parliamentary party, the administration of the executive branch, negotiation among the policy institutes of the major political parties, or the well-paid staff of the individual members of parliament or Congress. The insights of the elected representatives, in their roles as interlocutors with the people in their district, would inform that policymaking. In many democracies, this delegation of policymaking has already taken place to a great extent. Normative theory could recast the elected representative role accordingly, giving greater value to the representative as interlocutor.

Short of dramatically transforming how we conceive of the representative role, however, simply making representative-constituent communication a higher priority could lead theorists and empirical political scientists to look differently at the current components of democratic representative systems. If relatively homogeneous districts tended to promote communication between representatives and constituents, we might value them more highly despite their probable tendencies to foster extremism and lack of understanding across partisan differences. If long incumbencies allowed constituents to know their representatives' names and perhaps know other constituents who had contacted these representatives, making that process seem more possible, we might value long incumbencies more highly despite their probable tendency to dampen innovative political challenges and political activism among the citizens. In evaluating different models of representation, we might ask which models promoted the highest quality citizen-representative communication, judging that quality by deliberative standards. In toting up the pros and cons of different electoral systems, we might add to our list of criteria for judgment the capacity of these systems to foster recursive and creative communication between constituents and representatives.[63] In evaluating descriptive representation, we might focus more on how the perception of shared experience makes constituents more likely to contact a representative, the representative more likely to respond to the constituent, and each to understand the other's words.[64] In prescribing reforms for political parties, we might pay greater attention to the capacities of parties for engaging in recursive, deep, policy-oriented, and thoughtful conversations with ordinary citizens.[65]

This evaluative lens might also lead us to look more carefully at the ways political actors and parties communicate with citizens in campaigns. The 2017 campaign of Emmanuel Macron in France succeeded in part because his 5,000 or so "Grande Marche" volunteers knocked on as many as 300,000 doors, interviewing citizens and collecting more than 25,000 questionnaire answers. These interactions typically lasted only a few minutes but sometimes they were much longer, making the average of fourteen minutes per interview.[66] The questions were general: "What works in France?" "What doesn't work in France?" (for this question the top two answers were the education system and politics); "If you were to say one word about politics in France, what would it be?" "Tell us about the best/worst experience you had in the past year?" and "Can you tell us about a very concrete local initiative around you?" Macron then held three televised "town halls" on the subject, compiled the results in a 176-page document, and embedded responses in his political program. As one of the young entrepreneurs who thought up and executed this idea put it, "We want to use that to understand what is at stake in the country right now. But we also want to send a message that we are here to listen."[67]

The process did give that initial impression. Subsequently, some of the young volunteers who ran for Parliament in Macron's movement, En Marche!, became elected representatives for their district and possibly found ways of talking more than once with some of the citizens in their district. But the larger communicative effort was not itself recursive. When Macron's government passed some unpopular legislation, no one went back to any of the 25,000 interviewees to ask them how they reacted, to try to explain the legislation, or to listen to the reasons for their interlocutors' possibly negative reactions. The next move was simply a smaller version of the earlier effort, now entitled the "Grand March for Europe." For five weeks, volunteers again went door to door, asking the citizens, "What does the word Europe mean to you?" "How does Europe enrich your everyday life?," and "What do you think is going wrong in the European Union?"[68] The word "for" in the title of this new effort, however, reveals what may have been its underlying aim: to persuade rather than to listen.[69] In the end, such initially inspiring exercises may just create cynicism regarding the vehicle rather than serving as the entry point to a new communicative approach.

The many new uses of random selection (or "civic lottery") for deliberative assemblies of citizens provide another potential communicative device for connecting citizens fruitfully with the lawmaking process. Neblo and his colleagues have shown how one-hour Internet versions of these randomly selected assemblies can connect citizens with their elected representatives. Others have shown how the conclusions of longer, weekend-long assemblies can inform or even determine policy. As early as 1996, the Texas Public Utility Commission, an administrative agency, began a series of Deliberative Polls, each of more than a hundred randomly chosen citizens, to make recommendations for wind energy and conservation measures, eventually leading Texas to become the first of the fifty states in wind power. In 2006, the elected legislature of the Rome region in Italy used a Deliberative Poll to help make the difficult decision to reduce the number of hospital beds in the region. More recently, administrators in Uganda and Mongolia have used Deliberative Polls to decide on infrastructure priorities.[70] Some designs for randomly selected assemblies also make it more likely that citizens themselves suggest creative solutions to collective dilemmas.[71]

Some institutional innovations involve citizens more deeply in the representative process; others aim to substitute direct democracy for the representative process. The line between these two can sometimes become blurred, as indicated by the similarities between Michael Neblo's term "directly representative democracy" for Internet conversations between randomly chosen citizens and elected representatives, which he and his colleagues interpret as a support for representative democracy and Nadia Urbinati's term "direct representative democracy" for Beppe Grillo's web-based "virtual agora" interventions, which she interprets as a substitute for representative democracy.[72] Many innovations can play several roles. Randomly chosen citizens' assemblies, for example, can run the spectrum from those whose sole function is to advise the public to those whose decisions automatically become law, with the function of advising elected or administrative lawmakers falling in between.

The citizens who participate in these assemblies usually find them highly worthwhile. On average these citizens' subsequent political interest and participation also increase noticeably. Thinking constitutionally, citizens themselves might for good reasons choose a division of labor that in many cases placed them in an advisory rather than deciding role. Yet to provide the experience, however attenuated, of giving a law to oneself, these assemblies need some formal or strong informal tie to either the legislative or the administrative policymaking process. For the purpose of giving a law to oneself, the conclusions that a majority or supermajority of citizens reach in assembly must have arguably influential, although not necessarily dispositive, effects on policy outcomes, either through legislative or administrative representation.[73]

A SYSTEMIC APPROACH TO REPRESENTATION

In a large, complex, and interdependent society, the full system of political representation encompasses not only electoral representation but also representation in the administration of the laws, which inevitably includes lawmaking, at both the policy and the street level, and representation in the societal realm, which includes nongovernmental organizations and the media.[74] On the administrative front, earlier political theories tried to restrict the realm of lawmaking solely to the legislature.[75] This is no longer possible. Rather than denying this reality, we must face it and find ways for citizens to come closer to giving themselves the law that administrations produce.[76] On the societal front, we must also find ways for citizens to be heard, to be conscious of being heard, and to have their voices influence policy through the voluntary associations that today play such a large role in speaking for citizens.

Looking first at administrative representation, bureaucracies at both policymaking and street levels are torn among the multiple imperatives of trying to get their missions accomplished, doing so in ways that cannot be faulted for favoritism, and including many goals subsidiary to their mission that the public needs or wants.[77] Saddling administrators with the further imperative of redesigning their institutions and incentives to include more citizens' voices might be the final straw that could topple them into hopeless inefficiency. Despite these costs, however, excluding citizens' voices and ideas may have even more disastrous results.

In her study of nascent populism in the US Midwest, Katherine Cramer reports how her small-town respondents perceived the administration of the Wisconsin State Department of Natural Resources (DNR) as being out of touch with their strong concerns about hunting and fishing, even though employees of the department lived in these towns and consulted with local residents. When asked in public to agree or disagree with the standard survey question, "People like me don't have any say about what the government does," a man in a small group of loggers piped up: "A hundred percent. They don't care what we think. . . . You can go right with your DNR. They just have meetings around about, you know, the deer herd and everything else. You tell them, 'There ain't no deer around.' But they keep telling ya, 'Well, there's twelve thousand deer in Unit 6.' Well, we hunt in Unit 6. You know? . . . There aren't that many deer there. We tell them that. Oh no. 'Well, we're just gonna do what we wanna do.'"[78]

In this case many of the conditions for effective citizen-representative communication were in place. The DNR had tried to promote communication with its "meetings around." Those on whom the regulations were imposed had a chance to argue with the Department's facts and interpretations. The representatives of the public who worked for the DNR and acted as coercers were to some degree descriptively representative of those who experienced the coercion, in being generally of the same race, ethnicity, gender, and sometimes small-town background, although, crucially, their levels of education were higher than the average in the towns. The coercers and coerced were neighbors. Yet, despite these features of the administration that should have enhanced the recursive quality of its representation, this citizen perceived the central facts in counting the deer as impervious to his local knowledge. To him, the overall effect seemed a sham. Asked if people like him had a "say" in "government," this citizen thought not of the legislature but of the DNR and the issues so precious to his life. He concluded that he had no say in making some of the most important laws that affected him. Although a process that might reconcile his and the DNR's estimates of the number of deer might be too expensive in time and administrative effort to be worth instituting, that should be the communicative goal.[79]

Administrators in the United States and the European Union have worked out often elaborate processes for bringing major affected stakeholders into lawmaking and negotiating agreement on important policies—processes termed "negotiated rulemaking" (or "reg-neg") in the United States and "experimentalist governance" in the European Union.[80] Although the US process of negotiated rulemaking has not decreased the number of lawsuits,[81] it has probably made the resulting policies more responsive to the needs of the stakeholders on both sides. Some negotiations may even have resulted, as good negotiations can, in the needs of some parties being met not by the demands they originally made but by new solutions that imposed less cost on others. In the European Union, negotiation processes have been remarkably successful both in getting agreement from major stakeholders and in accustoming those stakeholders to an administrative culture that allows arguments from self-interest only as part of a larger public interest.[82] This is not "top-down technocracy" from Brussels. It is a flexible, iterative, and responsive process that proceeds experimentally and learns from its mistakes over time.[83]

One problem for democracy in these procedures, however, is that citizens below the level of the major stakeholders are not involved. This problem arises in the societal realm as much as in the administrative, with the two realms often deeply interwoven. A carpenters' union (societal) may engage in extensive deliberation and negotiation with construction companies (societal) and government experts (administrative) over the appropriate EU building code, and may even write subsidies and protections for workers or union members into that code. But without a greater interactive communicative apparatus within the union itself, the people who drive the nails into the wood never hear the arguments for the eventual regulations or have an opportunity to add their own insights to the process of making the laws that coerce them.

In some cases, a simple one-way explanation may make a great difference to the perception, if not of being heard, at least of being taken into consideration. One of my students, who came from a relatively poor East German town and had worked in the building trades before going to graduate school and rising in the EU bureaucracy, returned to his town one weekend and, over a drink with his buddies, listened to their grousing about some stupid EU building regulations. He mentioned that he had learned some of the reasons for those regulations, explained the reasons, and his friends replied with something on the order of, "Well, that makes sense. Why didn't anyone ever explain?" When a police officer stops you and gives you a ticket for speeding, it might help if he gave you a printed one-paragraph explanation of the reasons for the speed limit, perhaps comparing the number of people who die on the highways when cars travel at different speeds. When you have to wait a long time at a government agency, a printed apology and explanation on the wall for the long wait, giving the average number of clients, the number of agents, and the average time for each visit, might help you understand the pressures the agents are under and the reasons for the wait.[84] Explanations often diminish fury and may even elicit assent, in part because of the facts they impart, in part because of the respect they convey for the dignity of the individual coerced, and in part because in the best case they can usher the coerced, through imagination, down a path of seeing themselves as members of a public which, for good or at least contestable reasons, is giving this law (including the understaffing at the agency) to itself.

Two-way communication improves on one-way explanation. Citizens dissatisfied with an administrative ruling could be empowered, after collecting a certain number of signatures, to demand that an administrator meet with them to articulate the rationale for that ruling and listen to their complaints and suggestions. The more signatures, the higher could be the level of the official required to explain and listen.[85] A signature-collecting initiative process could also trigger a citizen assembly randomly selected from those affected by a proposed regulation, which could confer with the relevant administrators on the contested topic for a day, a weekend or perhaps a longer time.

Recursive communication improves on two-way communication. If genuine, it most fully brings citizens into the making of the law.

Decentralization also promotes giving the law to oneself. Consistent with the methods of "principled negotiation" used with major stakeholders, it might be possible for a superordinate legislature or agency to set a larger required goal (the principle) but allow some local discretion on how to meet that goal, as long as the local processes met reasonable democratic standards.[86] For example, if there were more than one way to protect a declining species of fish, different localities could perhaps discuss and decide on how to achieve the desired standard with whatever means best met local needs. Particularly on questions that are highly sensitive and central to the citizens' daily lives, such as jobs, driving habits, or the prized activities of hunting and fishing in the rural United States, administrative and legislative lawmakers should consider as many ways as are feasible for non-manipulatively bringing those who will be coerced into the process of making the law that affects them.[87]

Looking next at societal representation, today legislatures and administrations frequently reach out into the public sphere to consult, negotiate, and delegate authority. As representatives in the legislative and administrative realms seek greater capacity, expertise, and legitimacy in these ways, the interpenetration of legislation, administration, and societal organization deepens. Political parties are a relatively extreme example of organizations that in most democracies fall into the technically societal, nongovernmental realm, but have strong formal ties to legislative processes and are regulated by law. In neo-corporatist democracies, peak associations of labor and business negotiate mutually acceptable agreements that are then adopted as legislative or administrative law. In other democracies, administrative agencies directly delegate many powers to the societal sector. These agencies create new societal organizations, delegate powers to existing organizations, and even adopt as law on a regular basis the codes that private organizations have developed.[88] "Taken together," one set of experts concludes, "agency rulemaking and the policy decisions of private groups account for most policy-making in advanced societies."[89]

When societal organizations are directly involved in setting regulations that affect citizens' daily lives, and particularly when the regulation is likely to cause irritation and anger, it becomes especially important for both perceived and normative legitimacy to bring into the societal lawmaking process the citizens' own thoughts on whether state coercion is needed and what form it should take. To make the societal structure more open and egalitarian, a formal voucher scheme could let citizens choose which civil society organizations should represent them, giving those organizations both tax support and a guaranteed advisory role in legislation.[90] Yet even if such a system required such organizations to be internally democratic, they would probably have weak and low-quality processes of recursive communication with their constituents, particularly their less educated and less politically active constituents. The societal arena is thus unlikely to become a vehicle of egalitarian and recursive constituent-representative communication in the absence of significant reforms in almost every organization's processes. A good normative rule of thumb is that the more closely a societal organization is connected with the state, on a spectrum running from simple influence through consultation to direct delegation, the more right the public has to require that the organization's internal structure approaches some reasonable level on a set of democratic standards, including the standard of recursive communication with constituents.[91]

Shards, Threads, and Intimations

This chapter has offered several examples of how to strengthen both the perception and the reality of citizens giving the law to themselves within a representative system. I have argued that the impossibility of fully giving the law to oneself does not pose an insuperable normative problem because, although proposals should be realistic, principles need not be. For what I call "aspirational ideals"—ideals that are by definition impossible or almost impossible to reach—failure to achieve the ideal fully is built into the definition. The theorist's task then becomes understanding the possible elements in the ideal, the possible trade-offs and interactions among those elements, and the possible trade-offs and interactions between those elements and important elements of other ideals or goods. We now make sense of the ideals that people already have in their heads in somewhat inchoate form by clarifying those ideals and sometimes making suggestions for action based on those clarifications. Going forward, we might also let the cluster of aspirations and the "ideals behind the ideals" inform our evolving norms more imaginatively and indirectly. This process could allow the fundamental ideal of giving a law to oneself to emerge at various points *within* the representative system, not just in opposition to it.

In short, we can respond in several ways to the impossibility of fully giving a law to oneself in the representational system. We can try to replace the system of representation with direct democracy, following the precept, "The moment a people allows itself to be represented, it is no longer free."[92] This stance opposes representation and direct democracy. We can also try to replace parts—perhaps as many parts as possible—of the representative system with direct democracy, using instruments such as the initiative and referendum, direct primaries, and Internet mandates. This stance also opposes representation and direct democracy.[93] Or we can allow some of the "spirit" of the fundamental ideal—its shards, its threads, and its intimations—to inform both our ideals and our practices of representation. This stance is complementary to representation and intended to strengthen it.

Why "shards, threads, and intimations"? Autonomy is usually contrasted to heteronomy, that is, rule by one or more others. But the institution of political representation is not only rule by others. It centrally incorporates acts of citizen autonomy, most prominently the citizen's original vote for the representative and the later vote to maintain or replace that representative. In some moments, such as when the threat of sanction looms largest, those acts of citizen autonomy enter the representative's world violently, like shards of glass in an explosion. Scattered throughout the representative system, the shards of autonomy remind both representatives and citizens of the citizens' power. In other moments, such as when representatives meet and perhaps even discuss issues with their constituents, their mutual communications stitch the representatives' and citizens' worlds together in a strong fabric of delegated responsibility that could otherwise easily be torn apart. To see those threads, you may need to give the fabric a close, hard look. In still other moments the autonomy of citizens subtly informs, through hints and suggestion, the words the representative speaks and the thoughts the representative thinks, through motives on the representative's part that range from simple identity of interests and opinions with constituents through emotional solidarity and cognitive duty to the prudential anticipation of electoral sanctions. In this complex field, where the experience of being ruled in the representative process is riddled with the shards, threads, and intimations of the citizen's own autonomy, recursive communication between citizens and their representatives strengthens that autonomy and gives it life.

NOTES

1. See Jane Mansbridge, "What Is Political Science For?" *Perspectives on Politics* 12, no. 1 (2014): 8–17. See below, "A Communicative Turn," on the need for increasing state coercion and the corresponding increasing need to legitimate that coercion. As noted later, I define an "aspirational" ideal stipulatively as embodying inevitable or almost inevitable failure. For simplicity, in these sentences I use the word "inevitable" to mean "inevitable or almost inevitable." It is easiest analytically to assume inevitable failure on all the standards, although failure might not be quite inevitable, just extremely likely, for any given standard. In the context of representation, failure *is* inevitable (not just "almost" inevitable) on the standard on which I focus here, giving a law to oneself.

2. Jean Jacques Rousseau, *The Social Contract*, trans. Victor Gourevitch (Cambridge: Cambridge University Press, [1762] 1997), esp. Book I ch. 8, and Immanuel Kant, *Groundwork of the Metaphysics of Morals*, trans. Mary J. Gregor (New York: Cambridge University Press, [1785] 1998).

3. For a parallel, see the large literature on consent, especially A. John Simmons, *Moral Principles and Political Obligation* (Princeton, NJ: Princeton University Press, 1979). This literature tends to see consent as the sole source of democratic legitimacy; I argue for plural ideals in democracy and thus plural sources of legitimacy (e.g., Mansbridge, "What Is Political Science For?"). This chapter examines beyond consent the single, more stringent ideal of giving a law to oneself.

4. Jane Mansbridge, *Beyond Adversary Democracy* (New York: Basic Books, 1980), as discussed in Melissa Williams, "An Interview with Jane Mansbridge," in *Jane Mansbridge: Participation, Deliberation, Coercion* (New York: Routledge, 2018), on the goal of uncovering "the ideals behind the ideal" in order to approach those ideals more closely.

5. This chapter thus expands on earlier analyses in Jane Mansbridge, *Recursive Representation in the Representative System* (Harvard Kennedy School Working Paper No. RWP17–045, 2017), https://ssrn.com, and Jane Man-

sbridge, "Recursive Representation," in *Creating Political Presence: The New Politics of Democratic Representation*, eds. Dario Castiglione and Johannes Pollak (Chicago: University of Chicago Press, 2018). Both recursive communication and the larger ideal of giving a law to oneself are components in a concept of democratic legitimacy that is plural and non-dichotomous (see Mansbridge, "What Is Political Science For?").

6. See Kant on regulative ideals. Jane Mansbridge with James Bohman, Simone Chambers, David Estlund, Andreas Follesdal, Archon Fung, Cristina Lafont, Bernard Manin, and José Luis Martí, "The Place of Self-Interest and the Role of Power in Deliberative Democracy," *Journal of Political Philosophy* 18, no. 1 (2010): 65n3. I use the term "aspirational" to mean "unattainable or almost unattainable" only because it is more easily grasped in English than "regulative." The term "aspirational," however, has two significant drawbacks. First, all ideals are strictly speaking aspirational; we aspire toward both attainable and unattainable ideals. Second, and even more deeply problematic, to "aspire" in common usage means to "have a fixed desire, longing, or ambition for something *at present* above one" (*Oxford English Dictionary*, emphasis mine). That usage assumes an attainable goal. For these reasons, David Estlund, who coined the term "aspirational theory," *Democratic Authority* (Princeton, NJ: Princeton University Press, 2008, especially ch. 14), has begun to use the term "non-concessive" instead [see David Estlund, *Utopophobia; On the Limits (If Any) of Political Philosophy* (Princeton, NJ: Princeton University Press, 2020)]. For greater ease in reading I will continue to use the otherwise unsatisfactory term "aspirational" with the explicit stipulation that "aspirational" ideals as I define them are those that cannot be achieved, or are not likely to be achieved, in practice.

7. I thank David Estlund for this formulation. For the concept of "second best," see, inter alia, Richard Lipsey and Kelvin Lancaster, "The General Theory of Second Best," *Review of Economic Studies* 24, no. 1 (1956): 11–32; Robert Goodin, "Political Ideals and Political Practice," *British Journal of Political Science* 25, no. 1 (1995): 54; Estlund, *Democratic Authority*; Mansbridge et al., "The Place of Self-Interest"; and David Wiens, "Assessing Ideal Theories: Lessons from the Theory of Second Best," *Politics, Philosophy & Economics* 15, no. 2 (2016): 132–49 (although I do not accept Wiens's strong version of the theorem. because I am not concerned with "realizing" the ideal). I adopt what Wiens (2015) calls an "evaluative" view of ideals rather than a "benchmark" or "target" view. David Wiens, "Against Ideal Guidance," *Journal of Politics* 77, no. 2 (2015): 433–46.

8. I take this useful point on "ought implies can" from Estlund, personal communication.

9. I describe my position as "ultra-idealist" because I do not hesitate to recommend unachievable goals as ideals. Estlund, in the "idealist" camp,

takes a more cautious approach in his discussion of justice, focusing on standards the achievement of which is required and which therefore (allowing for "ought implies can") would have to be achievable. Nothing in Estlund's account rules out the possibility of ideals in my sense, which encompasses the problem of the "second best."

10. For example, consider Christ's injunction, "Be perfect as thy heavenly father is perfect" (Matthew 5:48). This choice of words makes the impossibility of the command absolutely clear. It would be sacrilegious to strive in this direction with the expectation of actually achieving the goal, because then one would expect to achieve being like God, and only God can be like God. We therefore know in this case that we *ought* never to expect to achieve the goal.

11. Estlund, *Utopophobia*, 10–11.

12. Ibid., xi–xii.

13. These statements and propositions all appear in William Galston, "Realism in Political Theory," *European Journal of Political Theory* 9, no. 4 (2010): 387–96, with references to several other theorists (e.g., on p. 387 he cites Bernard Williams, *In the Beginning Was the Deed: Realism and Moralism in Political Argument* [Princeton, NJ: Princeton University Press, 2005], 1–3 for "the moral prior to the political"). On the question of human nature, I assume non-pathology and thus a capacity to handle emotionally and rationally an ideal that is impossible to reach in its fullness. Not everyone has this capacity. Obsessive Compulsive Personality Disorder (OCPD) consists in general of "a preoccupation with orderliness, perfectionism, and mental and interpersonal control, at the expense of flexibility, openness, and efficiency." See Douglas Samuel and Thomas Widiger, "Conscientiousness and Obsessive-Compulsive Personality Disorder," *Personality Disorders: Theory, Research, and Treatment* 2, no. 3 (2011): 3. One form of OCPD, excessive "conscientiousness" in the moral realm, sometimes identified as "scrupulosity," is a particular "pathological guilt or obsession associated with moral or religious issues that is often accompanied by compulsive moral or religious observance and is highly distressing and maladaptive" (Chris Miller and Dawson Hedges, "Scrupulosity Disorder: An Overview and Introductory Analysis," *Journal of Anxiety Disorders* 22, no. 6 [2008]: 1042–58). The open-ended quality of an ideal that is impossible to attain in all its fullness might tempt overly scrupulous individuals or designers of institutions to over-reach in interpreting it. I see this as a failure in interpretation, not a failure in the casting of the ideal.

14. Galston, "Realism in Political Theory," 395.

15. Ibid.

16. Ibid., 401.

17. Full compliance is a feature of Rawls's ideal theory, not mine. See Valentini for a typology of forms of ideal theory (of which mine is the second, "Utopian," vs. "realist" theory) and for the sensible conclusion that "in situations of partial compliance, individuals ought to do what is *reasonably* within their power to respond to existing" infractions of the ideal, with "what counts as reasonable" depending on "the situation at hand" and the remaining crucial task being "to flesh out more concretely what the 'reasonableness' constraint amounts to" (Laura Valentini, "Ideal vs. Non-Ideal Theory: A Conceptual Map," *Philosophy Compass* 7, no. 9 [2012]: 654–64, emphasis in original).

18. For a recent claim regarding better conceived ideals, see the list of "first generation" and "second generation" deliberative ideals in André Bächtiger, John Dryzek, Jane Mansbridge, and Mark Warren, "Introduction," in *Oxford Handbook of Deliberative Democracy*, eds. André Bächtiger, John Dryzek, Jane Mansbridge, and Mark Warren (Oxford: Oxford University Press, 2018), based on Jane Mansbridge, "A Minimalist Definition of Deliberation," in *Deliberation and Development*, eds. Patrick Heller and Vijayendra Rao (Washington, DC: World Bank, 2015): 27–49. For "ideals behind the ideal," see note 4 above.

19. This is not Rousseau's view, as he opposed communication before the vote to prevent the emergence of factions and other ills (see Bernard Manin, "On Legitimacy and Political Deliberation," trans. Ellie Stein and Jane Mansbridge, *Political Theory* 15 no. 3 [1987]: 338–668). Independent judgment is also essential for the epistemic accuracy of the Condorcet Jury Theorem (CJT), in which the accuracy of the average estimate increases with the number of estimates of independent observers, each with a probability of more than .5 of being right. Independence may or may not require non-communication. See Hélène Landemore, *Democratic Reason: Politics, Collective Intelligence, and the Rule of the Many* (Princeton, NJ: Princeton University Press, 2013).

20. For deliberation, Joseph M. Bessette, *The Mild Voice of Reason: Deliberative Democracy and American National Government* (Chicago: University of Chicago Press, 1994); Amy Gutmann and Dennis Thompson, *Democracy and Disagreement* (Cambridge, MA: Harvard University Press 1996); for negotiation, Mark Warren and Jane Mansbridge, "Deliberative Negotiation," in *Political Negotiation*, eds. Jane Mansbridge and Cathy Jo Martin (Washington, DC: Brookings, [2013] 2016: 141–97).

21. See David Plotke, "Representation is Democracy," *Constellations* 4, no. 1 (1997): 19–34; Melissa S. Williams, *Voice, Trust, and Memory: Marginalized Groups and the Failings of Liberal Representation* (Princeton, NJ: Princeton University Press, 1998); Michael A. Neblo, Kevin M. Esterling, and David M. J. Lazer, *Politics with the People: Building a Directly Representative De-*

mocracy (Cambridge: Cambridge University Press, 2018); Mark E. Warren, "How Representation Enables Democratic Citizenship," in *Creating Political Presence: The New Politics of Democratic Representation,* eds. Dario Castiglione and Johannes Pollak (Chicago: University of Chicago Press, 2018).

22. Many deliberative theorists (excluding those in note 21) have the same failing. Rosanvallon notes that "Deliberative democratic theorists . . . have not paid much attention to exchanges between leaders [representatives] and citizens"; see Pierre Rosanvallon, *Democratic Legitimacy: Impartiality, Reflexivity, Proximity* (Princeton, NJ: Princeton University Press, [2008] 2011), 209. Rosanvallon's "interactive democracy," however, differs in many respects from the vision advanced here, in part by focusing on resistance and the "counterdemocratic" modes of "surveillance, veto, and judgment"; see also Pierre Rosanvallon, *Counter-Democracy: Politics in an Age of Distrust* (Cambridge: Cambridge University Press, [2006] 2008). For the contrast between a democracy of action and resistance, see Mansbridge, "What Is Political Science For?."

23. Coding legislators' answers to their open-ended question, "How would you describe the job of being a legislator—what are the most important things you should do here?" Eulau et al. placed most legislators (63%) in their category of "Trustee," only 14% in their category of "Delegate," and could not categorize the other 23% as either (see Heinz Eulau, John C. Wahlke, William Buchanan, and Leroy C. Ferguson, "The Role of the Representative: Some Empirical Observations on the Theory of Edmund Burke," *American Political Science Review* 53, no. 3 [1959]: 742–56). Burke's 1774 "Speech to the Electors of Bristol" did not use either term (see Edmund Burke, "Speech to the Electors of Bristol," in *The Works of the Right Honorable Edmund Burke, Vol. 2* [Boston: Little Brown, (1774)1889]. Pitkin, using different terms, made the "Mandate-Independence Controversy" central to her analysis, attempting in her concluding chapter to manage the issue with the formula that representing "means acting in the interests of the represented, in a manner responsive to them" (see Hanna Pitkin, *The Concept of Representation* [Berkeley: University of California Press, 1967], 209).

24. Burke, "Speech to the Electors of Bristol." The widespread early acceptance of the "principle of distinction" (Bernard Manin, *Principles of Representative Government* [Cambridge: Cambridge University Press, 1997]) primarily based on the imperative to "obtain for rulers men who possess most wisdom to discern, and most virtue to pursue, the common good of the society" [see James Madison, "Federalist 57," in *The Federalist Papers,* ed. Isaac Kramnick (New York: Penguin, [1788]1987)], also in small part reflects the difficulty of recursive constituent-representative communication.

25. In addition to Internet connection, ease of travel makes return to the constituencies more possible. In the United States, for example, the Republican leader Newt Gingrich after 1994 strongly urged the Republican representatives in Congress to return to their districts from Thursday to Tuesday and strongly disapproved of representatives moving their families to Washington (see Thomas E. Mann and Norman J. Ornstein, *It's Even Worse Than It Looks: How the American Constitutional System Collided with the New Politics of Extremism* [New York: Basis Books, (2012) 2013), 40]. Without structural changes in the rest of Congress to allocate policymaking to a semi-permanent and well-paid professional staff, the move to a three-day workweek with no families in Washington deeply undercuts the collegial interactions that in a past era helped facilitate bipartisan legislation.

26. See Nadia Urbinati, *Representative Democracy: Principles and Genealogy* (Chicago: University of Chicago Press, 2006). My goals and methods, however, are similar to Urbinati's intention to "understand those forms of *indirect* political presence that make contemporary government democratic" (3; also 5) and her non-opposition of direct and representative democracy. Nadia Urbinati, "A Revolt against Intermediary Bodies" *Constellations* 22, no. 4 (2015): 477–86, addresses new forms of constituent-representative interaction that she finds wanting, a move that opens the door to the application of deliberative standards to the quality of constituent-representative communication in different contexts, an empirically and normatively underexplored field. See Dawood (this volume) on context and Fuerstein (this volume) for the need to specify both the "norms and virtues that govern successful communication" and the structures that can support those norms and virtues. See also Vicki Jackson, "Pro-Constitutional Representation: Comparing the Role Obligations of Judges and Elected Representatives in Constitutional Democracy," *William & Mary Law Review* 57, no. 5 (2015): 1717–88, on the representative's duty "to listen, to respond, and to provide information" (1761) and the norm of "being in a conversation with constituents in which appropriate and better views are worked out" (1765).

27. Steven Levitsky and Daniel Ziblatt, *How Democracies Die* (New York: Crown/Penguin Random House, 2018), 72.

28. Katherine J. Cramer, *The Politics of Resentment: Rural Consciousness in Wisconsin and the Rise of Scott Walker* (Chicago: University of Chicago Press, 2016), 40, 52.

29. Jan-Werner Müller, *What Is Populism?* (Philadelphia: University of Pennsylvania Press, 2016), 43.

30. Madeleine Albright, with Bill Woodward, *Fascism: A Warning* (New York: Harper Collins, 2018), 160.

31. Müller, *What Is Populism?*, 35.

32. Katrin Bennhold, "A New Coalition with Merkel? Not So Fast," *New York Times*, January 19, 2018, www.nytimes.com.

33. "We say what you think" or similar words appear as slogans on the populist right in, e.g., Austria, Belgium, the Netherlands, and France. See Anna-Lena Lodenius, *Vi säger vad du tänker: högerpopulismen i Europa* (Stockholm: Atlas, 2015).

34. See Axel Honneth, *The Struggle for Recognition: The Moral Grammar of Social Conflicts* (Cambridge, MA: MIT Press, [1992] 1995). I am aware that Honneth did not have the populists in mind. Nor did Charles Taylor, "The Politics of Recognition," in *Multiculturalism: Examining the Politics of Recognition*, ed. Amy Gutmann (Princeton, NJ: Princeton University Press, 1992), 25–73, and Nancy Fraser, "From Redistribution to Recognition? Dilemmas of Justice in a 'Post-Socialist' Age," *New Left Review* I/212, July–August (1995).

35. This statement, made only once, has acquired legendary status. The single incident was reported in 2009 when a *Washington Post* writer quoted Representative Robert Inglis, a Republican from South Carolina, saying that at a "town-hall meeting" in the suburban town of Simpsonville, a man had told him to "keep your government hands off my Medicare." As Inglis told the story, "I had to politely explain that, 'Actually, sir, your health care is being provided by the government.' But he wasn't having any of it" (see Philip Rucker, "Sen. DeMint of S.C. Is Voice of Opposition to Health-Care Reform," *Washington Post*, 2009).

36. For a possible example of the subtle relationship between disregard and disrespect, in the United States many of the cosmopolitan elite rarely frequent the country's nine most popular restaurants. See the "Bubble Quiz" in Charles Murray, *Coming Apart: The State of White America 1960–2000* (New York: Crown Forum and Random House, [2012] 2013). Although Murray's test stresses only ignorance, one might read some slight lack of respect into that simple disregard. In any case, ignorance often generates inattention. See Cramer, *The Politics of Resentment*, 66, 71, 224, and citations on those pages. In Wisconsin, given the survey question, "How much *attention* do you feel the state government in Wisconsin pays to what *the people in your community think* when it decides what to do?," 70 percent of the non-metropolitan residents responded, "*only a small amount*" or "*none at all*" (105, emphasis mine).

37. One could perhaps imagine instances of constituent-representative communication that departed from deliberative ideals (for example, by reinforcing highly partisan information flows that would not meet the criteria for good reason-giving in deliberation), but in doing so nevertheless enhanced the deliberative quality of the entire deliberative system by

introducing new information and perspectives. The logic would follow that of the systemic justification for distorted and disrespectful enclave deliberation. See Jane Mansbridge, James Bohman, Simone Chambers, Thomas Christiano, Archon Fung, John Parkinson, Dennis Thompson, and Mark Warren, "A Systemic Approach to Democratic Deliberation," in *Deliberative Systems*, eds. John Parkinson and Jane Mansbridge (Cambridge: Cambridge University Press, 2012), 1–26. Yet these rare instances could be justified only by generating greater overall benefits than costs for the deliberative system as a whole (including the costs in the future of modeling such behavior). I thank Dawood, whose comment (this volume) encouraged me to begin to think through this issue.

38. For the United States, see Jane Mansbridge, "Rethinking Representation," *American Political Science Review* 97, no. 4 (2003): 520, citing William Bianco, *Trust: Representatives and Constituents* (Ann Arbor: University of Michigan Press, 1994), 50, and John Kingdon, *Congressmen's Voting Decisions* (New York: Harper Collins, 1981), 48, e.g., quoting one congressional representative on his support for a bill he considered bad public policy: "Very frankly, if I had a chance to sit down with all of my constituents for 15 minutes and talk to them, I'd have voted against the whole thing. But I didn't have that chance. They wanted [x]. If I voted against it, it would appear to them that I was against [x], and I wouldn't have had a chance to explain myself). Note the member's use of "talk *to*," not "talk *with*."

39. See Landemore, *Democratic Reason*, and Hélène Landemore, *Open Democracy: Reinventing Popular Rule for the 21st Century*, forthcoming, for evidence that, leaving negotiation aside, the incorporation of different points of view into a decision generally improves the quality of that decision.

40. Mary Parker Follett, "Constructive Conflict," in *Dynamic Administration: The Collected Papers of Mary Parker Follett*, eds. Henry C. Metcalf and L. Urwick (New York: Harper, [1925] 1942); Richard E. Walton and Robert McKersie, *A Behavioral Theory of Labor Negotiations: An Analysis of a Social Interaction System* (Ithaca, NY: ILR Press, 1965), 129; Roger Fisher, William Ury, and B. Patton, *Getting to Yes: Negotiating Agreement without Giving In*, 2nd ed. (New York: Penguin, 1991), 41–42.

41. Mansbridge, "What Is Political Science For?", "Recursive Representation," and, for the moral core/coercive periphery model, "A 'Moral Core' Solution to the Prisoners' Dilemma," in *Schools of Thought: Twenty-five Years of Interpretive Social Science*, eds. Joan W. Scott and Debra Keates (Princeton, NJ: Princeton University Press, 2001), 330–47. I use the term "free-use" goods because the economists' term "public goods" includes the component of non-rivalry, which is irrelevant to the logic I want to tap, and "non-excludable" is technically incorrect (Mansbridge, "What Is Political Science For?," 14, n.3).

42. James Q. Wilson, *Bureaucracy: What Government Agencies Do and Why They do It,* 2nd ed. (New York: Basic Books, [1989] 2000), xiv–xv.

43. Michel Crozier, Samuel P. Huntington, and Joji Watanuki, *The Crisis of Democracy: On the Governability of Democracies* (New York: New York University Press, 1975).

44. See Mansbridge, "What Is Political Science For?" and "Recursive Representation" for a fuller argument.

45. Ronald Inglehart, *Culture Shift in Advanced Society* (Princeton, NJ: Princeton University Press, 1990) and Pippa Norris and Ronald Inglehart, *Cultural Backlash: Trump, Brexit, and the Rise of Authoritarian Populism* (Cambridge: Cambridge University Press, 2018) for postmaterialism; see also Rosanvallon, *Democratic Legitimacy,* 11, for "heightened citizen demands," especially demands for "particularity," the desire to be treated as specific individuals, and the demand for "proximity" that a desire for particularity creates. Rosanvallon writes that "citizens . . . increasingly . . . want to be listened to and reckoned with. They want their views to be taken into account" (171). They want representatives who "are accessible, receptive and open . . . [who] react to what they hear and are willing to explain their decisions" (171). He further links what he perceives as a relatively new desire to be heard in the making of the law, in which desire I include the demand for a "politics of presence," to other desires for empathy, compassion, caring, special individual attention, and "the display of concern" (200), subtly implying in these possibly empirically linked desires a kind of weakness, infantilism, or perhaps even lack of virility. One could, by contrast, see these constituent desires as basic, and a representative's empathy, compassion, caring, individual attention, and concern (not just in display but in actuality) as components of a good communicative relationship that would allow the representative to hear what the constituent both said and meant.

46. In 2012, 67 percent of those polled in the United States said they believed that "Rich people buy elections," compared to 17 percent in Germany (American National Election Study [2012], www.electionstudies.org; World Values Survey [2013], www.worldvaluessurvey.org). For inequalities in campaign financing, see Lawrence Lessig, *Republic, Lost: How Money Corrupts Congress and a Plan to End It* (New York: Twelve/Hachette Book Group, 2011); Thomas E. Mann and Norman J. Ornstein, *It's Even Worse Than It Looks: How the American Constitutional System Collided with the New Politics of Extremism* (New York: Basis Books, [2012] 2013).

47. Martin Gilens and Benjamin I. Page, "Testing Theories of American Politics: Elites, Interest Groups, and Average Citizens," *Perspectives on Politics* 12, no. 3 (2014): 572.

48. The three major structural causes of polarization in the United States since 1980 are the increasing homogeneity in the political parties

after President Johnson signed the Civil Rights Act in 1964 and southern conservatives gradually left the Democratic Party (see Michael Barber and Nolan McCarthy, "Causes and Consequences of Polarization," in *Political Negotiation*, eds. Jane Mansbridge and Cathy Jo Martin [Washington, DC: Brookings, 2015]); the increasing competitiveness of the two parties after the Republican rise in 1980, making competition for majority control of Congress increasingly cutthroat (see Frances E. Lee, *Insecure Majorities: Congress and the Perpetual Campaign* [Chicago: University of Chicago Press, 2016] pointing out that the period of "bi-partisanship" from 1940 to 1980 was actually one of Democratic Party hegemony); and the steeply increasing economic inequality after 1980, giving the rich greater capacity to block inequality-reducing legislation (see Nolan McCarty, Keith T. Poole, and Howard Rosenthal, *Polarized America: The Dance of Ideology and Equal Riches*, 2nd ed. [Cambridge, MA: MIT Press, 2006], pointing out that the "dance" of causal interaction between inequality and polarization is complex and not fully understood).

49. On sorting, see, e.g., Bill Bishop, with Robert G. Cushing, *The Big Sort: Why the Clustering of Like-Minded America Is Tearing Us Apart* (Boston: Houghton Mifflin, 2008).

50. Pew Research Center, "Partisanship and Political Animosity in 2016 (June 2016), 5, comparing 17%/16% of Republicans/Democrats feeling "very unfavorable" to the opposite party in 1994 to 58%/55% in 2016. Within a shorter time, conclusions that "The [other] party's policies are so misguided that they threaten the nation's well-being" rose from 37%/31% in 2014 to 45%/41% in 2016. See Shanto Iyengar, Gaurav Sood, and Yphtach Lelkes, "Affect, Not Ideology: A Social Identity Perspective on Polarization," *Public Opinion Quarterly* 76, no. 3 (2012): 405–31 and Lynn Vavrek, "A Measure of Identity: Are You Wedded to Your Party?" *New York Times*, January 31, 2017.

51. Alina Mungio-Pippidi, *The Quest for Good Governance: How Societies Develop Control of Corruption* (Cambridge: Cambridge University Press, 2015) and Bo Rothstein and Aiysha Varraich, *Making Sense of Corruption* (Cambridge: Cambridge University Press, 2017).

52. Peter Mair, *Ruling the Void: The Hollowing of Western Democracy* (New York: Verso, 2013).

53. From the titles or subtitles, respectively, of Levitsky and Ziblatt, *How Democracies Die*; Yascha Mounk, *The People vs. Democracy: Why Our Freedom is in Danger and How to Save It* (Cambridge, MA: Harvard University Press, 2018); Galston, "Realism in Political Theory"; Mair, *Ruling the Void*; and Frances Rosenbluth and Ian Shapiro, *Responsible Parties: Saving Democracy from Itself* (New Haven, CT: Yale University Press, 2018).

54. See examples in, e.g., Landemore, *Open Democracy*.

55. See, e.g., the arguments in Rosenbluth and Shapiro, *Responsible Parties*. For how referenda may be designed or supplemented to become more deliberative, see Benjamin Barber, *Strong Democracy: Participatory Politics for a New Age* (Berkeley: University of California Press, 1984), John Gastil, *By Popular Demand: Revitalizing Representative Democracy Through Deliberative Elections* (Berkeley: University of California Press, 2000), and Mansbridge, *Recursive Representation in the Representative System.*

56. Eurobarometer, March 2018, http://ec.europa.eu/.

57. Quinton Mayne, *States of Satisfaction* (unpublished manuscript).

58. Mark Warren, personal communication from experience.

59. Cathie Jo Martin and Duane Swank, *The Construction of Business Interests: Coordination, Growth, and Equality* (Cambridge: Cambridge University Press, 2012).

60. See Landemore, *Democratic Reason* and *Open Democracy* on the policy outcomes.

61. Neblo, personal communication. Fewer interactions and smaller groups would reduce this percentage, but the overall effect could still be considerable.

62. William Minozzi, Michael A. Neblo, Kevin M. Esterling, and David M. J. Lazer, "Field Experiment Evidence of Substantive, Attributional, and Behavioral Persuasion by Members of Congress in Online Town Halls," *PNAS* 112, no. 13 (2015): 3937–42. Some of the direct recipients of these communications undoubtedly mentioned the process to others, creating further communicative waves.

63. Currently most empirical analyses of issues such as district composition, incumbency, and electoral systems omit the variable of constituent-representative communication. When they include it, it usually takes the form only of "constituency service," the current reigning form of representative-constituent connection (see, e.g., Pippa Norris, "Choosing Electoral Systems: Proportional, Majoritarian and Mixed Systems," *International Political Science Review* 18, no. 3 (1997): 297–312, comparing electoral systems). The book-length treatment of electoral systems in David M. Farrell, *Comparing Electoral Systems* (Hemel Hempstead: Prentice Hall/Harvester Wheatsheaf, 1997) is a partial exception, but it includes only four mentions of this connection: In "First Past the Post" (or Single Member Plurality) systems, "Each voter has a constituency MP who can be approached" (13). In 1997 Britain "constituency contact with MPs is significant and increasing" (29) and "The problem with national-level representation is that it reduces the contact between representatives and voters" (69). In the Single Transferable Vote (STV) system in Ireland, "Parliamentarians work their 'parish pumps,' attracting votes by a heavy emphasis on constituency social work and localist concerns" (132). To my

knowledge none of the work on the deliberative quality of representatives' interactions (e.g., Jürg Steiner, André Bächtiger, Markus Spörndli, and Marco R. Steenbergen, *Deliberative Politics in Action: Analyzing Parliamentary Discourse* [Cambridge: Cambridge University Press, 2004]) has been applied to the quality of constituent-representative communication. Future research could bring the standards developed for deliberative democracy to bear on the quality of that communication (see Dawood and Fuerstein, both in this volume).

64. See Williams, *Voice, Trust, and Memory*, for an important early analysis of the communicative dimension of descriptive representation. For contact, see Claudine Gay, "The Effect of Black Congressional Representation on Political Participation," *American Political Science Review* 95, no. 3 (2001): 589–602; Jane Mansbridge, "Should Blacks Represent Blacks and Women Represent Women? A Contingent 'Yes,'" *Journal of Politics* 61, no. 3 (1999): 627–57; David E. Broockman, "Black Politicians Are More Intrinsically Motivated to Advance Blacks' Interests: A Field Experiment Manipulating Political Incentives," *American Journal of Political Science* 57, no. 3 (2013): 521–36.

65. This dimension of the role of parties does not play a significant role in Mair, *Ruling the Void*; Nancy L. Rosenblum, *Membership and Morals: The Personal Uses of Pluralism in America* (Princeton, NJ: Princeton University Press, 1998) or Jonathan White and Lea Ypi, *The Meaning of Partisanship* (Oxford: Oxford University Press, 2016).

66. Emily Schultheis, "Can a French Political Upstart Ride Obama's Strategy to Victory?" April 21, 2017, www.theatlantic.com.

67. Chris O'Brien, "Meet the presidential candidate who's using the internet to reinvent French politics," *Venture Beat* online, last modified January 8, 2017, https://venturebeat.com.

68. Julia Amalia Heyer, "En Marche One Year On: How Macron's Movement Is Transforming French Politics," *Der Spiegel*, April 7, 2018, www.spiegel.de.

69. As one reporter put it, presumably echoing what the organizers had told her: "The action is designed to let people know what Europe can do for them" (Lisa Louis, "Emmanuel Macron: 'En Marche' to Brussels?," *Deutsche Welle*, April 17, 2018, www.dw.com).

70. For Texas and Rome, see James S. Fishkin, *When the People Speak: Deliberative Democracy and Public Consultation* (New York: Oxford University Press, 2009), 150–153. For Uganda and Mongolia, see James Fishkin, *Democracy When the People Are Thinking* (Oxford: Oxford University Press, 2018). Mongolia even passed a law requiring Deliberative Polling as one step in the procedure for constitutional amendments, projects funded by local development funds, and planning in cities and settlement areas

(100). For examples of empowered citizens' assemblies chosen by lot, see Yves Sintomer, *Petite histoire de l'expérimentation démocratique. Tirage au sort et politique d'Athènes à nos jours* (Paris: La Découverte, 2011) and John Gastil and Eric Olin Wright, *Legislation by Lot: Transformative Designs for Deliberative Governance* (London: Verso, 2019).

71. E.g., the 2018 Citizens Assembly on Brexit brought together fifty randomly selected citizens, representative of the nation in demographics and opinions on Brexit, for two sessions, the first primarily informational and the second, three weeks later, deliberative. From one of the expert speakers in the first session some participants were "interested to learn" that the UK government had made little attempt to remove EU residents who did not have a right to remain in Britain. Their feedback led the organizers to present in the second session an option they had previously not considered, namely, "Maintain free movement of labour [between the UK and EU], but make full use of available controls to prevent abuse of the system." That new option garnered the support of a majority of the participants at the end of the final deliberative session (Alan Renwick et al., *Report of the Citizens Assembly on Brexit* [UCL Constitution Unit, 2017], https://citizensassembly.co.uk, describing the emergence of "Option B"). Although this assembly was commissioned by neither a legislative nor an administrative body, its design, leading to an option that neither the government nor the organization sponsoring the assembly had previously offered, provided a greater opportunity than usual for citizens to move closer to giving a law to themselves.

72. Neblo et al., *Politics with the People*; Nadia Urbinati, "A Revolt against Intermediary Bodies," *Constellations* 22, no. 4 (2015): 477–86.

73. See Cristina Lafont, "Can Democracy Be Deliberative and Participatory? The Democratic Case for Political Uses of Minipublics," *Daedalus* 146, no. 3 (2017): 85–105 for reasons why citizens not chosen for such assemblies might not feel adequately represented; Genevieve Fuji Johnson, *Democratic Illusion: Deliberative Democracy in Canadian Public Policy* (Toronto: University of Toronto Press, 2015) on assemblies that have no visible effect on policy; and Sherry R. Arnstein, "A Ladder of Citizen Participation," *Journal of the American Planning Association* 35, no. 4 (1969): 216–24 on the manipulative uses of participatory consultation. Empowerment, however, is not the conclusive normative feature of good participatory design. Citizens assemblies with no formal tie to either a legislature or an administrative agency could still influence public opinion. Such influence could be enhanced in the future by public reports that gave greater attention to the reasons that citizens in these assemblies, particularly those who changed their minds, gave for their conclusions. Those reasons could be publicized with videos of typical members spelling out their reasons

in language that other citizens could understand and consequently envision themselves in the deliberative citizen's place. See also Christopher F. Karpowitz and Chad Raphael, *Deliberation, Democracy, and Civic Forums: Improving Equality and Publicity* (Cambridge: Cambridge University Press, 2014), 347, 356.

74. With the word "system" I mean not a mechanistic set of interactions, but only a set in which a movement or change in one part is likely to affect another, and which in some circumstances is likely to be judged as a whole, serving some broadly defined function. See Mansbridge et al., "A Systemic Approach to Democratic Deliberation," for a fuller explanation.

75. John Locke, *Two Treatises of Government*, ed. Peter Laslett (Cambridge: Cambridge University Press, [1679–1689] 1963), sec.141, "The legislative cannot transfer the power of making laws to any other hands," and, e.g., Jürgen Habermas, *The Structural Transformation of the Public Sphere: An Inquiry into a Category of Bourgeois Society*, trans. Thomas Burger (Boston: MIT Press, [1962] 1989). The standard Weberian account also follows this dichotomous model, as does the very term "bureaucracy," meaning rule by desks, not people. For a brief summary of this controversy, see Bernardo Zacka, *When the State Meets the Street: Public Service and Moral Agency* (Cambridge, MA: Harvard University Press, 2017), 37–47 and citations. For a discussion of why representation in administration is "representation," see Samuel Krislov and David H. Rosenbloom, *Representative Bureaucracy and the American Political System* (New York: Praeger, 1981), 21–26, and chap. 5. See also works cited in Mansbridge, "Recursive Representation" and "Recursive Representation in the Representative System," esp. appendix A.

76. Many studies and reforms in administration address this problem; my goal here is only to signal its place within a larger theory of representation.

77. See Wilson, *Bureaucracy* for the upper level bureaucracy; Zacka, *When the State Meets the Street* for the street level.

78. Cramer, *The Politics of Resentment*, 128.

79. The goal of recursive communication may not be well met by the standard "town hall" format exemplified by the DNA's "meetings around" and many of the meetings in Fuerstein's Minneapolis's "2040 Plan" (this volume) with their self-selected attendees and often confrontational styles of interacting. These "town halls" have important functions in deliberative systems, but a far lower quality of interaction than randomly selected citizens' assemblies with balanced background materials and good facilitators. An outstanding empirical question is when such randomly selected citizens' assemblies can serve as "trusted information proxies" for the citizens who do not attend (see Michael Mackenzie and Mark E. Warren, "Two Trust-Based Uses of Minipublics in Democratic Systems," in *Delibera-*

tive Systems: Deliberative Democracy at the Large Scale, eds. John Parkinson and Jane Mansbridge [Cambridge: Cambridge University Press, 2012), 95–124].

80. For an introduction to the concept, see Ian Ayres and John Braithwaite, *Responsive Regulation: Transcending the Regulation Debate* (Oxford: Oxford University Press, 1992), and for the EU, Charles Sabel and Jonathan Zeitlin, *Experimentalist Governance in the European Union: Towards a New Architecture* (Oxford: Oxford University Press, 2009).

81. Cary Coglianese, "Assessing Consensus: The Promise and Performance of Negotiated Rulemaking," *Duke Law Journal* 46, no. 6 (1997): 1255–1349.

82. Daniel Naurin, *Deliberation behind Closed Doors: Transparency and Lobbying in the European Union* (Colchester, UK: ECPR Press, 2007).

83. Sabel and Zeitlin, *Experimentalist Governance in the European Union*.

84. Slightly more recursively, street level agencies could install suggestion boxes or hand out to those waiting voluntary surveys that would explain the constraints under which the agency worked and asking for ideas on both how to make the line move more quickly and how to improve the services. The recursivity would be genuine only if the agencies tried to implement as many of the suggestions as possible.

85. Jane Mansbridge, "The Fallacy of Tightening the Reins," *Österreichische Zeitschrift für Politikwissenschaft* 34, no. 3 (2005): 233–47.

86. See Fisher, Ury, and Patton, *Getting to Yes*, for principled negotiation, and Lawrence Susskind, "How should you respond to the noisy health reform critics?" *The Consensus Building Approach* (blog), August 2009, http://theconsensusbuildingapproach.blogspot.com/ for processes in which local stakeholders set environmental law for themselves.

87. See, for example, the Finland legislature's experiment with crowdsourcing deliberation on whether to lower the permissible snowmobiling age (Landemore, *Open Democracy*).

88. In the United States, for example, the federal government adopts the accounting standards of the societal nonprofit Financial Accounting Standards Board and gives another societal nonprofit, the Financial Industry Regulating Authority, the power to discipline those who violate those standards. These two nongovernmental organizations have their own internal mechanisms for selecting their officers, unregulated by the state and almost entirely ignored by the public (Catherine E. Rudder, Lee Fritschuler, and Yon Jung Choi, *Public Policy-Making by Private Organizations* [Washington, DC: Brookings, 2016), 61–62 and ch. 4].

89. Rudder, Fritschuler, and Choi, *Public Policy-Making*, 1.

90. Phillipe C. Schmitter, "The Irony of Modern Democracy and Efforts to Improve Its Practice," *Politics and Society* 20, no. 4 (1992): 507–12.

91. See Mansbridge, "Recursive Representation," and "Recursive Representation in the Representative System," appendix B, for the relation between ties with the state and the normative requirement for internal democracy.

92. Rousseau, *Social Contract* III, 15. Rousseau himself intended no such a wholesale replacement, applying these words not to "government," i.e., administration, in which he thought citizens could be properly represented, but to sovereignty (see Judith Shklar, *Men and Citizens: A Study of Rousseau's Social Theory* [Cambridge: Cambridge University Press, 1969], 19–20).

93. See Stephen M. Griffin, "California Constitutionalism: Trust in Government and Direct Democracy," *University of Pennsylvania Journal of Constitutional Law* 111, no. 3 (2009): 551–95 on moves to direct democracy as often inspired by distrust (often justified) of representative government.

5

DEMOCRATIC THEORY AND
DEMOCRATIC FAILURE

A CONTEXTUAL APPROACH

YASMIN DAWOOD

The specter of democratic decline around the world poses two challenges for democratic theory: first, to diagnose and remedy democracy's apparent frailties; and second, to justify the very project of democratic theory itself. What role could democratic theory possibly play given the often deplorable state of political affairs? Does the practice of democracy not suggest that the theory is fundamentally mistaken?

For Jane Mansbridge, "failure is by definition inevitable" when it comes to the aspirational ideals that underpin democracy.[1] But the inevitability of failure does not mean that democratic theory ought to be jettisoned; to the contrary, Mansbridge urges a return to first principles. In light of the crisis of democracy, it is more urgent now than ever before to reconceptualize the basic principles of self-government. To this end, Mansbridge's chapter develops two interrelated themes. The first is concerned with the seemingly contradictory stance of returning to first principles while simultaneously acknowledging the impossibility of achieving them. The second is devoted to rethinking the ideal of giving a law to oneself.

This chapter focuses on the task of democratic theory in light of democratic failure. It is organized in three sections. The first part sets out Mansbridge's arguments about the ideal of giving a law to oneself. The second part investigates the question of what comprises the theorist's task in light of the inescapable failures of our political world. It identifies two kinds of democratic failure—democratic failure writ large and democratic failure writ small—and discusses the implications of each for democratic theory. The third part argues for a contextual approach to democratic theory. In particular, it claims that the theorist's dual task of articulating democratic principles in light of the two kinds of democratic failure is best achieved by taking context into account. A contextual approach pays attention to the particular configurations of power, institutions, incentives, and actors within which democratic principles are instantiated. The chapter then explores several dimensions of democratic theory and practice to which a contextual approach could be usefully applied.

Representation and Self-Government

A core ideal of democracy is the idea of giving a law to oneself. Not only does it encapsulate the commitment to self-government, it also serves to legitimate the coercion of law. Yet this ideal, which is arguably the very essence of democracy, has failure built right into it. We do not expect the ideal of giving a law to oneself to be fully realized in our political lives; indeed, we are content if it is only partially realized. As Mansbridge observes, during peaceful times, our system of representation strikes us as being sufficient despite its manifest failures, yet in troubled times, such failures seem unjustifiable and even dangerous.

While the general notion of "giving a law to oneself" is broad, Mansbridge focuses in particular on the communicative relationship between representatives and constituents. Yet she takes this one relationship, which has received far less attention in democratic theory than such topics as deliberation among elected representatives, and builds a multifaceted account that pays equal attention to ideal theory and the practical realities of democracy in action. It is impossible to capture all the detail of her account, but what follows identifies the key elements of her communicative theory of representation.

As a preliminary matter, Mansbridge argues that the ideal of giving a law to oneself should be viewed as lying at the center of the theory and practice of representation. Although such an ideal might appear at first glance to have a closer affinity with direct democracy, Mansbridge asserts that representation should be reconceptualized in order to contain within its theoretical apparatus a commitment to enabling citizens to give the law to themselves. While constituent-representative communication is crucial to democratic success and failure, it has not, with some important exceptions, been at the center of the literature on representation. Mansbridge's theory redirects our attention from deliberation among the representatives to communication between these representatives and the citizens they represent. This fundamental reconceptualization extends to practice as well: Representative institutions ought to be redesigned with the goal of strengthening both the perception and the reality of citizens giving the law to themselves.

In one sense, Mansbridge's account focuses on a single kind of interaction in the democratic sphere. A central objective is to improve the conditions for a healthy constituent-representative relationship. She argues that this relationship should be recursive, reciprocal, and iterative. The quality of the communication is key: "one feature of giving a law to oneself in a collective enterprise involves communicating one's views, being heard by other citizens and policymakers, and having what one says be adequately considered in both eventual policy and in the way that policy is expressed."[2] By making the constituent-representative communication more recursive, each party learns from and teaches the other. She argues that we ought to create incentives for decision-makers to provide reasons and justifications to citizens, and for citizens to share their thoughts, suggestions, and experiences. An improvement in the communication between constituents and their representatives enhances both the perception and the reality that the democratic order allows the giving of the law to oneself.

Yet, in another sense, the reach of her theory is broad. It extends the scope of representation to include not only legislative assemblies but also administrative agencies and societal organizations such as political parties, nongovernmental organizations, and social media. This "systemic account of representation" locates representative moments throughout a complex and interdependent society. According to Mansbridge, constituent-representative communication can be strengthened at all levels—national, subnational, and local. The local level in particular can benefit from "principled negotiation" with respect to those regulations that cause particular stress and frustration in the lives of citizens.

Not only does Mansbridge's account theorize the constituent-representative connection, it also provides a number of examples from around the world of democratic practices that embody this ideal. In addition, her chapter focuses on empirical and experimental research that has been conducted on the communication between representatives and their constituents. Mansbridge describes how it is possible for randomly selected citizens to engage with decision-makers in the elected, administrative, and social spheres.

The upshot of this imaginative theoretical and practical work is that we ought to fundamentally reconceive the project of representation. Representatives should devote greater energy to communicating rather than policymaking. The ideal of giving a law to oneself could be used to evaluate different models of representation with the goal of identifying which models promote the highest quality citizen-representative communication. In addition to setting forth the communicative dimension of representation, Mansbridge's theory has provided us with a vocabulary and conceptual framework that enriches our usual preoccupation with the trustee-delegate distinction; for, as she observes, neither trustees nor delegates were expected to communicate all that much with constituents.

What Is the Democratic Theorist's Task?

Democracy's failures—abuse of power, subjugation of the vulnerable, corruption, extreme polarization, hostility, incivility, and gridlock, to name but a few—raise serious questions about what it is that democratic theorists are doing and ought to be doing. Such introspection is particularly apt in these times when it seems as though the ideals and norms of the liberal, democratic, constitutional order are at best under siege and at worst eroding before our eyes.

Mansbridge is unapologetically in the ideal theory camp, yet she presents a view of ideal theory that is entirely compatible with democracy's frailties and failures. For Mansbridge, aspirational ideals are those "toward which we should strive but have little or no chance of actually achieving."[3] She adopts David Estlund's distinction between proposals that ought to be realistic and principles that are often unachievable; a distinction encapsulated by his theory of the stereoscopic view under which we are invited to simultaneously keep an eye on the ideal and things as they are.[4] The fact that democratic ideals are impossible to achieve is not fatal to a theory's ambition because, while proposals should be realistic, principles need not be. In addition, Mansbridge rejects the harms that some may associate with ideal theory. On her account, the embrace of ideals that will inevitably fail is fully compatible with paying attention to institutional failures, power, and conflict.

The inevitability of failure does not render ideal theory irrelevant. I shall suggest, however, that a democracy can fail in two distinct ways and that these two types of failure have different implications for the work of democratic theory. First, a democracy is inevitably a failure in the sense that it will never live up to its ideals. A wide array of ideals and principles are commonly associated with democratic self-government, including representation, participation, deliberation, equality, freedom, and accountability. There is no question, however, that democracies routinely fail to live up to these ideals in practice.

We can understand these deficiencies as democratic failure writ small. I suggest that democratic theory has a critical role to play with respect to this kind of failure. It is precisely the articulation and defense of democratic ideals and principles that allow us to identify deviations in practice. As such, the task of democratic theory with respect to failure writ small is to establish a baseline against which the practice of democracy can be judged. This baseline can be understood as a ceiling or upper limit. Democratic theories and principles demarcate this upper limit by identifying ideal values, institutions, processes, and policies. By so doing, they provide a crucial baseline against which democratic failures in the first sense can be identified and measured.

Second, a democracy can fail in a literal sense by collapsing into an authoritarian or hybrid regime. Several countries have experienced democratic backsliding via constitutional and legal means which leave a façade of democratic institutions while hollowing out democracy's substance.[5] These hybrid regimes have the features of both authoritarian and democratic systems.[6] In such systems, elected autocrats use the tools of constitutionalism to entrench themselves in power and reduce the efficacy of institutional checks.[7] While there is no single point in time in which a gradually eroding democracy can be said to have failed, the general direction or trend can be identified.

Democratic failure writ large is likewise a subject for democratic theory. The theorist's task is to articulate and conceptualize democracy's fundamental vulnerabilities, such as the abuse of power, institutional corruption, and inclinations to tyranny. In so doing, the theorist can demarcate a lower limit or floor, which can serve as a baseline below which a functioning democracy should not venture. Such theories can provide a measure against which a failing democracy can be judged.

The dual task of democratic theory, I suggest, spans the space between these two baselines. At the upper end, it defends the ideals and principles of democracy, while at the lower end it conceptualizes the dangers that can lead to the collapse of democracies. Democratic theory can also identify the connections between these two kinds of failure. Sufficient failures of the first kind can eventually lead to a failure of the second kind. The theory of democratic erosion, for instance, holds that democracies slowly collapse as representative and rule-of-law structures are undermined by power holders. Democratic theory should be viewed as inextricably linked to failure writ small and failure writ large.

DEMOCRATIC THEORY AND FAILURE IN CONTEXT

The theorist's dual task of articulating democratic ideals while simultaneously focusing on democratic failures is best achieved, I shall suggest, by adopting a contextual approach to democratic theory. There are several possible ways to conceive of a contextual approach and many theorists whose work could be described as contextual. A contextual approach situates abstract ideals within a particular context, that is to say, with attention to the particular configurations of power, institutions, incentives, and actors. On this view, the meaning, purpose, and impact of any given democratic ideal shifts and adapts to the particular context to which it is being applied.

Consider, for example, the ideal of deliberation. The role of democratic theory would be, in part, to provide an account of deliberation in its most ideal form, thereby establishing a ceiling that could serve as a baseline for the concept. A contextual approach to deliberation would recognize that the application of the ideal of deliberation in a particular context—say, in the context of hierarchical status structures, uneven material resources, or differences in education—could change our assessment of the value and suitability, as a normative matter, of deliberation as a means of decision-making. While deliberation would still remain a democratic ideal in an abstract sense, it may not be normatively appropriate within a given institutional and social context.

A contextual approach takes account of the immense complexity and diversity of democratic practice and thereby recasts democratic ideals as highly dependent and contingent rather than as fixed and unchanging. Such an approach also recognizes that democratic ideals are often in tension with one another and that there are trade-offs between democratic values, such as representation, accountability, and transparency. A contextual approach refashions the interplay between theory and practice, allowing each to be influenced by the other.

The contextual approach I describe here shares certain elements with the approach proposed by Joseph Carens, who argues that theorists should make abstract reasoning concrete by using examples and cases.[8] For Carens, the normative exploration of cases can enrich and even revise the theory. The use of the term "contextual approach" in this chapter shares Carens's focus on practice but differs in that normative ideals themselves are treated as contextual and highly contingent. For this reason, normative prescriptions may differ depending on the specific facts of a given situation.

Paying attention to context is crucial given that democracy is a vastly complex enterprise. Within any given democracy, there are innumerable moving parts—institutions, processes, actors, political parties, socioeconomic classes and conditions, cultural differences, population and geographic configurations, demographic shifts and so on—that interact within and are loosely contained by a legal superstructure of constitutional provisions, electoral laws, conventions, and norms. Within each democracy, this internal complexity is constantly changing and in flux. This complexity is multiplied when we consider democratic nations as a collective, each with their own histories, institutional configurations, cultures, and values. The field of comparative political theory, for example, exemplifies the importance of context.[9] Under a contextual approach, the complexity and diversity of democracy in practice can inform the development of theory.

A contextual approach pays attention to the particular configurations of power, institutions, incentives, and actors. For example, theorists have examined the structure of elections, political institutions, representation, deliberation, partisanship, and constitutional configurations such as federalism.[10] A contextual approach recognizes that the meaning and value of a given democratic ideal may change depending on the institutional context within which that ideal is being realized. Likewise, particular institutional contexts may make the realization of certain ideals more likely than other institutional contexts.

The contextual approach is indispensable for illuminating democratic failure writ small and democratic failure writ large. By paying attention to the ways in which various democratic principles and ideals manifest within particular situations, a theorist can shed light on the vulnerabilities that are inevitable in democratic practice. Democratic failures are recognizable as such once the configurations of power, interest, institutions, and actors are interpreted. Context also matters because failures both large and small can be presented as democracy-enhancing successes. As an example of failure writ small, voter identification laws are justified on the grounds that they ensure electoral integrity, but a contextual approach reveals that such rules often suppress voting and participation. Likewise, democratic erosion, or failure writ large, can take place through democratic and constitutional changes, which often have the appearance of being consistent with democratic ideals but which in practice serve to concentrate power and eliminate accountability. A contextual approach to democratic theory is essential for the proper diagnosis of failures writ large and small.

Mansbridge's arguments about the ideal of giving a law to oneself are acutely sensitive to the issue of context. One aim of the chapter is to "introduce contingency and context into decisions about when to emphasize and deemphasize an ideal."[11] Mansbridge observes that there is a tension between those practices that enlarge democracy and those practices that sustain democracy. In some contexts, "expanding the practices of democracy to more closely approach their core ideals is the best way of sustaining democracy itself."[12] But in other contexts, practices that are meant to expand democracy could undermine it instead. When faced with such a choice, Mansbridge argues that sustaining democracy should take precedence. As a more general matter, the task at hand, according to Mansbridge, is to understand "the possible elements in the ideal, the possible trade-offs and interactions among those elements and elements of other ideals or goods."[13]

Once we take context into account, the communication between representatives and constituents in many established democracies can amount to a double-edged sword. Mansbridge acknowledges the downside of communication in many of the examples she provides, noting instances of power inequity, bias, strategic ploys on the part of politicians, and the like. As Mansbridge rightly observes, a common theme in populist movements in Europe and the United States is the experience of not having been heard; thus, the solution is to enhance the communication between representatives and constituents. A contextual approach would suggest, however, that while failures in constituent-representative communication may have been one of the sources of resentment that culminated in a populist movement, it is less clear that such communication is an unmitigated good once populism has taken hold. On the one hand, it could be argued that this kind of communication is the very epitome of democratic discourse. Yet when that discourse becomes laced with hatred for those who are vulnerable in our society, democracy could become destabilized over time. To be sure, Mansbridge addresses this worry, writing that "we may refuse to meet racist or xenophobic demands . . . because our ideals make meeting such demands nonnegotiable."[14] She argues further that "we may be able to find ways of responding to some of the interests behind those demands that do not require forsaking or even compromising our own ideals."[15] Yet the very expression and amplification of such demands in the context of populism, even when such demands are not met, arguably erodes the fabric of our common life. Recursive communication between constituents and representatives could equally well fan the flames of xenophobia; indeed, the electoral incentives facing representatives may make it tempting to exploit underlying fears and even amplify or create them. The question, then, is whether we want such views to be expressed and normalized. While enhancing constituent-representative communication during pre-populist times may avert the problem of people feeling that they are not heard, the enhancement of such communication during a populist move-ment may lead to other difficulties for the democratic polity.

A contextual approach also sheds light on the circumstances and trade-offs that are inherent to democratic practice. For example, in the United States, constituent-representative communication takes place in the shadow of the campaign finance regime. Representa-tives spend most of their time fund-raising rather than making pol-icy, and their communication with certain constituents—wealthy donors—is robust. The influence of the wealthy on the formation of public policy raises the question of whether the communication between certain constituents and their representatives is actually *too* successful. In recent decisions, the Supreme Court has treated activity that was once deemed to be corruption as amounting to "participation" on the part of donors and "gratitude" on the part of representatives.[16] That is to say, speech in the form of donations that influences representatives' decision-making is no longer viewed by a majority of the Court as amounting to corruption. In this way, one very rarified kind of constituent-representative communication is undermining the ideal of citizens giving the laws to themselves because the laws that are adopted reflect the interests of the wealthy rather than the interests of the average citizen.

A contextual approach also illuminates the trade-off between the ideals of liberty and equality that lie at the heart of the debate over campaign finance regulation.[17] Removing campaign finance restrictions enhances the freedom of speech but simultaneously serves to further entrench political and economic inequality. The outsized influence of the wealthy on the formation of public policy in the United States directly challenges a central precept of democracy that all citizens are political equals.[18] A contextual approach recognizes not only the circumstances in which demo-cratic principles operate but also the complex interplay between and among such principles when instantiated in practice.

Attention to context is also useful given the dynamic nature of democracy. New technologies, including social media, have changed the possibilities for democratic discourse. For example, Mansbridge notes that recursive communication between representatives and ordinary constituents (as opposed to donors) has been impossible given the sheer size of the United States. Yet she suggests that new innovations, such as the e-townhalls experiment conducted by Michael Neblo et al., raise the possibility of communication between a majority of citizens and their elected representatives.[19] These innovations may give rise to the perception that citizens are giving the law to themselves—in itself a valuable and important goal.

Yet other innovations, most notably social media, also raise challenges for democratic theory. It is undoubtedly true that social media provides citizens with a venue and a voice. Social media, however, is also subject to a host of problems including echo chambers, bias, and manipulation.[20] In recent times, there have been credible reports of companies and foreign governments using social media to target and manipulate citizens with fake news.[21] Fears of manipulation are more serious than our usual concerns about the formation of echo chambers in deliberative spaces. Manipulation on social media can lead to increased polarization in the citizenry and can exacerbate xenophobia and racism. The use of social media, particularly by populist leaders, is viewed as undermining the traditional party structure and the moderating role that big-tent political parties play with respect to extreme views.[22] A contextual approach would allow for a nuanced assessment of the benefits and drawbacks of social media for democracy.

The issues explored above all serve to demonstrate a central contribution of Mansbridge's chapter, which is that while democratic ideals have failure built into them, it is nonetheless crucial to continue to strive toward achieving these ideals. Her theory of representation has shed fresh light on the dynamic between constituents and their representatives, opening the door to new possibilities in democratic theory and practice.

CONCLUSION

Democracies inevitably fail by not living up to their ideals. They may also fail in the more dramatic sense by eroding or collapsing into a non-democratic regime. The task of democratic theory is to establish baselines—ceilings and floors—by which such failures can be identified, conceptualized, and judged. The task of the democratic theorist is thus twofold: to articulate the ideals and principles of democracy while simultaneously considering its failures writ large and small. This dual task, I have suggested, is aided by the adoption of a contextual approach. A contextual approach views democratic principles as being located within particular configurations of power, institutions, actors, and incentive structures. A contextual approach takes account of the fact that the practice of democracy is highly complex, diverse, and dynamic. When applied to particular circumstances, democratic ideals are contingent and are often in tension with one another. A contextual approach to the dual task of democratic theory is attentive to both the promise and the perils of democracy.

NOTES

1. Jane Mansbridge, "Representation Failure" (this volume). I would like to thank Michael Fuerstein, Jane Mansbridge, Melissa Schwartzberg, Mark Tushnet, and Daniel Viehoff for very helpful discussions.

2. Jane Mansbridge, "Representation Failure" (this volume).

3. Ibid.

4. David Estlund, *Utopophobia; On the Limits (If Any) of Political Philosophy* (Princeton, NJ: Princeton University Press, 2020), as cited in Jane Mansbridge, "Representation Failure" (this volume).

5. For theories of democratic erosion, see Tom Ginsburg and Aziz Z. Huq, *How to Save A Constitutional Democracy* (Chicago: University of Chicago Press, 2019); Steven Levitzky and Daniel Ziblatt, *How Democracies Die* (New York: Crown, 2018).

6. Steven Levitsky and Lucan Way, *Competitive Authoritarianism: Hybrid Regimes After the Cold War* (New York: Cambridge University Press, 2010); Andreas Schedler, ed., *Electoral Authoritarianism: The Dynamics of Unfree Competition* (Boulder, CO: Lynne Rienner, 2006); Kim Lane Scheppele, "The Rule of Law and the Frankenstate: Why Governance Checklists Do Not Work," *Governance* 26:4 (2013): 559–62.

7. David Landau, "Abusive Constitutionalism," *University of California Davis Law Review* 47 (2013): 189–260, at 191; Mark Tushnet, "Authoritarian Constitutionalism," *Cornell Law Review* 100 (2015): 391–461, at 396.

8. Joseph H. Carens, "A Contextual Approach to Political Theory," *Ethical Theory and Moral Practice* 7 (2004): 117–32.

9. See Diego von Vacano, "The Scope of Comparative Political Theory," *Annual Review of Political Science* 18 (2015): 465–80.

10. Dennis F. Thompson, *Just Elections: Creating a Fair Electoral Process in the United States* (Chicago: University of Chicago Press, 2004); Jeremy Waldron, *Political Political Theory: Essays on Institutions* (Cambridge, MA: Harvard University Press, 2016); Melissa Williams, *Voice, Trust, and Memory: Marginalized Groups and the Failings of Liberal Representation* (Princeton, NJ: Princeton University Press, 1998); James S. Fishkin, *Democracy and Deliberation: New Directions for Democratic Reform* (New Haven, CT: Yale University Press, 1991); John Parkinson and Jane Mansbridge, eds., *Deliberative Systems* (New York: Cambridge University Press, 2012); Nancy L. Rosenblum, *On the Side of the Angels: An Appreciation of Parties and Partisanship* (Princeton, NJ: Princeton University Press, 2008); Jonathan White and Lea Ypi, *The Meaning of Partisanship* (Oxford: Oxford University Press, 2016); Jacob T. Levy, "Federalism, Liberalism, and the Separation of Loyalties," *American Political Science Review* 101:3 (2007): 459–77.

11. Mansbridge, "Representation Failure" (this volume).

12. Ibid.

13. Ibid.

14. Ibid.

15. Ibid.

16. See, e.g., *McCutcheon v FEC*, 134 S. Ct. 1434 (2014).

17. Yasmin Dawood, "Democracy and the Freedom of Speech: Rethinking the Conflict Between Liberty and Equality," *Canadian Journal of Law and Jurisprudence* 26:2 (2013): 293–311.

18. Martin Gilens, *Affluence and Influence: Economic Inequality and Political Power in America* (Princeton, NJ: Princeton University Press, 2014).

19. Michael A. Neblo et al., *Politics with the People: Building a Directly Representative Democracy* (Cambridge: Cambridge University Press, 2018).

20. Cass Sunstein, *#Republic: Divided Democracy in the Age of Social Media* (Princeton, NJ: Princeton University Press, 2017).

21. Alexis C. Madrigal, "What Facebook Did to American Democracy," *The Atlantic* (October 12, 2017).

22. For a particularly stark example (Brazil), see Zack Beauchamp, "Social Media Is Rotting Democracy from Within: How Social Platforms Enable Far-right Politicians' Campaigns to Undermine Democracy," *Vox*, January 22, 2019.

6

DEMOCRATIC REPRESENTATIVES AS EPISTEMIC INTERMEDIARIES

MICHAEL FUERSTEIN

As a newly appointed member of the Fulton Neighborhood Zoning Committee in Minneapolis, I recently had my first inside glimpse—albeit extremely limited—of the democratic process.[1] Our little group participated in sometimes heated deliberations over Minneapolis's "2040 Plan," a legally required document that lays out a vision for the city over the next couple of decades. It spells out commitments to goals such as social equity, economic growth, livability, and sustainability, and articulates in somewhat broad terms a series of initiatives toward reaching those goals.

After submitting an initial draft of the plan to the public, the city created an extensive open-comment period, seeking feedback through various forums and media. Public input in this process has been voluminous: The last time I checked, citizens had submitted 1,682 comments through online forms, along with another 250+ emailed comments, and presumably many more comments at in-person forums.[2] A very large share of these comments consist in poorly informed rants rather than thoughtful positions supported by evidence. Citizens pick out specific details and attack them without considering the broader context. They badly misrepresent what is in the plan. They ignore the interests of other constituents with compelling concerns. They make assertions about complex empirical matters without, apparently, consulting any credible research. What is the effect of building luxury housing on housing prices overall? What kinds of housing subsidies are most likely to promote an increase in affordable housing supply?

How do changes in parking supply downtown affect commuter patterns? Hypocrisy and lazy/inconsistent arguments abound, and the incentives for responsible engagement are pretty weak. To be sure, one can also find thoughtful and well researched perspectives. But that is the exception rather than the norm, and the general perspective one gets on citizen-representative interchange does not flatter the democratic process.

For better and worse, the comments will surely have some effect on the ultimate outcome. Yet a large share of the people who have submitted comments will come away with the view that the politicians and planners are "not listening" to them. They will think this because those who must weigh all of the relevant considerations will realize that acting on the stated concerns of most citizens would (for various reasons unfamiliar to the citizens themselves) be a really bad idea and because, in any case, there are too many incompatible objectives in play to accommodate all of those concerns practically. But when confronted with the difference between what they as individuals called for and the policy that resulted, many citizens will complain that their elected agents are contemptuous of the public.

The example draws our attention to some important tensions in the practice and ideal of democratic representation. On the one hand, the guiding idea of a representative system is that, in order to reliably serve citizens' interests, we need to create mechanisms through which their input is sought. Input is important on the presumption that we cannot really understand what serves citizens' interests without an egalitarian process of regular and extensive consultation. On the other hand, democratic citizens are frequently ill-informed and narrow in their sympathies and motivations. The first consideration explains, at least in part, why serving citizens' interests requires a representative system rather than technocracy. The second consideration explains, at least in part, why it requires a representative system rather than direct democracy.

My suggestion in this chapter is that a representative political system presents a solution that navigates two different kinds of epistemic problems: first, the risk that citizens will be ignored; second, the risk that they will be ignorant. The first risk pulls us toward more delegate-like systems of representation: more direct forms of citizen involvement and greater deference among official representatives. The second pulls us toward more trustee-like models: less direct citizen involvement and more independence of representatives. Admittedly, the trustee/delegate distinction is a bit worn. Nonetheless, it offers a useful rubric for representing this fundamental tension in democracy—between citizen involvement on the one hand and expertise on the other. From an epistemic point of view, I suggest, democratic representatives are best modeled as epistemic intermediaries who facilitate the vertical integration of knowledge between policy experts and non-experts, and the horizontal integration of knowledge among diverse non-experts. The primary analytical payoff of this model is that it provides a clear rationale for variation in the norms and institutionalization of representative behavior. Sometimes a delegate-like approach is the right one, and sometimes a trustee-like approach is better. The key determinant is the effect of these models on the epistemic quality of outcomes under different circumstances. Toward the end of the chapter, I apply the model to the present case of populism and consider its implications in that context.

One caveat before moving forward: Quite plausibly, there are significant non-epistemic considerations of procedural fairness and legitimacy that bear on the justification and character of representative institutions. Below, my working assumption is that, while procedural considerations may constrain or in some cases trump epistemic concerns, these two approaches are normally compatible. Indeed, one important upshot of my argument is that epistemic considerations are generally supportive of a system of democratic representation and, in this way, do not push us toward non-democratic models of elitism (as has frequently been argued[3]).

THE DISTINCTIVE EPISTEMIC CHALLENGE OF DEMOCRACY

Epistemic models of democracy hold that democracy is to be recommended at least in part based on its tendency to produce decision outcomes that "track the truth."[4] Democracy's characteristic norms and procedures can then be explained and justified by reference to their contribution to this outcome. Some epistemic democrats, for example, have appealed to formal work on the wisdom of crowds to explain why democratic decision-making would beat aristocracy under the right conditions.[5] The idea of political truth invites a variety of worries that have been addressed elsewhere,[6] but on my view its significance has been overstated among epistemic democrats. In Joshua Cohen's classic formulation of epistemic democracy, the key notion is not political truth but, instead, the idea of a "standard of correct decisions" that is independent "of current consensus and the outcomes of votes."[7] On this view, the key consideration is a certain notion of objectivity in our understanding of good decision outcomes, i.e., a measure of normative distance between whatever decision it is that citizens actually endorse or decide upon through the political process and what it is that would constitute a correct decision.[8] That kind of independent standard might be provided by some sort of strongly realist notion of political truth; but it might also be provided by constructivist alternatives, according to which correct outcomes are the ones that would be agreed upon under idealized conditions of deliberation, for example.[9]

In any case, for present purposes, let us say that an *epistemic* notion of democracy is one that recommends democracy, at least in part, based on its tendency to produce decision outcomes that correspond to the right objective standard. Why would democracy tend to do that? It would tend to do that, most crucially, if the kind of knowledge required to best approximate objectively correct outcomes were very widely dispersed among the citizenry. And that assumption looks quite plausible at least on certain baseline liberal assumptions: First, a basic principle of equality according to which no one's interests are intrinsically worthy of more weight in decision-making than anyone else's. And, second, the idea that citizens have a fundamental interest in their own liberty, i.e., at a minimum, a life that reflects their own non-coerced values and ambitions, consistent with a similar scope of liberty for others. Respecting these two basic principles might in principle be possible with some non-democratic model. However, as I explain below, it looks nearly impossible to attend effectively and fairly to disparate interests without a process of intensive, ongoing, and egalitarian consultation.

So the general appeal of democratic systems lies in their capacity to integrate widely and asymmetrically dispersed knowledge about political matters.[10] Yet neither of the two dominant mechanisms of democratic agency—voting and deliberation—is likely on its own to succeed in this regard. Voting is inadequate because, on its own, it has a frequent tendency to amplify rather than remedy ignorance. If citizens individually know a fraction of what they need to know about climate policy to make good decisions, for example, the majority perspective is unlikely to represent a rational outlook. On its own, voting also does a poor job of integrating disparate information. If four voters know about four different successful business deals conducted by Donald Trump, and the fifth knows about a fifth deal in which he ripped off his suppliers, went into bankruptcy, committed tax fraud, and got bailed out with a $50 million gift from his father, then a substantial majority will conclude that he is a brilliant and ethically upstanding businessman. Aggregating their knowledge through an election will not yield epistemic benefits. This point extends to complicated policy problems in which developing an informed view requires attending to disparate considerations. Whatever its epistemic merits, voting on its own is not a reliable route to the "wisdom of crowds" in political contexts.

Inclusive deliberation is a tempting solution to this problem, since deliberation enables individuals to upgrade their perspective in the light of asymmetrically dispersed information.[11] But even under the best of circumstances, there are severe practical limitations to the prospects of universal deliberation given the size of contemporary democracies and the range of challenges they face. The "deliberative systems" approach presents an important move toward addressing that challenge within deliberative democracy,[12] but remains an incomplete solution at best. Relatedly, the ideal of inclusive egalitarian deliberation at best abstracts away from the inevitability, and utility, of epistemic hierarchies. The division of cognitive labor is essential when matters become complex, and no system of decision-making can succeed without some rational, structural reliance on expertise.[13]

From an epistemic point of view, then, representation most naturally enters this picture as a means of assimilating disparate input about citizens' interests into a process of shared decision-making. Representatives play a particular role in the democratic system that works in tandem with voting and deliberation to improve epistemic outputs. Andrew Rehfeld characterizes the "standard" understanding of political representation in terms of what he dubs the "interest and responsiveness" account. This involves two components:

(i) to advance, seek, or pursue another person's or group's interests; and/or
(ii) to act in a manner responsive to that other person or group.[14]

I will treat this "standard" account as a baseline for present purposes.[15] From a procedural point of view, a moral good is achieved by giving individuals a say in decision-making. The key point is that, in a political context, there is no authoritative vantage point from which to identify correct decisions. Thus it is essential to avoid unjustly privileging any particular individual's view(s).[16] In this respect, there are clear merits, on grounds of fairness, to having a democratic representative system.

Nonetheless, even though the correct outcome of political processes may be essentially contested, we can legitimately critique that process for failing on epistemic grounds: The majority opinion may be supported by fallacious reasoning, it may hinge on lies or misrepresentations, it may be premised on overconfidence about poorly understood information, and it may blatantly ignore the vital interests of particular groups with a stake in the process. These are all essentially epistemic considerations, because they recruit normative criteria of reasoning and justification which are independent of actual beliefs and procedural outputs and, for that matter, moral characteristics of procedures, such as the extent to which all individuals have an equal say.

From a procedural point of view, representation is a way of realizing the equal moral status of citizens in political decision-making. In epistemic terms, designating people to advance the interests of particular groups of citizens helps ensure that the full spectrum of considerations that are relevant to justifying policy outcomes are in fact considered. Economic policy that only consults wealthy people is unlikely to fairly and effectively serve all citizens' interests. Parallel points apply to education policy that only consults city dwellers, technological regulation that only consults industry, and so forth. This rationale has long been a pillar of democratic thought.[17]

In particular, it is worth noting a couple of crucial reasons why—given the presumption of liberty and equality—producing correct outcomes is likely to depend on wide egalitarian consultation.

The first reason is that the content of any individual's legitimate interests is *desire-sensitive*. That is, following a standard liberal understanding of well-being, what is good for me depends to a large degree on what I actually desire and aspire to. Religious believers, for example, have a compelling interest in the capacity to practice their religion in virtue of their subjective attitudes toward religious doctrine and practice; caring about and engaging with these things in a particular way gives them an interest in the capacity to practice their religion. Likewise, same-sex couples have a compelling interest in the right to marriage in significant part because of the existence of genuine and deep-seated desires to participate in that institution. The defense of same-sex marriage would be incomplete without this fact about contingent human attitudes and affections. All things held equal, getting what we desire is generally good for us, and the contingent shape of human desires plays a fundamental constitutive role in determining our interests.

The second reason that producing correct outcomes depends on wide egalitarian consultation is that interests are *fact-sensitive*. That is, what is good for me depends substantially on features of the world beyond my subjective state of mind. If I am allergic to penicillin, then it is against my interests to take penicillin, even if I desire it or believe that it's good for me. On a political scale, manufacturing workers may believe that tariffs are going to be good for them while, in fact, they will produce unforeseen consequences that make them worse off. Wide consultation tends to be important, therefore, because citizens have an incomplete epistemic perspective on the facts relevant to their interests. A process that is properly sensitive to our interests should be one that ensures the chance for all relevant factual information to receive uptake.

The fact sensitivity of interests entails that democracy requires an enormous body of scientific knowledge, where this encompasses natural and social-scientific as well as other bodies of technical knowledge.[18] Democracy requires, we might say, the *downward vertical integration* of knowledge from experts into the decision-making process. The Minneapolis 2040 plan illustrates this well, since competently assessing the plan requires drawing on a vast array of economic, sociological, and ecological concerns and integrating them coherently and intelligently. There are undoubtedly some types of policy questions for which more mundane forms of knowledge suffice (How should we renovate park facilities? Should the school system expand its investment in the arts?). Nonetheless, many core legislative issues hinge on complex scientific matters. The present debate surrounding healthcare reform in the United States is a telling example. This debate tends to inspire strong positions on all sides, even though there is enormous uncertainty about the ultimate results, costs, and trade-offs of different policies. The difficulty of the underlying issues surpasses that of string theory so far as I can tell, yet voters are practically screaming at their representatives (and each other) about what ought to be done.

At the same time, citizens tend to know factual qualities of their local situation that are relevant to their interests but are not well known by elites operating at a remove. Democracy thus requires *upward vertical integration*—from non-experts into the decision-making process—of knowledge as well. The efficacy of healthcare policy, for example, is sensitive to highly localized needs and sociological dynamics: Who winds up in the emergency room and why? Where are the cost overruns most extreme? What kinds of care are most needed and for which populations? How do racial and economic inequalities play out in the provision of care? There is a long history of poor decision-making by policy elites who are not sufficiently familiar with the localized conditions under which policy is to be implemented, and with the concerns of those most directly affected by it. Education policy provides a particularly rich abundance of examples on this point. High-level reforms, such as "No Child Left Behind" in the United States, impose sweeping measures to address problems that are enormously heterogeneous at the local level. The inevitable result is a variety of perverse incentives and unintended consequences, of which "teaching to the test" is (in this case) only the most notorious example.[19]

In the Minneapolis 2040 case, citizens tend to offer perspectives grounded in what is likely to happen on their block without weighing the needs of those in neighborhoods that are different in their demographics, housing stock, transportation needs, and economic prosperity. Voters defending gun rights in a rural context seem at best dimly aware of the consequences in poor urban neighborhoods. Voters angry about environmental regulations on water usage tend to forget or ignore what happens downstream. The challenge in a political system that is supposed to treat all citizens equally is to assimilate their interests across a heterogeneous population. This is the problem of the *horizontal integration* of knowledge. We need an interchange between experts and non-experts, but we also need an interchange among different types of experts and, especially, among diverse non-experts. In this context, the problem is not only to generate a sufficient awareness of the diversity of interest-relevant facts, but also the diversity of interest-relevant desires across the population. Here again the same-sex marriage case looks like an important example. The compelling interest of same-sex couples in marital rights, I noted above, derives to a significant degree from the particular set of aspirations and attitudes attached to the institution of marriage by a substantial portion of the gay community.

To summarize: Democracy is epistemically demanding because serving interests fairly and effectively requires integrating knowledge across a large and heterogeneous population. This integration concerns both interest-relevant facts—about scientific matters and also local practical constraints—and contingent desires that generate interests as a function of variable plans, attitudes, and commitments. The integration required must flow from experts toward the broader system of decision-making (*downward vertical integration*), from non-experts toward that system (*upward vertical integration*), and between non-experts at different social locations (*horizontal integration*). If, on the standard account, the fundamental task of representation is the advancement of interests, then we can understand representatives as occupying a distinctive role that facilitates these different kinds of epistemic integration. That is the suggestion I pursue in the next section.

DEMOCRATIC REPRESENTATIVES AS EPISTEMIC INTERMEDIARIES

The Minneapolis 2040 website describes a variety of means through which the public is being engaged to provide feedback on the plan throughout its development, but it does not offer much detail on the actual steps by which a draft was produced. Still, we can imagine what Mansbridge calls in her chapter in this volume a "recursive" process of deliberation among council members, the public, and the planners. A somewhat simplified version of the ideal goes like this: The perspective of elected council members is informed by their engagement with citizens; the council members in turn make some judgments about collective priorities of their constituents and channel those to the planners; the planners draw on their expertise to identify crucial practical issues, constraints, and tensions; the council members channel those points back to their constituents in public forums; the public then has a chance to respond; and so forth. Although, in this case, there will be no public referendum vote on the plan, it is reasonable to assume that the City Council would be unlikely to move forward with the ratification of any particular plan until a draft garners substantial public support across a range of constituencies.

The role of the public in this case is primarily one of providing feedback which is then integrated by planners, along with various technical considerations, into crafting further drafts of the plan. Taking this as a fairly standard case of democratic representation, two aspects of public input in this case are worth noting.

First, public input is collectively valuable but highly incomplete at the individual level. The value of public input tends to emerge through the accumulation of diverse perspectives that are individually incomplete on their own. In Minneapolis, developers have one particular set of issues in mind; African American renters on the North side of town have another; white homeowners in the affluent neighborhoods in the southwestern part of town have yet another; businesses downtown will raise yet another; those who commute to work every day have a different perspective on transportation issues than those who work from home; and so on. A good planning document will integrate all of these perspectives along with a broad spectrum of technical considerations. But that is principally the task of the technocrats in the planning department—in dialogue with City Council members—rather than one for individual citizens. Most individual citizens will be poorly positioned to perform this integrative task, due to inevitable deficiencies of both scientific knowledge and knowledge of other citizens' interests. This corresponds to the need, described earlier, for horizontal and downward vertical integration.

Second, much of the process that determines the final document takes place off stage, in the nitty gritty technical deliberations of the technocrats who set the agenda. By the time the general public reaches a point where it is positioned to exercise some kind of direct authorization, the considerations in play, the kinds of measures proposed, and the defining aims of the document will have already been substantially framed and narrowed down. There will be no direct public vote on the planning document. Still, even if there were such a vote, the public's choice would be substantially shaped by the construction of available options.

Both of these considerations underscore the fundamental difficulty with the idea that representative democracy is an attempt to approximate, within practical constraints, an ideal of self-rule or, as Mansbridge puts it (see her contribution in this volume), "giving a law to oneself." The idea of citizens giving laws to themselves depends on a parallel idea of citizens adequately informed and engaged to do this competently, that is, to meet democracy's epistemic demands. That model of democracy looks most plausible in contexts like Ancient Greece, Rousseau's Geneva, or perhaps Mansbridge's small-town New England.[20] In these cases, the democratic franchise applied to a manageably small group of citizens, and the geographic and population units over which authority had to be exercised, were comparatively miniscule. Likewise, the kind of scientific knowledge required for policy in these contexts does not match its degree of sophistication in contemporary national contexts.

The defining features of the 2040 plan process are that individual citizens tend to be poorly positioned to make complete legislative judgments on their own. Likewise, the choices that individuals make in this case—even technical experts—are highly shaped and constrained by distributed processes of agenda-setting, theory-building, and knowledge production. The conclusions of urban planners, engineers, and school administrators are themselves premised on a broader web of background theories and assumptions that have been developed within those fields, and that serve to shape decision-making in fundamental ways. From this point of view, the input of individual citizens is best understood as a certain kind of participation in a collective, but highly distributed process of inquiry and choice.[21] We shouldn't aspire to be authors of the laws because civic and political maturity requires understanding ourselves as participants in a collective, systemic process, rather than as direct authors of outcomes. The goal of democratic participation, on this view, is not that citizens be heard or exercise oversight exclusively for its own sake; the goal is that citizens be heard because and to the extent that doing so will create policies that fairly respect the interests of all.

Yet, though democratic decision-making is by nature an output of the system, rather than individuals, it also clearly depends on individuals within the system who play a crucial role in bringing together disparate bodies of knowledge. My suggestion is that democratic representatives occupy an institutional location that makes them distinctly well suited to play such a role. Representatives have formal power to participate in policy decisions and are at the same time accountable to constituents via elections. This puts them in a natural mediating position between experts and non-experts. The nitty-gritty of policy depends on scientific knowledge and, therefore, representatives must have a grip on the relevant technical considerations. At the same time, their accountability to constituents generates incentives to bring these technicalities into dialogue with the perspective of citizens "on the ground." Likewise, they must communicate the technical perspective of experts so that policy is seen by non-experts to serve their interests. Representatives also must engage in a substantial deliberative negotiation with representatives of other constituents. In this respect, they must fairly assimilate the interests of other groups in a way that is, once again, seen by their own constituents as interest-advancing.

It is important to note that the role that representatives play in this context is both informational and motivational. As described above, their informational role is evident enough: Representatives create an institutional channel through which asymmetrically dispersed information is circulated. But circulating information, on its own, is only part of the challenge in improving the epistemic quality of decisions. In a variety of familiar ways, political officials, expert technocrats, and non-expert citizens are all highly imperfect in the way that they process and act on information. Most obviously, self-interest has a tendency to crowd out a due regard for the interests of others, even given full information about the stakes. But even where naked self-interest is not the rule, implicit biases, motivated reasoning, and narrow group-based affections and antipathies tend to work against the epistemic reliability of individuals. Political representatives act as significant focal points for a process of contestation that enables individuals, not only to represent information, but also to give it salience and some measure of motivational significance. Of course, as the present case of populism reveals, political representation is hardly a fail-safe in encouraging epistemic responsibility (more on this below). Nonetheless, a system of representation, backed by egalitarian norms and basic civil liberties, creates mechanisms that enable citizens to mobilize reasons and hold one another to account on their basis.

Thus, the formal power of representatives, combined with their accountability to constituents, makes them natural epistemic intermediaries: entities that facilitate the vertical and horizontal integration of politically vital knowledge. That kind of role appears to be indispensable in the context of contemporary democracy given the epistemic inadequacy (as I argued earlier) of mass voting or deliberation on its own. When representatives perform well in their role they will succeed, not only in persuading constituents that they are fairly and effectively advancing their interests, but also in fairly and effectively advancing their interests as a matter of objective fact. It is in this latter respect that the epistemic perspective is important. The ultimate criterion of whether the representative system is failing or succeeding, on this approach, is to look at the extent to which decisions correspond to objective standards of fairness and efficacy. And the appropriate norms governing representatives take on a strictly functional character: They can be assessed and calibrated by reference to their tendency to achieve epistemic improvements in the system's outputs. It is possible that there are alternatives to the representative system that might perform better from an epistemic point of view.[22] But as I argued above, the presumption of liberty and equality as foundational values creates very strong pressures toward an approach that balances wide consultation with rational deference to experts.

Thinking about representatives as epistemic intermediaries offers us a fresh way of approaching some of the debates that have surrounded representation in democratic theory. As I noted earlier, the classic formulation of that debate lies in the "trustee" versus "delegate" dispute. The essential question in that context is this: To what extent does good representation entail deference to the expressed desires and judgments of constituents on the one hand, versus the autonomous exercise of a representative's own evaluations on the other? Are representatives obliged principally to pursue their independent judgments about how to advance constituents' interests, tutored by their own informed understanding of the common good (a trustee model), or are they obliged principally to bring forth the concerns of their constituents as understood and articulated by the constituents themselves (a delegate model)? From an epistemic point of view, the answer is that "it depends." In some contexts, very substantial deference to the expressed views of constituents is the best way of contributing to the fair and effective service of their interests while, in others, a more independent mode of judgment and deliberation is appropriate.[23]

One obvious consideration favoring a more trustee-style role would be the relevance of highly technical considerations that are difficult for non-experts to competently assimilate to their perspective. The complex fact sensitivity of interests pushes us toward granting representatives greater autonomy of judgment and behavior. Again, the recent debate about healthcare reform in the United States hinges on enormously complicated economic and human interactions among different components of the system. Should we be asking non-experts for their judgments about the proper role of re-insurance, for example? What about the determination of formularies, or the proper term of orphan drug exclusivity under patent law? Plausibly, a tutored mini-public of non-experts with access to curated information could form credible judgments on such issues.[24] But simply bringing forth the voice of the mass public—serving as their "delegate"—is unlikely to serve anyone's interests. Those interests will be better served by representatives who can operate in relative (though not complete) insulation from the opinions of their constituents, because that kind of insulation is a better route to the integration of interest-relevant facts in this context.

On the other hand, interests with a high level of desire sensitivity would favor a more delegate-like approach. A trivial type of case might involve decisions about how to invest in different kinds of communal amenities. Should the local park have tennis courts or a swimming pool? Here, barring the existence of unusual complications, the interests of the community will be best served primarily by satisfying the contingent desires of the majority, such as it is. Here the representative should function largely as a mouthpiece for the community. The Minneapolis 2040 plan illustrates a more complex variant on this sort of example. Urban planning visions must rely on expert knowledge. Yet they also cannot abstract away from the particularities of what people want from their city, what amenities they expect, what problems they see as most significant, and what kind of community life they see as valuable.

Even in a seemingly trivial case like "swimming pool versus tennis courts," things can quickly become complicated. Tennis courts and swimming pools may cater to different kinds of people with different kinds of class interests and identities. These options may have different social implications for the neighborhood in which they are constructed. What if more people in the neighborhood want tennis courts, but there is a dearth of access to swimming for low-income residents? Do public parks have an obligation to provide amenities for the underserved? How should that be weighed against the majority view? Likewise, where will the resources come from to build the pool/tennis court? Is this community in competition with another community for these resources? Who has the more compelling claim and why? Representatives who simply channel whatever is believed by the better portion of their constituents are unlikely to attend adequately to the broader context as they consider how to advance those constituents' interests.

From an epistemic point of view, most policy matters of interest will require moving between a trustee- and delegate-style role of deliberation. The particular interest that citizens have in a good education, for example, depends in part on their conception of the good life and where/how education fits within that. For this reason, successful representation requires channeling and understanding citizens' core desires as they relate to a good life. At the same time, designing a good education policy also requires attending to an institutional and scientific understanding of teaching models, the social dynamics of the classroom, budgetary and other practical constraints, and competing demands on resources.

Similar kinds of points can be made in the context of healthcare, economic, or housing policy.

Contributing to system outcomes that fairly and effectively serve interests in most cases requires moving between delegate- and trustee-styles of behavior. A rigid dichotomy between these two approaches is difficult to reconcile with the wide variation among policy challenges and the kinds of intuitions that these disparate cases generate. An epistemic understanding of representation offers a clear account of this variation, and a justification for pluralism in our approach: If the goal is policy outputs that fairly and effectively serve interests, then different combinations of these two models are called for on different policy occasions among different publics. Epistemic output has fact-sensitive dimensions, which is why simply channeling public attitudes will not do. At the same time, it has desire-sensitive dimensions, which is why pure trustee models will not do either.

Similar points apply in reference to other proposed models of representation. For example, drawing on Mansbridge's terminology, is the proper approach to representation "anticipatory," "promissory," "gyroscopic," or "surrogacy"?[25] As she herself suggests, the answer is plausibly that "it depends." In some cases, it may be best for representatives to act as "gyroscopes" who are selected on the basis of core values and dispositions, and who then act more or less independently of their constituents' day-to-day judgments. That model sounds most plausible in contexts where a more trustee-like mode of engagement is appropriate. "Promissory" models of representation—in which representatives are accountable to the particular set of commitments on which they were elected—may be most appropriate in cases where warranted confidence in the motives of representatives is low. "Surrogate" representation—in which the shared social identity of representatives and constituents is particularly significant—is attractive in contexts where there are strong identity-based disparities in power and interests, and where there are strongly desire-sensitive interests in play.

Does good representation, as Suzanne Dovi suggests, fundamentally require preserving and promoting the autonomy of constituents to contest the decisions of representatives?[26] From an epistemic point of view it undoubtedly does, primarily because such contestation facilitates a regular transfer of knowledge between constituents and their representatives. Nonetheless, the idea of autonomy on its own substantially underdetermines the form and extent of contestation. To what degree should citizens be directly involved with the legislative process as opposed to granting appointed technocrats the discretion to operate behind closed doors? Thinking about representation in epistemic terms allows us to answer this question by looking at the epistemic quality of the system's decision outputs and provides a clear justification for variation in the norms and institutional structure of representation.

THE EPISTEMIC FAILURES OF THE NEW POPULISM

In the terms considered above, one way of thinking about representatives who "don't listen" is to say that there have been important failures of upward vertical integration in the epistemic system. This is at least very plausibly true in the context of recent populist movements. The core populist grievances have revolved around the economic and social effects of globalization. And while these grievances are partially grounded in falsehoods or severe distortions, there is also some legitimacy to them. In the United States, a cluster of familiar considerations include: the increasing economic precariousness of lower- and middle-class workers,[27] labor displacement resulting from technology and globalization,[28] rising social and economic inequality,[29] the dismantling of unions,[30] and the asymmetric (Wall Street versus "Main Street") political response to the 2008 financial crisis.[31] The idea that Donald Trump offers a credible remedy to these problems is at best highly problematic, but the underlying grievances themselves reflect genuine failures of representation. In general, the American representative system has been systematically unresponsive toward the concerns of lower-income voters.[32] There is truth in the view that Trump's voters—at least the less affluent and less educated among them—have been "forgotten."[33]

What explains this representational failure? In puzzling over the massive under-representation of working-class voters in American policy, Larry Bartels finds little support for what might otherwise seem to be plausible explanations of this phenomenon: that the wealthy are more informed or that they vote more. The most straightforward explanation of available data, he speculates, may simply be the overpowering significance of money in funding electoral campaigns (though he notes the lack of clear evidence on this point).[34] Nicholas Carnes observes that working-class citizens have never held more than 2 percent of congressional seats in the United States.[35] Pointing to systematic differences in the values and policy outlook of rich and working-class citizens, he argues that the US government has long been, in effect, a government "by the rich for the rich."

And why do the rich govern "for the rich"? There are undoubtedly both motivational and informational issues in play. Motivationally, class affiliation shapes our values and our perceptions of what matters and why. Those who are more affluent and educated are likely to develop substantially different views about the appropriate policy course.[36] And yet the more and less economically well off are also likely to have different pools of information about economic policy and its effects, insofar as that information is drawn from life experience and social networks. These informational and motivational effects are not independent: Caring more about the predicament of low-wage manufacturing workers is likely to induce one to gather more information about that predicament; and having more information about that predicament makes it more likely that one will care about it.

One example of particular relevance here concerns the economic consequences of low-skilled immigration in sectors such as farming and manufacturing. Here is a somewhat speculative account of what is going on in that case. On the one hand, the policy establishment tends to emphasize the positive benefits of low-skilled immigration for economic growth.[37] On the other, populists focus on wage suppression, arguing that immigrants are "stealing jobs." As George Borjas argues, however, both of these arguments are in some sense right: Low-wage immigration is beneficial to the economy in the aggregate but also tends to reduce the wages of low-skill native workers in the relevant industries by a few percentage points.[38] To an affluent citizen, of course, a 2 percent drop in the wages of poultry plant workers may look like a small price to pay for higher aggregate growth. For those already struggling to make ends meet, however, a 2 percent wage cut may be very significant indeed. The approach of US economic policy appears to have been much more sensitive to the perspective of a typical affluent citizen in this regard.[39] And that plausibly reflects an interplay between motivational elements on the one hand—more affluent citizens just don't find a 2 percent wage drop among the working class to be particularly significant, and informational on the other—those who haven't felt the acute economic vulnerabilities of low-skill workers may easily dismiss their concerns as mere racism without attending carefully to the economic facts.

In this respect, the representative system is very clearly failing in its role as epistemic intermediary, and the rise of populism reflects that failure. Recent economic policy has not fairly and effectively served the interests of less educated and less skilled workers, and in this respect those workers are not being heard. However, there is a second problem at work in this context. The problem is that the people complaining about not being heard are themselves not listening to others. On any number of issues, scientific and social-scientific authority is conveniently ignored or twisted in politically convenient ways. Journalists who report ideologically inconvenient facts are disparaged and threatened, and the idea of truth itself is often treated as a sort of political game.[40] Indeed, this attitude toward experts, facts, and expertise is one of populism's definitive features,[41] and particularly of American populism. The epistemic quality of voters has always been shaky at best.[42] What's particularly striking about the present moment is the extent to which ignorance is a kind of willful and explicitly endorsed state.

Most obviously, there is ignorance among populist voters of important scientific facts that bear on interests. Believing that climate change is a "hoax" does not make it any less harmful to future generations. There is also ignorance of the disparate desires and particularities that define interests across much of the population. Populists tend to focus on the concerns most salient to a particular demographic group of "true" Americans (or English, Hungarians, Italians, etc.) with little regard, and often active contempt, for the expressed concerns of large classes of their fellow citizens.[43] To some degree, this can be seen as a failure of sympathy or moral motivation as much as ignorance. But the complex of strong out-group hostility also sustains patterns of cognition and epistemic negligence that are constitutive of ignorance. Populism is to a large degree defined by patterns of affect and epistemic cognition that are mutually reinforcing.[44] This point supports the idea that, as I have noted, systems of representation produce epistemic goods through both informational and motivational mechanisms: They create a means for disseminating information, but they also create a system of friction and contestation that encourages some measure of deliberative accountability.

Thus, if it is problematic that policymakers and representatives are out of touch with important concerns of certain sectors of the public, then it is at least as problematic that "ordinary" constituents are themselves proudly ignorant of essential scientific facts, and likewise seem unable to represent the pressing concerns of other social groups. This point applies broadly across democratic citizens, but is particularly compelling in the case of populism, which (a) explicitly rejects the authority of scientific experts and (b) is organized around forms of out-grouping that degrade and marginalize the concerns of entire social classes. So ignorance works in both directions between the "elites" who populist voters resent and those voters themselves. The policy outlook of elites has not been adequately shaped by the concerns of populist voters and, at the same time, those voters have not been adequately informed by elites' knowledge. These voters are ignored, but they are also ignorant. This dynamic is one central driver of the present democratic failure.

Contrary to Pepe Grillo and other populists, representatives are not and should not be a direct voice box for "what you want." That is because the epistemic challenge of democracy entails a correlative duty of listening and absorbing information from technical experts, along with others outside one's district and/or social group. As I have been suggesting, institutions of representation work well when they counter the inherently limited perspective of both non-expert constituents and technocratic policy designers.

How should we think about these observations in light of the epistemic model of representation that we have been considering? Mansbridge points to Michael Neblo, Kevin Esterling, and David Lazer's work with e-townhalls as an example of how high-quality constituent-representative communication could be implemented.[45] She also mentions deliberative polling as an important model along these lines. Both of these examples involve highly structured forums for input in which citizens engage with high-quality expert information and are obliged to listen and respond in a thoughtful manner. The benefit of communication in these contexts depends as much on the pro-social incentives and engagement created as the way in which information is transferred. In other words, the primary problem solved is not that citizens are ignored but that they are ignorant. The deliberative forum encourages them to become engaged and informed, and to exercise appropriate deference to those who know more than they about technical matters.

The examples of deliberative polling and e-townhalls suggest that there are potentially powerful complementarities between institutional mechanisms that facilitate upward, downward, and horizontal epistemic integration at the same time. The complementarities exist because the institutional structure of high-quality deliberation strongly encourages the disposition both toward listening and toward rational deference to credible authority. Democratic representation is not intrinsically necessary to facilitate that kind of process. Nonetheless, as I noted earlier, representatives create a formal target for the uptake of relevant perspectives into the decision-making process. In that way, the existence of representatives creates an institutional context for mutual engagement that would not exist in an undemocratic system, but that would also not be scalable and sustainable in a purely plebiscitary democracy.

However, the general lesson of this chapter has been that there is no completely generalizable model for an epistemically healthy model of representation, and this clearly applies to an assessment of recent populism. Those critical of populist movements tend to emphasize ways in which the participants in those movements are ignorant, while those supportive of those movements tend to emphasize the ways in which they are ignored. The first of these perspectives tempts us with a push toward more technocratic and trustee-like models of democratic governance, while the second of these perspectives tempts us with more direct and delegate-like models of democratic rule.

From an epistemic point of view, we should look with skepticism toward both of these proposals. When technocratic policy-making becomes badly decoupled from the everyday perspective of citizens, failures of interest representation are inevitable, and the plight of low-wage workers in advanced economies illustrates this point well. Yet sometimes the issues at hand are sufficiently complex that it is epistemically rational to keep the public at a certain technocratic remove. Establishing more robust forms of public input, engagement, and contestation is not always instrumental to improving the fair and effective representation of interests, and this explains why Grillo's "mouthpiece of the people" model of representation is a mistake.

It is likely that, in some cases, a purely epistemic approach would push us past the dividing line between democracy and something more elitist. In those instances, as I noted in my introduction, I accept that considerations of procedural fairness might take effect as a valid constraint on epistemic objectives. A culture in which officials are accountable to citizens and obliged to explain and justify their use of power is plausibly quite valuable even if it is epistemically suboptimal.[46] The argument above is not premised on any precise view about how the interaction between procedural and epistemic concerns operates. I will only note that, at least conventionally, the general mandates of democratic procedural fairness are compatible with enormous variation in the degree and type of technocratic delegation. Even apart from concerns about procedural fairness, the case of Grillo illustrates more pragmatic reasons for ensuring that citizens have some basic measure of voice in the process: When people believe that no one is listening to them, they will get angry and obstruct the democratic process. Therefore, my point against Grillo is not that we should ignore the intrinsic and pragmatic value of citizens' participation in the process; it is that we should not treat these as definitive of our model of representation.

If citizens learn to embrace a democratic ideal that treats their involvement and direct authority as always and everywhere desirable, then achieving a healthy division of cognitive labor will become difficult, and society will need to continually soothe anxieties from the perceived unheard. Populism thrives on a misguided epistemic egalitarianism and transforms one important mechanism in democracy—citizen input and oversight—into a singular objective that crowds out other goods worth protecting. Political and civic maturity require a recognition that it is sometimes imperative to speak and be heard, and other times better to stand back and listen. A theory of representation should be able to accommodate and explain this point.

NOTES

1. I am grateful to Jane Mansbridge and Daniel Viehoff for helpful feedback on this chapter. I also benefited from comments and discussion among the participants at the 2018 NOMOS Conference on "Democratic Failure" at the Boston University School of Law.

2. See the website, https://minneapolis2040.com, for additional information

3. E.g., Jason Brennan, *Against Democracy* (Princeton, NJ: Princeton University Press, 2016).

4. Robert E. Goodin and Kai Spiekermann, *An Epistemic Theory of Democracy* (Oxford: Oxford University Press, 2018); Hélène Landemore, *Democratic Reason: Politics, Collective Intelligence, and the Rule of the Many* (Princeton, NJ: Princeton University Press, 2013); David M. Estlund, *Democratic Authority: A Philosophical Framework* (Princeton, NJ: Princeton University Press, 2008); Joshua Cohen, "An Epistemic Conception of Democracy," *Ethics* 97, no. 1 (1986): 26–38.

5. Landemore, *Democratic Reason.*

6. Estlund, *Democratic Authority.*

7. Cohen, "An Epistemic Conception of Democracy," 34.

8. Michael Fuerstein, "Democratic Consensus as an Essential Byproduct," *Journal of Political Philosophy* 22, no. 3 (2014): 282–301.

9. Estlund, *Democratic Authority.*

10. Michael Fuerstein, "Epistemic Democracy and the Social Character of Knowledge," *Episteme* 5, no. 1 (2008): 74–93.

11. Elizabeth Anderson, "The Epistemology of Democracy," *Episteme* 3, no. 1–2 (2006): 8–22.

12. John Parkinson and Jane Mansbridge, *Deliberative Systems* (Cambridge: Cambridge University Press, 2012).

13. John Hardwig, "The Role of Trust in Knowledge," *Journal of Philosophy* 88, no. 12 (1991): 693–708. Alfred Moore, *Critical Elitism: Deliberation, Democracy, and the Problem of Expertise* (Cambridge: Cambridge University Press, 2017).

14. Andrew Rehfeld, "On Representing," *Journal of Political Philosophy* 26, no. 2 (2018): 216.

15. Rehfeld's objective, in fact, is to argue that, for various reasons, these conditions are neither necessary nor sufficient for representation. However, his particular concerns do not bear significantly on the approach developed here.

16. Estlund, *Democratic Authority.*

17. John Stuart Mill, "Considerations on Representative Government," in *On Liberty and Other Essays,* ed. John Gray (Oxford: Oxford University Press, 1991).

18. Michael Fuerstein, "Epistemic Trust and Liberal Justification," *Journal of Political Philosophy* 21, no. 2 (2013): 179–99; Moore, *Critical Elitism*; Philip Kitcher, *The Ethical Project* (Cambridge, MA: Harvard University Press, 2011).

19. Linda Darling-Hammond, "Race, Inequality, and Educational Accountability: The Irony of 'No Child Left Behind'," *Race Ethnicity and Education* 10, no. 3 (2008): 245–60.

20. Josiah Ober, *Democracy and Knowledge: Innovation and Learning in Classical Athens* (Princeton, NJ: Princeton University Press, 2008); Helena Rosenblatt, *Rousseau and Geneva: From the First Discourse to the Social Contract 1749–1762* (Cambridge: Cambridge University Press, 1997); Jane Mansbridge, "Reconstructing Democracy," in *Revisioning the Political: Feminist Reconstructions of Traditional Concepts in Western Political Theory*, ed. Nancy J. Hirschmann and Christine Di Stefano (Boulder, CO: Westview Press, 1996).

21. Fuerstein, "Epistemic Democracy and the Social Character of Knowledge."

22. Brennan, *Against Democracy*; Daniel A. Bell, *The China Model: Political Meritocracy and the Limits of Democracy* (Princeton, NJ: Princeton University Press, 2015).

23. Goodin and Spiekermann offer their own very helpful discussion of this issue and endorse a similarly pluralistic conclusion in *An Epistemic Theory of Democracy*, 244–59; "Epistemic Aspects of Representative Government," *European Political Science Review* 4, no. 3 (2012): 303–325, though that discussion arises within the specific context of the Condorcet Jury Theorem. They are primarily concerned with the epistemic advantages of larger versus smaller bodies and do not address the way in which variations in the sources and types of politically relevant knowledge might imply advantages to one approach or another.

24. Annabelle Lever, "Democracy, Deliberation, and Public Service Reform," in *Public Services: A New Reform Agenda*, ed. Henry Kippin and Gary Stoker (New York: Bloomsbury Academic, 2012); Philip Kitcher, *Science in a Democratic Society* (Amherst, NY: Prometheus Books, 2011); James S. Fishkin, *When the People Speak: Deliberative Democracy and Public Consultation* (Oxford: Oxford University Press, 2009).

25. Jane Mansbridge, "Rethinking Representation," *American Political Science Review* 97, no. 4 (2003): 515–28.

26. Suzanne Dovi, "Good Representatives Foster Autonomy," *PS: Political Science and Politics* 51, no. 2 (2018): 303–26.

27. Jacob S. Hacker, *The Great Risk Shift: The New Economic Insecurity and the Decline of the American Dream*, 2nd ed. (Oxford: Oxford University Press, 2019).

28. David Autor, "The Polarization of Job Opportunities in the US Labor Market: Implications for Employment and Earnings," *Community Investments* 23, no. 2 (2010): 11–16.

29. Thomas Piketty and Emmanuel Saez, "Inequality in the Long Run," *Science* 344, no. 6186 (2014): 838–43.

30. Megan Dunn and James Walker, "Union Membership in the United States," US Bureau of Labor Statistics [online], www.bls.gov/.

31. Neil Barofsky, *Bailout: An Inside Account of How Washington Abandoned Main Street While Rescuing Wall Street* (New York: Free Press, 2012).

32. Larry M. Bartels, *Unequal Democracy: The Political Economy of the New Gilded Age*, 2nd ed. (Princeton, NJ: Princeton University Press, 2016).

33. Not all of Trump's support is working class, of course. In the general election, only 35% of Trump voters had household incomes less than $50,000 annually, and some have argued on this and related grounds that the idea that Trump's base is working class is a myth. See Nicholas Carnes and Noam Lupu, "It's Time to Bust the Myth: Most Trump Voters Were Not Working Class," *Washington Post*, June 5, 2017 [online], www.washingtonpost.com. However, Trump's political narrative is undeniably pitched in important respects toward the white working class, and his victory was critically propelled by shifts in support among this group. Nate Silver's analysis, for example, supports this claim with a focus on education levels: "Education, Not Income, Predicted Who Would Vote for Trump," *FiveThirtyEight*, November 22, 2016 [online], https://fivethirtyeight.com/. See also Stephen L. Morgan and Jiwon Lee, "Trump Voters and the White Working Class," *Sociological Science* 5 (2018): 234–45.

34. Bartels, *Unequal Democracy*, 267.

35. Nicholas Carnes, *The Cash Ceiling: Why Only the Rich Run for Office and What We Can Do About It* (Princeton, NJ: Princeton University Press, 2018).

36. Nicholas Carnes, *White Collar Government: The Hidden Role of Class in Economic Policy Making* (Chicago: University of Chicago Press, 2013).

37. See, for example, Eduardo Porter, "The Danger from Low-Skilled Immigrants: Not Having Them," *New York Times*, August 8, 2017 [online], www.nytimes.com; Lena Groeger, "The Immigration Effect," *ProPublica*, July 19, 2017 [online], https://projects.propublica.org.

38. George J. Borjas, *We Wanted Workers: Unraveling the Immigration Narrative* (New York: Norton, 2016).

39. For a particularly rich analysis along these lines, see Michael Lind, "The New Class War," *American Affairs* 1, no. 2 (2017): 19–44.

40. Lee McIntyre, *Post-Truth* (Cambridge, MA: MIT Press, 2018).

41. Jan-Werner Müller, *What Is Populism?* (Philadelphia: University of Pennsylvania Press, 2016).

42. Ilya Somin, *Democracy and Political Ignorance: Why Smaller Government Is Smarter*, 2nd ed. (Stanford, CA: Stanford University Press, 2016).

43. Pippa Norris and Ronald Inglehart, *Cultural Backlash: Trump, Brexit, and Authoritarian Populism* (Cambridge: Cambridge University Press, 2019); William A. Galston, *Anti-Pluralism: The Populist Threat to Liberal Democracy* (New Haven, CT: Yale University Press, 2018). While the more racist and xenophobic corners of Trump's constituents are egregious in this respect, I don't think they are alone in their ignorance of other citizens' interests. Cosmopolitan urbanites surely have their own failings to understand the origins of rural, working-class anger at the social and economic status quo. For a particularly compelling account, see Joan C. Williams, *White Working Class: Overcoming Class Cluelessness in America* (Boston, MA: Harvard Business Review Press, 2017).

44. Richard C. Fording and Sanford F. Schram, "The Cognitive and Emotional Sources of Trump Support: The Case of Low-Information Voters," *New Political Science* 39, no. 4 (2017): 670–86.

45. Michael A. Neblo, Kevin M. Esterling, and David M. J. Lazer, *Politics with the People: Building a Directly Representative Democracy* (Cambridge: Cambridge University Press, 2018).

46. I thank Daniel Viehoff for pressing this concern on me.

7

POLITICAL PARTIES AND PUBLIC POLICY

CHRISTIAN SALAS,
FRANCES MCCALL ROSENBLUTH,
AND IAN SHAPIRO

History, it was once alleged, "ended" in the happy and permanent state of democratic prosperity.[1] Since World War II, the world's democracies had demonstrated superior powers to achieve both economic development and national security, forcing other regimes to struggle to keep up. Following the Cold War and the collapse of Soviet Communism, adopting democratic institutions became the price of entry for former East European countries into NATO and the European Union. Even Vladimir Putin insisted that Russia was a "sovereign democracy." Ignoring such euphemistic claims, by the turn of the twenty-first century there were nonetheless more democracies than non-democracies in the world for the first time, and academics, disinclined to teleology, were prone to grant democracy an exception to the rule. China remained stubbornly authoritarian, but much of the Western commentary focused on how long the regime would be able to resist modernizing pressures to democratize—not whether it would ever happen.

That optimism has gone. Not only have authoritarian strongmen eroded democracies in Turkey, Latin America, and much of Eastern Europe. Resurgent authoritarian regimes in the Middle East and North Africa leave Tunisia as the only remaining harvest of the Arab Spring of 2010–2011. To a degree and extent once unthinkable, many Western democracies show signs of internal fragility. Even global leaders and democracy exporters such as the United States and Britain no longer appear immune from regime dysfunction. Book titles like *How Democracies Die, How Democracy Ends*, and *The Road to Unfreedom* capture a new sense of gloom about democracy's prospects.[2]

We do not offer a crystal ball about democracy's future. We argue, instead, that democracies have the best chance of thriving if they can provide policies that are good for most voters over the long run, and we suggest why programmatic competition between disciplined political parties is the best way to choose good policies, as Joseph Schumpeter recognized almost eight decades ago.[3] Policies aimed at the voter in the political middle may not always be optimal, particularly when extreme income inequality leaves many people in poverty, or enduring prejudice harms ethnic and racial minorities. But strong parties, by resisting populist tricks, are less likely to divide and disempower these voters in the first place. The choice of policies, in other words, depends on the structure of political competition. This logic is lost on advocates of identity politics; minority disenfranchisement and disadvantage are real, but they are man-made blights exacerbated by internally weak parties that cannot deliver on prosperity.

In what follows we discuss why political competition is important for prosperity, but we also explain why not all forms of competition are equally conducive to good public policy. How political competition is structured has discernible consequences for policy. More than we may have realized, the internal structure of political parties as well as the number of parties that compete for votes also have bearing on the viability of democratic governance itself. We describe the deleterious effects on policy of weak party discipline and of party system fragmentation. Informed citizens should resist the temptation to wrest the steering wheel from political parties. Instead, they should seek ways to strengthen parties, enhancing their ability to formulate and implement good public policy.

WHY TWO STRONG PARTIES

Our argument echoes E. E. Schattschneider's classic scholarship on political parties. Schattschneider's central insight was that "parties do not need laws to make them sensitive to the wishes of the voters any more than we need laws compelling merchants to please their customers. The sovereignty of the voter consists in his freedom of choice . . . Democracy is not found in the parties but between the parties."[4] Electoral competition between two large parties that straddle the political middle achieves what no amount of "democratizing" of parties (through primaries) or proliferating of parties could accomplish: It forces parties to take turns at offering, and then implementing, policies that benefit most voters. And because parties, unlike individual politicians, have reputations that go into the indefinite future, competition between parties pushes them to offer policies that will be good for voters in the long term.

In line with Schattschneider, Carey and Shugart elaborated on the corrosive effects of competition within parties.[5] Their core insight was that party backbenchers who are electorally accountable as individuals rather than as members of a disciplined party would be unable to commit to policies that, for the sake of the party's long-term reputation and strength, would benefit most of the voters most of the time, over the long haul. Carey and Shugart's contribution was to rank-order electoral systems by features most conducive to party discipline and, by extension, by their ability to deliver good public policy.

But Carey and Shugart, and indeed much of the academic mainstream, depart from Schattschneider in one important respect: They do not share his admiration of two large parties. We agree with them that postwar European social democracy was superior to the obsession with limiting the taxpayer's burden that often resulted from the Anglo-American competition for the median voter.[6] European Proportional Representation (PR) democracies excelled at combining economic prosperity with social equality throughout much of the postwar period. Not only Scandinavia, where social democracy was strongest, but other European PR countries as well, outperformed the United States and United Kingdom in providing unemployment insurance and job retraining for those left behind in the global economy.[7]

If, like Carey and Shugart, we consider the effects of strong party discipline alone, closed-list proportional representation systems might produce better policies than district-based systems that cater to some degree to narrowly based and self-serving groups anchored in geographic districts.[8] Large portions of the population in western Europe were unionized workers in well-paying and stable industrial jobs, and because these jobs depended on trade competitiveness, workers restrained their wage demands. Social democrats representing these workers were a regular and moderate presence in government. Coalition governments across the political spectrum underwrote a kind of political cartel between representatives of workers and employers to ensure export-led growth with egalitarian benefits.[9]

Europe's golden formula of class compromise might, however, have rested on a rare and lucky confluence of circumstances. Democracy confronts big challenges everywhere. One source of them is that, as the proportion of workers in stable industrial jobs has declined, the number of parties in PR systems in particular has proliferated. This, in turn, strains parties' ability to forge the famously moderate coalitions of yore that were able to balance short-term and long-term benefits to the citizenry. Preliminary evidence suggests that, under these new conditions, the growing fragmentation in PR systems will push more countries toward ill-advised clientelism.

Note, moreover, that Westminster's strong two-party competition produced single-payer health insurance, strong transportation infrastructure that has survived successive nationalizations and denationalizations, and impressive climate change policies to rival those of continental Europe. In the United States, by contrast, weaker party discipline has robbed the American electorate of those policies, despite their popularity. Britain's strong parties have also protected ethnic and racial minorities better than the weak parties in the United States, notwithstanding America's Bill of Rights and independent judiciary to enforce it. Nor do minorities in Britain need to live in fear of the growing presence of far right, often flagrantly racist and xenophobic parties that have been gaining footholds in many European legislatures over the past decade.

Westminster has the additional advantage over PR countries in offering voters a clear choice between two broad visions of the public good that can hold governments accountable for policy outcomes. Coalition governments can hypothetically deliver policies in the political middle just as well as a center-posturing majoritarian party through post-election bargaining.[10] To the extent this is true, proportional representation systems have the edge over majoritarian systems. Proportional representation systems that are based in large rather than small geographic districts can aggregate interests at or close to the national level, considering the costs and benefits of a given policy on the entire population. Moreover, large, encompassing political parties such as Germany's SPD and CDU/CSU have aimed, in the past, at the broad interests of voters in the ideological middle, eschewing policies desired by narrow groups that would be costly to many others.

This configuration would appear nearly ideal for the adoption of policies designed to promote broadly beneficial outcomes, and to predict inclusive and long-term prosperity. Germany performed so admirably over the postwar decades that many countries in the second and third waves of democratization emulated Germany's mixed-member electoral system, which was anchored in PR but had an element of single-member districts to foster large parties that would aim at the middle. But even in Germany the felicitous combination seems to be breaking down. It took Angela Merkel seven months to cobble together a government after the 2017 elections, and even then she only managed to entice the SPD back into it because polls showed that the AfD would do even better if the country went to another election—as was confirmed in the regional elections in Hesse and Bavaria the following year. As we will see, Germany's capacity to deliver the kinds of encompassing policies for which it is so well known is now in doubt.

The upshot is that Schattschneider's argument about the countervailing advantages of majoritarian electoral systems may have been right after all. Forcing two large parties to compete for the political middle reduces the hold that smaller, niche parties might have on final coalition building in legislative politics.[11] When only two parties compete for votes, political competition will be more likely to converge on economic policies aimed at the broad interests of the nation. By contrast, if parties in a PR system join a government coalition and then logroll the intense preferences of their respective constituencies, the population at large might well pay for the costs of those logrolls in the form of higher prices for protected industries, higher taxes for privileged recipients of redistribution, and possibly lower long-term growth.[12] It is an empirical question whether and under what conditions separately elected parties in PR systems can and will subordinate the interests of their respective constituencies to those of the coalition government.[13] The preliminary empirical results that we present below suggest that current economic conditions may undermine the ability of parties in coalition governments collectively to internalize the costs of their respective constituents' interests, to the detriment of good economic policy.

Democracy everywhere faces bigger challenges than in the rapid growth years following World War II. But as the proportion of workers in stable industrial jobs has declined, the number of parties has proliferated in PR systems, straining the ability of even strong parties to forge the famously moderate coalitions of yore that balanced short-term and long-term benefits of the citizenry. Preliminary evidence suggests that, under those new conditions, the growing fragmentation in PR systems may push more countries toward ill-advised clientelism.

EMPIRICAL STRATEGY AND FINDINGS

Understanding how democratic systems work requires measuring both party discipline and party fragmentation and studying how they work in combination. The interaction effects are complex because the more parties there are, the smaller each will be—rendering internal party discipline less consequential for policymaking. But increased fragmentation can play out in contradictory ways: The larger number of smaller parties might limit any given party's bargaining power, but parties that turn out to be indispensable will be able to extract disproportionate rents for keeping a government afloat. We undertake this study in two steps: First, we explore the connection between the decline in industrial jobs and party fragmentation under different electoral rules. Prosperity underpinned political moderation by giving the mass of voters a stake in the status quo. Many voters have abandoned traditional parties on the left, perhaps from frustration at their inability to stem the tide of job loss in the face of automation and foreign replacement of domestic manufacturing jobs. Second, we examine how party fragmentation and party discipline, in combination, shape policy outcomes.

Our empirical study suggests that party fragmentation, which in PR systems follows a drop in industrial jobs, decreases spending on public goods and increases spending on individual transfers. Strikingly, this change in budget priorities occurs more in disciplined systems than in weak party systems.[14] On the other hand, party fragmentation had no effect in undisciplined systems. Put another way, party discipline did not inoculate countries against the potent and negative effects of party fragmentation on a government's ability to offer good public policy. Because the data we employ cover several decades and many countries, they likely understate the effects of today's accelerating deindustrialization.

TABLE 7.1. Industrial Jobs and Voter Support

| | Left | | Right | |
| | Traditional | Non-Traditional | Traditional | Non-Traditional |
	(1)	(2)	(3)	(4)
Ind Jobs	0.41	-0.89**	0.54	-0.24
	(0.57)	(0.43)	(0.32)	(0.18)
SMD	0.12	-0.02	-0.11*	0.05
	(0.10)	(0.07)	(0.05)	(0.05)
Open List	-0.03	0.05	0.06**	0.01
	(0.05)	(0.03)	(0.02)	(0.03)
Presidential	-0.02	0.03	0.02	-0.09***
	(0.03)	(0.02)	(0.02)	(0.02)
GDP per cap	0.05	0.03	-0.01	0.04
	(0.08)	(0.06)	(0.04)	(0.05)
R2	0.907	0.646	0.927	0.822
N	222	222	222	222
Mean of Dep Var	0.272	0.060	0.298	0.047

Statistical significance: *0.10 **0.05 ***0.01

Tables 7.1 and 7.2 offer quantitative details. Table 7.1 shows that a shift in votes from the traditional postwar left-leaning parties to new parties on the left increased the number of parties. In table 7.2 we show that a 10 percent drop in the share of industrial jobs is associated with an increase in the number of effective parties, principally on the left, by about half a party across all of these country-years. In Germany, for example, the Social Democrats (SPD) lost votes to their left, to Die Linke and the Greens, forcing the SPD in turn to move leftward or at least to spread out ideologically. The CDU under Chancellor Angela Merkel took tactical advantage of their move by staking a larger claim to the political middle, which in turn may have spawned AfD activism on her right as she did so. Fragmentation on the left, in response to fewer industrial jobs, appears to have unleashed spatial strategies that increased fragmentation across the political spectrum.

TABLE 7.2. Industrial Jobs and Fragmentation on Left Parties

	Left	
	By Vote (5)	By Seats (6)
Ind Jobs	-4.73*	-5.73**
	(2.59)	(2.50)
SMD	0.47	0.30
	(0.72)	(0.64)
Open List	0.68**	0.55**
	(0.27)	(0.25)
Presidential	0.25	0.25
	(0.36)	(0.40)
GDP per cap	0.60	0.52
	(0.75)	(0.60)
R2	0.792	0.795
N	221	222
Mean of Dep Var	1.821	1.697

Statistical significance: *0.10 **0.05 ***0.01

Column 1 in table 7.3 shows that fragmentation occurred mostly in non-SMD systems, as we would expect. Majoritarian systems, even if beset with the same loss of industrial jobs, put up barriers to a political strategy of launching smaller parties to capture the disaffected.

Column 2 in table 7.3 shows the same substantive results if we measure the effects of majoritarian systems by the minimum share of votes within a district necessary for a party to secure one seat (rather than SMD). At very high levels of electoral system proportionality, a 10 percent loss of industrial jobs increases the number of parties by more than one-half on average (0.71). With every 10 percent increase in the minimum share of votes needed to win a seat, approaching the 50 percent of SMDs, the number of parties decreases by about a quarter of a party on average. Column 3 shows that in PR systems with open or closed lists— that is, irrespective of internal party discipline—the decline in industrial jobs is significantly associated with left party fragmentation. For reasons we do not explore in this chapter, but which we speculate may have something to do with clientelism in the presidential systems of Latin America that are also in this data set, column 4 shows that the connection between the loss of industrial jobs and left party fragmentation only exists in parliamentary systems.

TABLE 7.3. Industrial Jobs and Fragmentation on Left Parties, Heterogeneous Relation

| | Effective Number of Left Parties | | | |
	(1)	(2)	(3)	(4)
Ind Jobs	-5.21**	-7.19***	-5.87**	-5.46**
	(2.39)	(2.57)	(2.55)	(2.50)
Ind Jobs × SMD	8.91**			
	(4.01)			
Ind Jobs × Min %		25.51**		
		(11.51)		
Ind Jobs × Open List			1.76	
			(3.50)	
Ind Jobs × Presidential				11.40***
				(3.91)
R2	0.799	0.803	0.795	0.800
N	222	212	222	222
Mean of Dep Var	1.697	1.685	1.697	1.697
+ p-value	0.445	0.505	0.032	0.232

Statistical significance: *0.10 **0.05 ***0.01

Party Fragmentation and Economic Policies

The splintering of parties on the left in response to dissatisfaction reduces these parties' support for moderate policies that benefit the political middle- and long-term interests for most voters. A decrease in left-vote cohesiveness away from the median voter is likely to shift policies toward smaller and more dispersed groups of voters.

Table 7.4 offers suggestive evidence for that trend, that left fragmentation reduces spending on public goods (community services) when the left is in government. By contrast, agricultural producers' support, which is an example of spending on narrower groups in the population, increases with fragmentation. Spending on redistribution, the hallmark policy of the left, increases with fragmentation when the left is government and decreases when the right is in power. This suggests that fragmentation is likely to reduce long-term growth and prosperity while increasing political fragmentation. Public goods provision is superior to redistributive transfers favoring insider groups; and while transfers designed to reduce inequality are desirable, fragmented political systems tend not to transfer income to the weak.

TABLE 7.4. Fragmentation on Left Parties and Policy Choice and Outcome

	Gov Spend Community (1)	Agric Producer Support (2)	Gov Spend Redistribution (3)	Unemployment Rate (4)
Left Frag	-0.03	0.25***	-0.42**	0.01
	(0.04)	(0.06)	(0.19)	(0.20)
Left Frag × Left Gov	-0.15**	0.06	1.01**	1.02***
	(0.07)	(0.08)	(0.39)	(0.37)
Left Gov	0.18***	-0.32**	-0.06	0.30
	(0.05)	(0.13)	(0.22)	(0.27)
R^2	0.544	0.913	0.948	0.746
N	478	302	478	639
Mean of Dep Var	0.759	1.430	15.370	7.165
+ p-value	0.008	0.000	0.107	0.030

Statistical significance: *0.10 **0.05 ***0.01

In more bad news, when the left is in government, fragmentation increases unemployment: One additional left party causes an increase of 1 percent in the share of workers who are unemployed. We speculate that the fall in industrial jobs forces the left to continue serving well-organized workers with employment benefits and protection at the expense of workers who have lost their jobs and who find it hard to get a new job given the high costs of employment.

Postwar prosperity generated political moderation that masked institutional differences that have since begun to reveal themselves. Large and well-organized groups such as unionized workers, able to support a strong party of the left, moderated their demands for higher wages because organized labor was such a large proportion of the total population to encompass their interests as consumers and exporters as well as workers.[15] Majoritarian electoral systems by contrast forced parties to aim at broader coalitions than industrial workers alone, but the governments and policies produced by majoritarian and PR systems would be much the same if industrial workers encompass the median voter. As organized labor shrinks as a percentage of the population, its interests have diverged from those of voters in the middle, pulling labor parties to the political left. Because PR systems make it easy for parties to fragment and gain elections as small parties, deindustrialization has produced left-party fragmentation in PR but not in majoritarian countries.

Majoritarian Systems: Strengths and Weaknesses

The disciplined, PR systems of Europe have been hard hit by the decline in industrial jobs. The United States and Britain have not fared so well either, but each in its own way. National parties in the United States are weak by design because they share control over policy levers with each other and with different levels of government. Gary Cox and Mathew McCubbins point out the status quo bias of the US system, which perhaps was an advantage in good times.[16] The tendency for citizens to blame politicians for bad economic fortunes has produced an accretion of reforms, including legislative party primaries and referendums that further weaken the ability of parties to craft and implement programmatic electoral platforms aimed at the country's best interest. State legislatures' drawing of congressional district lines to favor incumbents or, worse yet, one party's incumbents over another's, have skewed the results of primaries toward extremists and party activists who bother to turn out in primary elections. Voters respond to the resulting congressional polarization and policy gridlock with even more fury than that which has fueled Trump's executive adventurism.[17]

Britain's Westminster system that combines single member districts with parliamentary democracy has been synonymous with strong party competition. But in Britain, too, the decline in industrial jobs has produced a growing divide between London's service-sector prosperity and the rest of the country. The parties have weakened internally, as constituencies from one kind of district share fewer interests with the other. These demographic changes overwhelmed Britain's very strong institutional incentives, giving vent to the demand for Brexit and the subsequent assaults on the system of internal party control.

Misguided Solutions

Previous scholarship has shown that, separately, party fragmentation and party indiscipline contribute to the under-provision of public goods and the over-provision of private goods. Our principal contribution is to consider how these institutional features interact. Strongly disciplined parties are less able to provide public goods as their number increases; and transfers to individuals, which we take as a proxy for inefficient clientelism, increase for disciplined parties as their number increases. Conversely, the less internally disciplined political parties are, the less important are party labels and their fragmentation for policymaking. This finding offers no endorsement for low party discipline, however, since these systems have a lower capacity for public goods provision to begin with.

To the extent that traditional parties are fragmenting in established democracies, especially in Western Europe, we should expect increased budget allocation to individual transfers, decreased allocation to public goods, and increased allocation to future consumption, especially in disciplined systems. It is striking that party discipline in this circumstance offers no cure and may actually worsen the ills of party fragmentation.

The impulse to "democratize" parties by weakening party discipline by means of open lists and primaries, however, is equally misguided. Neither party discipline nor indiscipline can guard against the potent and negative effects of party fragmentation on a government's ability to offer good public policy.

Industrial jobs have disappeared in rich democracies, undercutting political moderation. Nowhere has this occurred more dramatically than in the proportional representation countries of Europe where small, extremist parties have grown with astonishing speed and effectiveness. In the UK, by contrast, neither the racist British National Party nor the anti-European UKIP have made significant parliamentary inroads. With 12.6 percent of the vote in the 2015 UK election, under proportionate representation, UKIP would have netted eighty-six seats in the House of Commons instead of the solitary seat it won.[18] (Similarly, in the 1920s and 1930s, when extremist parties exploited economic stagnation to make major inroads in many other countries, the fascist Mosleyites got nowhere in British electoral politics.)

Reforms in many proportional representation countries have moved in the wrong direction: Opening list systems to let voters select individual representatives on party lists and using primaries to draw up lists. These measures produce intra-party competition that rewards small groups with intense preferences, and undermine healthy competition over national programs. It would be far better to increase thresholds, forcing small parties to combine, retain closed lists to strengthen party leaderships, and use counting rules that tilt in favor of the largest parties.

Internally disciplined and hierarchical parties have an undemocratic ring. The key to democratic accountability is for leaders' authority to be conditional on parliamentary backbenchers' preference for strategic moderation. If party members know they are better able to get and stay elected when they offer coherent policies, they can choose new leaders who can—as the swift departures of Margaret Thatcher in 1990 and David Cameron in 2016 underscore. Parties that are broad-gauged, encompassing an electoral majority, and are disciplined enough to enforce majority-enhancing deals give voters clear signals of what the party stands for and what it will implement in the event that it wins the election and becomes the government.

Populism in the United States and United Kingdom has corroded the major parties, to be sure. But first-past-the-post electoral rules in these countries force groups like the Tea Party to fight for prominence within the established parties rather than to establish separate political parties. Electoral competition in Single Member Districts has blunted the force of extremist groups, though decentralizing reforms have rendered them more vulnerable to hostile takeovers—as underscored by Jeremy Corbyn's reelection by the membership in September 2016 following an overwhelming no-confidence vote from the Parliamentary Labour Party, and Donald Trump's hostile takeover of the Republicans.[19] The more electoral districts remain competitive between the two major parties, the more electoral competition benefits the average citizen. Parties forced to compete for the political middle must be strategically moderate or fail.

Better Pathways for Reform

Democratic accountability rests on political competition between strong parties that can craft and deliver good policies. In proportional representation systems, raising the electoral threshold for legislative representation would reduce the toehold of small extremist parties and force party leaders to bundle policies at the level of aggregation that benefits most voters over the long term. Eliminating open lists and primaries would give party leaders the levers of control with which to enforce this kind of strategic moderation. Scrapping runoff elections would also promote moderation by robbing narrow interest groups of a source of power—their ability to swing elections in the second round of voting in exchange for special favors. Proportional representation countries, which have an advantage over district-based systems in controlling backbenchers to offer nationally competitive platforms, forfeit that advantage when they succumb to the false promises of decentralizing forms of "party democratization."

District-based systems such as those in the United States and Britain need radical restructuring in the direction of national competition. Ideally, every electoral district would be diverse in ways that mirror the nation's diversity across the range of issues that voters care about. Given the wealth and prosperity differentials between New York and London and many other parts of their respective countries, an ideal system would include a sliver of cities, suburbs, and rural areas in every constituency. The median voter in each constituency would then better resemble the national median voter, and their elected representatives would find it comparatively easy to agree on policy priorities. Backbenchers in the legislature would be willing to delegate authority to their party leaders in order to get legislative work done and protect the party's brand into the future. In Britain, this would also mean substantially increasing the size of constituencies and correspondingly reducing the number of MPs. The average British constituencies are a third the size of Germany's single member districts and a tenth of the size of the typical US congressional district.

American geographic diversity is locked into constitutional powers of the Senate that pose even bigger challenges. One realistic reform would be redistricting in favor of competitive congressional elections. State legislatures have relentlessly redistricted with exactly the opposite purpose: to create the maximum number of districts for their own party while wasting as many votes for the opposite party as possible with super-safe districts. In most districts this means that the primary election is the only contest of any consequence, fostering Tea Party takeovers and other kinds of extremism.

Majority-minority districts have, ironically, reduced partisan competition and thereby failed to serve the interests of the minority voters that they are intended to benefit. Alternative ways to achieve diversity in legislatures include the reservation of seven out of New Zealand's 120 parliamentary seats for Māoris, or the comparable provision in India dating back to the Poona Pact of 1934, which reserves 84 out of the parliament's 543 seats for Untouchables and other scheduled castes. Requiring parties to nominate a diverse field of candidates could also enhance gender and other forms of diversity without diluting democracy's competitive lifeblood. Making every district accountable to the preferences of voters in the political middle would moderate the stances of American legislative parties by strengthening their leaders at the expense of the shrinking number of outliers. There may be some vulnerable minorities that will not be adequately protected by any electoral arrangements, particularly when ethnic and racial inequalities consistently map onto inequalities of income.

Even in that case, vulnerable minorities would be better served when politicians are given incentives to campaign on political platforms defined by economic interests rather than ethnicity and race. Identity politics tends to breed identity politics, as the scramble to benefit from set-asides and other benefits for scheduled casts in India and the recent rise of white identity politics in the United States underscore. African Americans in the United States would be better served if both major parties had incentives to compete for their voters, rather than the current status quo in which Democrats can take them for granted and Republicans' main incentive is to find ways to suppress minority turnout.[20]

American checks and balances, hailed as antidotes to tyranny, have often fallen prey to powerful groups rather than working to protect weak ones. Most advances that vulnerable minorities have achieved in the United States have come through legislatures, not the courts—protestations by lawyers to the contrary notwithstanding.[21] Comparative evidence suggests that separation-of-powers systems with independent courts do no better than parliamentary democracy at protecting vulnerable minorities. Indeed, courts have undermined democratic competition in the United States since 1976 by declaring money to be speech protected by the First Amendment to the Constitution, disproportionately empowering the well-heeled to work their will in the American political process.[22]

Plebiscites and referendums undermine rather than enhance democratic accountability. Britain had never had a referendum before Harold Wilson called one in 1975 over remaining in the European Union. In those pre-Thatcherite days, it was Labour that was divided over Europe, which was considered less hospitable than Britain to workers' legal protections under UK law. Rather than do the hard work of fighting it out within his party, Wilson put it to a referendum in which Remain beat Leave by 67.2 percent to 32.8 percent. Pleased with himself as a Cheshire cat, Wilson opined in his autobiography: "It was a matter of some satisfaction that an issue which threatened several times over thirteen years to tear the Labour movement apart had been resolved fairly and finally . . . all that had divided us in that great controversy was

put behind us."[23] Five years later, in 1980, a referendum split the
Labour Party nevertheless. When Michael Foot, having retracted
his earlier acceptance of the Referendum result and declaring that
Britain should leave Europe without another referendum, won the
leadership contest in 1980, the Gang of Four—Roy Jenkins, David
Owen, Shirley Williams, and Bill Rodgers—stormed out to form
the Social Democratic Party. Had Dennis Healey not defeated
Tony Benn for the Deputy Leadership, the exodus would have
been a lot larger. Thirty-five years later, David Cameron made a
comparable blunder as the path of least resistance to avoid con-
fronting the Tory rifts over Brexit.

It is the job of political parties to bundle issues, so that voters
discount the things that they want against the other things that
they also want. American voters support unilateral tax cuts when
asked about them in Referendums such as Proposition 13 in California in 1978, limiting property taxes to 1 percent of assessed
value. The downstream effect was to decimate California's public
schools and local government. Polls show that voters will support
any tax cut when asked about them in isolation, but not if they are
told that a particular cut will be accompanied by losing a popular program such as free medical prescriptions.[24] Then they are
forced to discount their preference for lower taxes by their preference for free medical prescriptions.

Parties are better positioned than individual voters to consider
the costs and benefits of alternatives when they bundle policies
into programs. They must discount everything they propose by
everything else they propose in ways that they hope will appeal to
as large a swath of the population as possible. The larger the parties, the more voters they must consider. This is why both Labour
and the Tory parliamentary parties strongly favored remaining in
Europe. When they discounted the costs of leaving against everything else they knew most voters wanted, Remain made better
sense. Considering one issue at a time in a referendum creates an
artificial choice for voters, as in the case of the Brexit vote.

Weakening parties in favor of increasing local and diverse
voices has a democratic ring to it. This has been the dominant
response to rising insecurity. Unfortunately, decentralized control
also undermines the ability of parties to work out the tradeoffs
among policies in a complex world. As E. E. Schattschneider said

in 1942, "the condition of the parties is the best possible evidence of the nature of any regime."[25] Whatever the system, political parties play a vital role in identifying, competing over, and defending the broad interests of the voting public. Strengthening rather than weakening political parties is democracy's best hope.

APPENDIX

Data

We collect data on electoral rules, electoral results of legislative elections, and economic performance of the thirty-five OECD countries for 1945 to 2017.

For every election held democratically in this sample, we record the rules regarding: parliamentary or presidential system, district system (majoritarian, proportional or mixed), district magnitude, PR formula (Danish, Hare, Sainte-Lague, LR-Droop, D'Hondt, LR-Imperiali, Imperiali highest averages), list system (Open or preferential, Closed), PR legal threshold (minimum percentage of votes required for a party to be admitted into parliament), number of districts, and number of seats available or filled.

For every election we record whether the election was scheduled beforehand or called early, the number of rounds, and the turnout for each round. Only France has two rounds, we record the second round whenever a choice needs to be made. In the case of countries that use two different votes with different electoral systems, such as Germany and Mexico, we code the PR one. We record the vote share and seat share obtained by every party elected to parliament, recording which parties were "traditional" and which "non-traditional" and which parties were right-leaning and which left. Finally, we record the vote share for parties not elected to parliament if categorized as non-traditional (e.g., far right, far left).

In general, we follow standard coding rules such as those of Carey and Hix (2011).[26] We use several sources, including previous publications containing such information, official records (in print and online), and unofficial online sites (e.g., Google, Wikipedia).[27] Economic indicators such as the share of employment accounted for the industrial sector, GDP, unemployment, and inflation were obtained from the public databases of the OECD, the ILO, and the World Bank. All variables containing monetary amounts are measured in real terms, and with purchasing power parity when available; when used in estimation, these variables are logged.

Data availability varies with variable. The estimations shown in the text use the maximum number of years and countries for which data are available for our main variables, namely, party fragmentation and the share of employment accounted for the industrial sector. Since some potentially relevant controls are available only for a subset of years and/or countries, in the text we present estimates using only those controls available for the maximum sample.

Research Design

To examine the effect of the fall of industrial jobs on the support for different political factions and party fragmentation, we estimate

$$y_{it} = \alpha_i + \lambda_t + \beta \, IndJobs_{it-1} + X_{it-1} \, \Pi + \varepsilon_{it} \quad (1)$$

where i indexes countries where, and t indexes years when, an election was held. Given the data limitations and the year of elections, we are able to consider all thirty-five OECD countries but two, South Korea and Latvia, and all years from 1966 until 2015. With the exception of eight years where no election was held, in every year elections are held in a median of 4.5 countries, with as few as 1 (e.g., 1995) and as many as 13 (in 2011).

Our dependent variable y_{it} will measure an electoral outcome, of which we will consider two sets: (i) share of votes obtained by a political faction (traditional left, traditional right, non-traditional left, non-traditional right) and (ii) the resultant party fragmentation in parliament, as measured by the number of parties and by the classic *effective number of parties* measure, which basically weights each party by its share of seats.[28] Our preferred measure for fragmentation is *effective number of parties*, because it better accounts for actual fragmentation of forces in parliament.[29] Our main coefficient of interest is β, which accompanies $IndJobs_{it-1}$ the share of employment that corresponds to the industrial and manufacturing sector. Since some elections are held in the middle of the year and in order to avoid reverse causality issues, we measure $IndJobs_{it-1}$ the year prior to the election. All standard errors are clustered at the year level to correct for non-independence of observations across countries within a year, for example due to global political or economic trends.[30]

The specification includes country fixed effects α_i and year fixed effects γ_t. The country fixed effects capture any time-invariant differences across countries, such as persistent differences in ideological stigma or in corruption. Year fixed effects control for global trends that affect all countries similarly.

To account for the fact that the timing of election may be endogenous, we restrict the sample to exclude elections that were called ahead of the next scheduled election, about 13 percent of all elections in our sample. To control for country-specific time-varying unobservables, the specification includes a vector of covariates X_{it-1}, including GDP per capita of the year prior to the election to avoid reverse causality issues, and a collection of controls for the political system valid the year of the election. Political controls include indicator variables for parliamentary, vis-à-vis presidential, system, for closed-list systems, and for electoral systems with single-member districts (SMDs). We also include a variable we call *Min %* that calculates for each election the minimum percentage of votes within a district that a party requires to secure at least one seat. This variable intends to measure the degree of proportionality of an electoral system, and it is constructed using three pieces of information: the median district magnitude, the formula used to allocate seats to parties in a proportional system (e.g., D'Hondt), and the PR legal threshold, if one exists.

Finally, in addition to equation (1), for our main variable of interest—fragmentation on the left—we estimate (1) including an interaction of industrial jobs with SMD and *Min %* in order to test whether the result differs across degrees of proportionality.

To examine the effect of fragmentation of the left on labor policy choice and outcomes, we estimate

$$y_{it+1} = \alpha_i + \lambda_t + \beta\ LeftFrag_{it} + \gamma\ LeftGov_{it} \times LeftFrag_{it} + X_{it}\ \Pi + \varepsilon_{it} \quad (2)$$

where i indexes countries and t years. Given the data limitations and the year of elections, we are able to consider all thirty-five OECD countries but South Korea, and all years from 1966 until

2015. Fragmentation changes only at elections, and elections are held in different years for different countries. This staggered nature of elections allows us to employ a differences-in-differences design to test how left fragmentation $LeftFrag_{it}$ has affected policy choice and outcome, when the left was in government ($LeftGov_{it}$) as opposed to when it was not.

Depending on the country, elections are held at various times of the year, and some countries hold elections every two or three years. Thus, to focus on the effect of the recent fragmentation change without contaminating the results with future political phenomena, we measure all outcomes in the year posterior to the election, which inevitably limits our analysis to short-run policies.

As part of the differences-in-differences design, equation (2) includes country fixed effects α_i and year fixed effects γ_t. The main identifying assumption in this design is the parallel trends assumption, which requires that the trajectory of our dependent variable in a country where an election was held would, if it hadn't been held, have been similar to that of a country where no election occurred. Here again we exclude from the sample elections that were called ahead of the next scheduled election, about 13 percent of all elections in our sample. To account for omitted country-specific time-varying factors, the specification also includes a vector of covariates X_{it}, containing the same covariates as the first research design, together with an indicator variable of whether the governing party or coalition is from the left and a variable that measures the fragmentation of the right parties, which allows us to isolate the effect of left fragmentation alone, as opposed to general parliament fragmentation, on the policy outcome. Results are robust when using the full sample and, for the restricted and full sample, including linear time trends for each country, a parametric way of relaxing the parallel trends assumption allowing each country to have a unique trend over time.

Notes

1. Francis Fukuyama, *The End of History and the Last Man* (New York: Free Press, 1992).

2. Steven Levitsky and Daniel Ziblatt, *How Democracies Die* (New York: Crown, 2018), David Runciman, *How Democracy Ends* (New York: Basic

Books, 2018), and Timothy Snyder, *The Road to Unfreedom: Russia, Europe, America* (New York: Duggan Books, 2018).

3. Joseph Schumpeter, *Capitalism, Socialism and Democracy* (London: George Allen and Unwin, 1943), 250–83.

4. E. E. Schattschneider, *Party Government* (New York: Farrar & Rinehart, 1942), 53.

5. John Carey and Matthew S. Shugart, "Incentives to Cultivate a Personal Vote: A Rank Ordering of Electoral Formulas," *Electoral Studies* 14, no. 4 (December 1995): 417–39.

6. Eric C. Chang, Mark Andreas Kayser, Drew A. Linzer, and Ronald Rogowski, *Electoral Systems and the Balance of Consumer-Producer Power* (New York: Cambridge University Press, 2011).

7. Proportional representation (PR) is an electoral system, widely adopted in Europe and Latin America, in which parties gain electoral seats in proportion to the votes cast for them. As a result, PR systems tend to have numerous, smaller parties as compared to majoritarian systems.

8. Bruce Cain, John Ferejohn, and Morris Fiorina, "The Constituency Component: A Comparison of Service in Great Britain and the United States," *Comparative Political Studies* 16, no. 1 (1983): 67–91; Bruce Cain, John Ferejohn, and Morris Fiorina, "The Constituency Service Basis of the Personal Vote for U.S. representatives and Members of the British Parliament," *American Political Science Review* 78, no. 1 (1984): 110–25.

9. Peter A. Swenson, *Capitalists against Markets: The Making of Labor Markets and Welfare States in the United States and Sweden* (New York: Oxford University Press, 2010); Torben Iversen and David Soskice, *Democracy and Prosperity: Reinventing Capitalism through a Turbulent Century* (Princeton, NJ: Princeton University Press, 2019); Torben Iversen and David Soskice, "Electoral Institutions and the Politics of Coalitions: Why Some Democracies Redistribute More than Others," *American Political Science Review* 100, no. 2 (May 2006): 165–81.

For evidence that some countries such as Germany were able to establish rules within the cabinet to inhibit interparty logrolling, see, for example, Mark Hallerberg and Jurgen von Hagen, "Electoral Institutions, Cabinet Negotiations, and Budget Deficits in the European Union," NBER Working Paper No. 6341, National Bureau of Economic Research (December 1997); Lanny W. Martin and Georg Vanberg, *Parliaments and Coalitions: The Role of Legislative Institutions in Multiparty Governance* (New York: Oxford University Press, 2011).

10. Bingham G. Powell, *Elections as Instruments of Democracy: Majoritarian and Proportional Visions* (New Haven, CT: Yale University Press, 2000).

11. Druckman and Warwick argue that small parties are less likely to be pivotal in government formation—and therefore distorting of legislative

politics—when the existence of a large number of small parties reduces the value of their bids to join the government coalition. See Paul V. Warwick and James N. Druckman, "Portfolio salience and the proportionality of payoffs in coalition governments," *British Journal of Political Science* 31:4 (October 2001): 627–49. On the other hand, small religious parties in Israel seem to maintain out-sized influence in coalition politics on the dimension of religion and territorial aggrandizement to the extent they all agree on those points.

12. Kathleen Bawn and Frances Rosenbluth, "Short versus Long Coalitions: Electoral Accountability and the Size of the Public Sector," *American Journal of Political Science* 50, no. 2 (April 2006): 251–65; Torsten Persson, Gerard Roland, and Guido Tabellini, "Electoral Rules and Government Spending in Parliamentary Democracies," *Quarterly Journal of Political Science* 2, no. 2 (2007): 1–34. On the association between strong parties and economic growth, see Fernando Bizzarro et al., "Party Strength and Economic Growth," *World Politics* 70, no. 2 (April 2018): 275–320.

13. Bingham G. Powell, "PR, the Median Voter, and Economic Policy: An Exploration," Paper presented at the annual meeting of the American Political Science Association, 2002; Martin and Vanberg, *Parliaments and Coalitions*; Mark Hallerberg, Rolf Rainer Strauch, and Jurgen von Hagen, "The Design of Fiscal Rules and Forms of Governance in European Union Countries," *European Journal of Political Economy* 23, no. 2 (June 2009): 338–59.

14. To study the increasingly complicated institutional incentives of a changing labor force, we employed a data set of internal party structure and number of parties in thirty-four OECD countries from 1970 to 2017. We exploited the arbitrary timing of scheduled elections to gauge within-country variation in party structure over time and across democracies. Note that the countries in the sample with larger numbers of parties (the party fragmentation variable) were mostly in Latin America and Eastern Europe, where economies were less prosperous and stable.

15. Lars Calmfors and John Driffill, "Bargaining Structure, Corporatism and Macroeconomic Performance," *Economic Policy* 3, no. 6 (April 1988): 13–61; Iversen and Soskice, "Electoral Institutions and the Politics of Coalitions."

16. Gary W. Cox and Mathew D. McCubbins, *Setting the Agenda: Responsible Party Government in the U.S. House of Representatives* (New York: Cambridge University Press, 2005).

17. Sarah Binder, *Stalemate: Causes and Consequences of Legislative Gridlock* (Washington, DC: Brookings Institution Press, 2003).

18. "Election 2015: What Difference Would Proportional Representation Have Made?" BBC News, May 9, 2015, www.bbc.com/.

19. Frances Rosenbluth and Ian Shapiro, *Responsible Parties: Saving Democracy from Itself* (New Haven, CT: Yale University Press, 2018), 62–127.

20. Ibid., 42–61.

21. Gerald N. Rosenberg, *The Hollow Hope: Can Courts Bring About Social Change*, 2nd ed. (Chicago: University of Chicago Press, 2008).

22. Ian Shapiro, *Politics against Domination* (Cambridge, MA: Harvard University Press, 2016), 93–102.

23. Harold Wilson, *The Final Term: The Labour Government 1974–76* (London: Weidenfield & Nicholson, 1979), 109.

24. Mayling Birney, Ian Shapiro, and Michael Graetz, "The Elite Uses of Public Opinion: Lessons from the Estate Tax Repeal," in *Divide and Deal: The Politics of Distribution in Democracies*, eds. Ian Shapiro, Peter Swenson, and Daniela Donno (New York: New York University Press, 2008), 298–40.

25. Schattschneider, *Party Government*.

26. John M. Carey and Simon Hix, "The Electoral Sweet Spot: Low-Magnitude Proportional Electoral Systems," *American Political Science Review* 55, no. 2 (April 2011): 383–97.

27. Ibid.; Cesi Cruz, Philip Keefer, and Carlos Scartascini, *The Database of Political Institutions 2015 (DPI 2015)* (Washington, DC: Inter-American Development Bank, 2016).

28. Formally, effective number of parties is equal to one over the sum of the shares of each party squared, where shares are measured in decimals.

29. We wish to use a measure that captures the fact that a parliament consisting of four parties with equal share of seats is far more "fragmented" than one consisting of four parties with shares 45%, 45%, 5%, and 5%. Number of parties would indicate that both parliaments have four parties, while *effective number of parties* would indicate that the first has four parties while the second 2.44, exactly what intuition calls for.

30. Findings are similar when clustering by country. We use year clusters as the preferred method since the number of countries (33) is low (lower than 42 years), and we worry that our standard error estimates may be biased with small number of clusters.

PART III

FAILURES OF KNOWLEDGE

8

DU BOIS'S DEFENSE OF DEMOCRACY

DERRICK DARBY

The beginnings of the present failure of democracy in America was the repudiation of the democratic process in the case of black American citizens in the South.

—W. E. B. Du Bois, "Democracy Fails in America"[1]

The question which you and I have to settle is this: can we envision and do we want a democracy where the rights of all citizens are equal? It is not necessary to meet this clear statement by the trite remark that all people are not and probably never will be equal and similar in their abilities, their gifts and their accomplishments. The problem which is now proposed is a problem of legal rights to recognized political, civil and social equality for every citizen.

—W. E. B. Du Bois, "No Second-Class Citizens"[2]

Ignorance has been used to justify excluding certain citizens from political rule. Once a common justification for denying women and blacks the ballot in the United States, it was said that they did not know enough about society, politics, business, or even about their own good to be entrusted with the vote. Some contemporary writers—laboring under the dubious presumption that "ignorant" whites of low education are primarily responsible for his 2016 victory—have floated this as a reason for disenfranchising Donald Trump supporters. Consider, for example, a recent article in *Dissent*: "If majorities rally to a blustering, bullying, conspiracy-minded, bigotry-stoking joke of a candidate and turn him into no joke at all," the author asks, "is majority rule really any way to run a country?"[3]

W. E. B. Du Bois flatly rejected appeals to ignorance as justification for excluding citizens from political rule. The arguments he
used in the early decades of the twentieth century, which turn on
taking the right to vote to be a necessity, not a privilege, are still
valid today. Although we can use his arguments to answer anxious
liberals willing to entertain drastic measures to guard against the
harm that some "deplorable" voters may do, the main reason to
revisit Du Bois is that he supplies invaluable insight into how to
save democracy from failure. The solution he offers takes seriously
the threat to democracy posed not only by political elites but by
the great mass of citizens—women, blacks, the poor, working-class
whites, and other historically subordinated groups—who rightly
worry that the system is not working for them.

Democracy can fail in different ways. It can do so when its fundamental foundations—the right to vote, freedom of the press,
the rule of law—crumble. Since these are basic institutions, we can
call this *institutional failure*. It can also fail when self-proclaimed
democratic nations do not realize certain normative ideals such
as freedom and justice for all. Since these are basic aspirations,
we can call this *aspirational failure*. Both kinds of failure, which are
obviously related, can stem from the action or inaction of political elites including elected officials and administrative appointees.
But one can also link democratic failure to the action or inaction
of citizens whose decision to vote or to refrain from voting for a
certain candidate can create the opportunity for elected elites to
engineer institutional and aspirational failure.

Du Bois's solution addresses the threat to democracy from
below, that is, from the submerged masses who may use what little
political power they have to propel us toward democratic failure.
His solution speaks to how we can address the masses' legitimate
complaint that democracy is not working for them but for the
elites, the wealthy, and the powerful. The hope is that by doing this
we can decrease the odds that the masses will give political elites
an opportunity to engineer institutional and aspirational failure.

If we are committed to achieving a more perfect democracy—
one that moves us closer to securing the broadest measure of justice for all—we have a political duty to address the circumstances
that contribute to the masses potentially doing us harm by securing for them certain legal rights. Rights to education, economic

opportunity, and protection from discrimination are normative safeguards against democratic failure. Unfettered access to the ballot is essential because the right to vote helps the masses secure these other rights. Du Bois proposes that the way to avert democratic failure is to guarantee civil and political rights, social equality, and economic justice for every citizen. Of course this is no guarantee that democracy will endure. Other factors can contribute to democratic failure. Nevertheless, offering a solution that makes it less likely that the masses will use their votes to hand aspiring autocrats and political elites an opportunity to engineer democratic failure is an important safeguard worth pursuing.

We are living through times of worry about the future of democracy here in America and abroad. To be sure, democracy is not the only way to organize political society, and democracies are certainly not blameless when taking stock of atrocities around the globe. And while Du Bois's political thought also addresses imperialism, exploitation, and racism, which are global problems not limited to democratic societies, questions of democracy loom large for him. Three of them are featured in what follows: Why have some citizens been denied the right to vote? How does this contribute to democratic failure? How can we avert it?[4] For fresh insight into how democracy can survive, we should consult visionary voices that attend to the plight of persons on the dark side of the color line. What they have to teach us is not just relevant for blacks but for all of American democracy's outcasts. This chapter reconstructs Du Bois's defense of democracy as presented in "Of the Ruling of Men," a chapter of his neglected yet important work *Darkwater: Voices from Within the Veil.*[5]

DEMOCRACY'S DILEMMA

The presidential election of Donald Trump in 2016 stirred up heightened anxiety about the fate of American democracy. White liberals have been especially worried. It is a rare dinner party with this group where Trump and his grave threat to democracy is not the main topic of conversation.

But scholars who have been brought up on the wisdom of Frederick Douglass, Anna Julia Cooper, Ida B. Wells, W. E. B. Du Bois, Zora Neale Hurston, Langston Hughes, Ella Baker, Fannie Lou

Hamer, Malcolm X, Martin Luther King, Jr., Audre Lorde, and Angela Davis are no more anxious than usual. These students of past and present social movements that have placed the suffering and democratic aspirations of black folks at center stage have lower expectations about American democracy given its checkered track record.[6] And there is reason to believe that this skepticism is also justified when viewing Western democracy through a global historical lens.[7]

The heightened state of alarm among anxious white liberals is really about a lamentable lack of historical perspective regarding the black experience in America and the experiences of people of color more generally. Appreciating Du Bois's critical reflections on the promises and practices of American democracy, as well as the wisdom of black folks that came before and after him, accounts for why many students of black social and political thought do not think that the Trump presidency, and the precarious state of American democracy today, amounts to anything more than business as usual. The players may have changed but the game is the same one Du Bois criticized roughly one hundred years ago. America is an imperfect democracy rigged to benefit the few—"the Rich, the Privileged, the Powerful"—at the expense of the many.[8] And the color line remains an obstacle to the working-class unity needed to make the game more fair and less exploitative.

This is not to say that we should surrender to tyranny of the few without a good fight. Nor is it to deny that there are relative differences in value among imperfect democratic regimes. And I agree with the late Richard Rorty and with Cornel West that we must certainly not let political nihilism tempt us to lose all hope for achieving our country—an America that is worthy of its democratic aspirations. My point is that Trump's victory gives us no novel reasons to be alarmed today. Trump's rise to power is a symptom not a cause of much deeper problems with American democracy. To appreciate this insight, we must take up the political thought of figures like Du Bois who have been largely neglected in mainstream public and academic discussions of democracy.[9]

Philosophers have long argued for the value of democracy. Some have defended democracy as something to be valued for its own sake, while others have argued that its value lies in all the valuable things it affords us, not the least of which are freedom, equality, and security. We assume that, when the masses are entrusted with political power to rule themselves, freedom, equality, security, and whatever else of value that democracy is thought to bring us will follow straightaway. But this is certainly wishful thinking.

A cursory reflection on the history of America's experiment with democracy suffices to highlight what can go wrong, and how rule by the people can deliver unfreedom rather than freedom, inequality rather than equality, and terrorism instead of security. As we know, some of the masses served up black chattel slavery, lynch mobs, and American Apartheid. And whether we attribute these products of American democracy to racial prejudice, white ignorance, a principled commitment to states' rights or to capitalist greed, these results hardly constituted a realization of the valuable ideals that justify democracy on instrumental grounds.

In America's defense, some have insisted upon democracy's instrumental value not by claiming that these atrocities were aberrations. Instead, they draw specious distinctions between persons based on racial membership and other arbitrary characteristics such as gender. And they use them to qualify who was fit to rule, who to serve, who was meant to benefit from the ideals safeguarded by democracy, and who was not. Others have noted that democracy in its most inclusive form—rule by all not just some of the masses—has yet to be realized in world history.

For example, one writer tells us: "The democracy of Athens was a rather exclusive government of intellectuals based on slavery; the republican cities of the Adriatic and even the Swiss cantons were administered in accordance with aristocratic principles; even Cromwell's commonwealth was a modified dictatorship."[10] Du Bois makes a similar observation about America: "Because you can imagine in a democracy democratic principles being overthrown and the power being put into the hands of a few men; but that has not happened in the United States. What you have in the United States is that the power still, supposedly, rests with the masses of the people, but the right to exercise it has been taken by a few men."[11]

With the election of Trump, many Americans, especially white liberal ones coming off of an eight-year Obama high and now fearing the demise of a democratic world order, have had to confront a question that Du Bois and countless black folks, women, and poor people have asked many times before: *What should we do when American democracy fails us?* Blacks have asked: When democracy renders us what Du Bois calls "second-class citizens," should we flee? Should we fight? Should we tear the whole thing down? And if we stand and fight, should we play by the existing rules of democracy to transform our fortunes or should we rely upon non-democratic means? Should we fight alone or join forces with others? These questions are vexing a significant majority of the American electorate today.

Democracy is commonly understood as government of the people. But when the masses (or some might say the "deplorables") have the right to vote in a democratic society, the results of elections can be utterly unpredictable. They can also be detrimental to the general welfare of losers and winners. After the votes are tallied the masses might entrust our collective fate to tyrants that threaten the very existence of democracy. They can be hostile to a free press, the rule of law, basic liberties, and voting rights, which they perceive as a threat to their rule. This outcome, which I earlier defined as institutional failure, is arguably the most destructive consequence of rule of the masses in a self-proclaimed liberal democratic society. And it encapsulates democracy's dilemma: *Giving power to the people empowers them to disempower themselves and to empower those wanting to rig the rules to serve selfish interests.*

How should we guard against this prospect of the people undoing democracy democratically? One solution—which Du Bois and I favor—is to make the masses less vulnerable to selecting representatives likely to undermine democratic rule. Perhaps making the people smarter, more rational, and less partisan can do this. Or maybe we need to improve their material circumstances and recognize the rights they need to contribute to realizing this outcome. Another solution, which is anti-democratic and anti-egalitarian, is to take away or diminish their political power and place such power in the hands of a so-called knowledgeable elite said to possess characteristics and knowledge about policy and policymaking deemed vital for democratic governance. In a tradition of thought that goes back to Plato, an elite class of such citizens has been considered better stewards of democracy. Even liberals, most famously John Stuart Mill, have entertained this option.

More recently, epistocracy has been defended by Jason Brennan in his provocative book, *Against Democracy*.[12]

America's current encounter with democracy's dilemma has made epistocracy tempting to some theorists worried about ignorant voters and the damage they can do. One theorist, who finds inspiration in China for an alternative to democracy, puts his cards directly on the table: "The uncomfortable truth is that the best (perhaps only) way to reduce the political influence of ignorant voters is to deprive them of the vote."[13] For different reasons, rooted in concerns that blacks were gaining too much political power and whites were at risk of losing it, many Americans were also seduced by restricting political rule to an allegedly more knowledgeable class of citizens during the end of the nineteenth and start of the twentieth century.

As I will argue, Du Bois resisted epistocracy.[14] Not only did he believe that a genuine democracy had an imperative to make the masses fit to rule, he believed that it was important to take the steps needed to make the masses less discontent with democracy and, it was hoped, less prone to rejecting it and relinquishing political rule to tyrants and plutocrats. This requires securing for the masses a set of universal legal rights including education, economic security, and protection against discrimination.

Why Democracy?

Du Bois's philosophical engagement with democracy extends over five decades in books, essays, articles, speeches, and correspondence. Although he touches on the topic of democracy earlier, it gets his undivided attention for the first time in chapter 6 of *Darkwater*, published in 1920. But here he does not advance an ideal theory of democracy—dwelling on the meaning, implications, and justification of its basic principles, which may prompt some to mistakenly dismiss what he has to say as irrelevant to political philosophers and political theorists. Instead, he draws on a way of understanding the normative function of democracy and develops his thoughts on why America falls short. Due to this deficiency one can say that the nation is not a genuine democracy or, as I will say, that it is an imperfect one.[15]

In what follows I will use "Of the Ruling of Men," which is essentially an essay about democratic failure, as the primary text for my reconstruction of Du Bois's defense of democracy, incorporating other works only to elucidate and expand upon what he says there. For Du Bois, the widest possible distribution of political rule is the democratic default position: *As many citizens as possible should have the right to vote.* Yet history shows that exclusion, which always benefits the interests of a select few, has been supported on different grounds, including by claiming that the excluded are too ignorant to rule. On my reading of this insightful chapter, Du Bois defends democracy by rebutting this and other justifications for less inclusive political rule.[16] But here, and elsewhere, he says things that acknowledge there are other ways to proceed with a defense grounded in taking democracy to have both instrumental and non-instrumental value. Let us briefly consider some of what Du Bois has to say about the nature and value of democracy, more generally, before considering his rebuttal of the ignorance justification in the next section.

In an ideal democracy, political rule should benefit everyone—the high and low classes, the powerful and powerless, the rich and poor, men and women, white and black alike. But being far from ideal, for much of its history political rule in America has only aimed at the good of a select few. One hypothesis for this is that many people have historically been excluded from political rule, or if not excluded entirely, have been afforded diminished and unequal political power. Because of this, those in power have used it largely for their own benefit rather than for the benefit of all. And under these nonideal conditions all people have not been beneficiaries of political rule.

To be clear, to say that *all* people should be beneficiaries of political rule is not to say that all the people should rule. The work of politics, which includes enacting policy, can be assigned to public officials. The point is that everyone should have a say in who occupies these roles, and this can be the result of affording all people an equal opportunity to select their government representatives through voting.[17] On this popular sovereignty model of democracy the people—all the people—should have real political power over their rulers and government. This is something that Du Bois espoused in some of his earlier and later reflections on democracy.

In a 1907 speech delivered at Carnegie Hall in New York City, for example, Du Bois says: "We believe not that every man should rule, but that every man—black and white, high and low—should have power over the rulers and that every man's personal desires, personal ideals, personal powers, should be counted in the great workings of the nation."[18] Affording every citizen such power is, on his view, essential for establishing democratic authority and sovereignty. Failure to do this can have grave consequences and avoiding them supplies an instrumental justification for democratic rule: It allows us to avoid certain bad results.

Forty-three years later, Du Bois lamented that the great mass of American people did not have such sovereignty and that political rule in the nation was effectively controlled by a small class of plutocrats. In a 1950 radio broadcast, after defining democracy as "the form of government in which each citizen has a voice in all decisions of policy and action," Du Bois observes: "We entered the 20th century, not as a democracy ruled by the votes of the people but as a plutocracy ruled by wealth and for wealth. The slave power was replaced by the money power and under neither can democracy flourish."[19] Unfortunately, this still rings true today. The super wealthy have a disproportionate share of political power, and as historian Nancy MacLean has powerfully argued, they are using it to put democracy in chains.[20]

With this more modest conception of democratic political rule in hand, where each citizen has a voice that counts and exercises real political power over rulers and the nation, we can say that rule of all the people for the greatest good of all is the ideal of *perfect democracy*. Rule of the few for the benefit of some is the nonideal reality of an *imperfect democracy*. Struggles for ideal democracy, usually led by the lower, less powerful, and more impoverished classes, aim to change things by expanding the beneficiaries of political rule to include all the people. They aim to move a society from an imperfect state of democratic rule to a more perfect one by securing a share of political rule for the downtrodden, dispossessed, and despised. They seek to afford all citizens, not merely the wealthy, a voice in determining government policy and action. In sum, democratic movements seek to give real political power to the people. Du Bois's earliest and most sustained reflections on the nature and value of democracy begin with these thoughts.

"Of the Ruling of Men" starts with the claim that the greatest good of all should be the aim of the ruling of people. Du Bois calls this the *universal good*. Democracy, when perfectly realized, is a form of political rule that organizes the actions of all persons who are subject to political rule to realize this end. A form of rule seeking the good of fewer persons or that organizes the actions of few persons to achieve this aim is imperfect. So from this vantage point, were we to ask, "Why Democracy?," the answer is that it is instrumental for realizing the universal good. This normative ideal admits of different interpretations, and two are at work here.

On the one hand, Du Bois adopts an instrumentalist interpretation of democracy that is essentially utilitarian, where utility maximization is about aggregating the political preferences or interests of the greatest number of citizens in setting government policy and directing government action. When more people participate in democracy, he tells us, "the appearance of new interests and complaints means disarrangement and confusion to the older equilibrium. It is, of course, the inevitable preliminary step to that larger equilibrium in which the interests of no human soul will be neglected."[21] And then he concludes: "The problem of government thereafter would be to reduce the necessary conflict of human interests to the minimum."[22]

However, as the argument unfolds, he introduces another description of the normative aim of democracy, which invites a deontological interpretation of the universal good. Du Bois writes: "Democracy is a method of realizing the broadest measure of justice to all human beings."[23] And we accomplish this, he says, by affording the ballot to excluded groups such as women, not as a privilege, but as something they need "to right the balance of a world sadly awry because of its brutal neglect of the rights of women and children."[24] These thoughts suggest that democracy seeks the universal good by recognizing the rights of all citizens so that they can advance their interests.

In "Of the Ruling of Men" there are, therefore, at least two readings of Du Bois's instrumentalist justification of democracy—one that puts a utilitarian spin on what realizing the universal good amounts to, and another that gives this a deontological twist. I will not attempt to reconcile these two interpretations. But I will adopt the latter one in my reconstruction of his defense of democracy

(§4), and in thinking through what needs to happen for American democracy to survive (§5).

One might suppose, as Du Bois does, that the more people involved in political rule, where this means having a voice that counts, and having real political power over government policy and action, the more likely the case that the broadest measure of justice for all will be secured. He also supposes that "the right to vote is the only effective weapon of democracy" and that "disfranchisement deprives any individual or group of its opportunity to realize and guide democracy."[25] Thus, if voting constitutes a way to give people a hand in political rule, then we have a straightforward instrumental justification for affording as many people as possible access to the ballot. Du Bois sums this up as follows: "if All ruled they would rule for All and thus Universal Good was sought through Universal Suffrage."[26]

It might be objected that this instrumental justification puts the case for democracy on too weak a footing. What if we could achieve the universal good without inclusive or maximally inclusive political rule? If popular sovereignty is only valuable because it helps us secure this good, and we can secure it with something less than rule of all, and there are compelling reasons for wanting to do so, then we should opt for imperfect democracy or no democracy at all. Du Bois entertains this possibility but flatly rejects it. For one, he thinks human history shows that this is not a realistic possibility, that is, no nation that excludes citizens from political rule has secured the broadest measure of justice for all.

But even if this were possible, we have additional reasons for embracing a popular sovereignty model of democracy to achieve this aim. Democracy helps us secure valuable collective goods such as the progress of culture and civilization. It also secures the individual goods of self-development and self-knowledge. Du Bois makes and connects these points quite elegantly. He writes:

> The vast and wonderful knowledge of this marvelous universe is locked in the bosoms of its individual souls. To tap this mighty reservoir of experience, knowledge, beauty, love, and deed we must appeal not to the few, not to some souls, but to all. The narrower the appeal, the poorer the culture; the wider the appeal the more magnificent are the possibilities.[27]

Insofar as some of these goods might be said to have non-instrumental value, Du Bois can say that popular sovereignty, apart from being instrumental for securing the broadest measure of justice for all, is also good for us even if it does not lead to this outcome.[28] So if we could secure the justice benefit with less inclusive political rule, the non-instrumental benefits of inclusive democracy would be loss. And these are good for us regardless of whether they lead to justice. Thus we see that Du Bois values democracy both instrumentally and non-instrumentally.

However, as valuable as it is, democracy does not require specific policy outcomes. As he puts it: "The theory of democracy does not call for equality of gift, universal college education or absolute individual integrity; but it does depend upon the widest possible consultation with the mass of citizens on the theory that only this way can you consult ultimate authority and ultimate sovereignty."[29] History has shown that failure to do this can have dire consequences for democracy, which include chaos and even revolution. In addition, undemocratic rule denies all citizens—both those excluded and included—the benefits that are non-instrumentally good for each and every one of us.

Du Bois's conception of the nature and value of democracy is rich with insights. It offers us various ways of defending democracy. We can argue that it helps us secure benefits that are valuable instrumentally and non-instrumentally, and that we should avoid burdens that are bad because of their effects and regardless of them. But the main burden of his *Darkwater* essay on democratic failure is not to unpack these philosophical claims about democracy's nature and value. Rather, it is to offer a defense of democracy that turns on rebutting justifications for excluding some citizens from democratic rule. And conceding that citizens are not omniscient is central to this task.

IGNORANT CITIZENS

The general thrust of Du Bois's pre- and post-*Darkwater* writings on democracy is to contrast perfect and imperfect democracy, to document how and why Western democracies and American democracy in particular have been so imperfect, and to offer guidance on how to move from our grossly imperfect democracy to a more perfect one. His primary purpose in "Of the Ruling of Men," as I read it, is to identify, interrogate, and invalidate familiar justifications for not giving power to all of the people—so that they may pursue the broadest measure of justice for all.

Because of his lifelong focus on America's problem of the color line, Du Bois keenly appreciated how the presumption that excluded citizens were ignorant was a significant obstacle to moving from an imperfect to a more perfect democracy. His writings dwell upon this and other acute challenges including poverty and prejudice that subvert our democratic aspirations. However, the problem of ignorance looms large in his 1920 assessment of democratic failure, though this problem was on his radar long before then.[30]

For example, as early as 1898, in laying out a general plan for the study of social problems affecting American blacks, Du Bois notes that this group was largely ignorant due to the legacy of slavery and its aftermath. Of all the groups in the nation at the time, he writes: "the Negro is by far the most ignorant; nearly half of the race are absolutely illiterate, only a minority of the other half have thorough common school training, and but a remnant are liberally educated."[31]

Du Bois cautioned his readers against thinking that the social problems raised by the color line were new. At the dawn of the nineteenth century, America was struggling with the question of what to do with a class of persons—American Negroes[32]—who were subordinated, exploited, and rendered second-class citizens. But a century before, the nation was fixated on how to deal with "the great mass of its ignorant and poor [white] laboring classes." Hence, the problem of this earlier age was the political rights of the masses, which raised some of the same social questions as the race issue.

One such question was whether the so-called ignorant classes (of white laborers) should be afforded a voice in democratic rule. The Enlightenment ideal that the rule of the people, and the legitimacy of government authority, is based on the consent of the governed has long been considered a feature of all "civilized" societies. Yet there have been people who have always sought to make exceptions, as Du Bois observes:

> There were men—and wise men, too—who believed that democratic government was simply impossible with human nature in its

\

present condition. "Shall the tail wag the dog?" said they; shall a brutish mob sway the destinies of the intelligent and well-born of the nation? It was all very well for Rousseau to sing the Rights of Man, but this civic idealism must make way for calm criticism.[33]

In many self-proclaimed democratic societies, it is likely that some class of persons will be declared too ignorant to share in democratic rule. Of course, these people will be expected (unreasonably in my view) to pay taxes, to obey the laws, and to pledge allegiance to the flag. But when it comes to political governance, they will be expected to hold their tongues. Therefore, if we take a broader historical view of democracy, as Du Bois urges, we will find that a pretext for excluding persons of different class, race, or gender from political rule has been to declare them too ignorant to rule.

Today, when we hear that some Americans are entertaining the thought that the ignorant masses—who are willing to entrust our democratic future to leaders with bad intentions—should be excluded, we should know that the epistocracy solution is not new. We have been down this road before and Du Bois thought we should resist epistocracy. But he did not do so, in the first instance, by denying the premise that the masses are ignorant. Rather, he partly conceded, contextualized, and co-opted it to defend democracy, and to supply a normative understanding of the duties of democratic rule.

According to Du Bois the great majority of people—with and without smarts—are ignorant of many things that must be known for ruling to serve the good of all. Obviously, the masses lack knowledge about other individuals as well as groups of individuals. For example, we live in close proximity to our neighbors, yet many of us know little about their interests, fears, and pains. Similarly, we encounter individuals in our daily lives who share certain faiths, class status, and who are marked differently by race and ethnicity, but we know little, if anything, about what interests they share in common by virtue of these group-based identities.

But, even more important, as Du Bois intimates, reflecting on the predicament of late nineteenth- and early twentieth-century America, the masses did not know enough about the complex set of issues and problems such as poverty, inequality, and discrimination associated with a growing industrial society, or, most important, about how the titans of industry—plutocrats and their political stooges—used the industrial age to serve their narrow interests. He argues that the rapid growth of industry in America at the time created "an invincible kingdom of trade, business, and commerce," which placed the fate of democracy in the hands of "the Captains of Industry and their created Millionaires," which proved difficult for the masses to understand.[34] This lack of understanding, and corresponding lack of control over their well-being, created discontent among those who labored the hardest but reaped the least during the Industrial Revolution.

During the first reconstruction America had a chance to secure a more inclusive democracy, and it took some steps with amendments, education, and setting up federal oversight to make sure that the newly acquired legal rights of black Americans were respected. But the former slave-owning class conspired with captains of industry to establish white rule and block the formation of a unified class of black and white laborers to challenge the industrial order. And this was done largely through voter disfranchisement and unequal schooling, and by using racial hatred to gain broad support for sustaining a democracy ruled by whites to benefit whites.

But worker-class whites saw the handwriting on the wall and sought to use what little political power they had to secure their rights from being trampled by the captains of industry. However, as Du Bois astutely observes, their battle was doomed to fail because they tried to secure a share of rule for themselves while leaving black laborers on the outskirts of democracy, which would allow industrialists to undercut their efforts by threatening to use cheaper black labor. Thus, many whites were willing to stifle the pursuit of a more perfect democracy, including making industry democratic, to maintain their privileged place in an imperfect racial democracy where whiteness was the currency of the realm.

So, to be sure, the masses are ignorant of many things. And this was certainly true of blacks, who at the start of 1900, were less than four decades removed from having suffered through a brutal slave system that criminalized literacy.[35] Thus, it was no surprise, as Du Bois noted, that when it came to society's understanding of the Negro problem, and the thinking of some that blacks were unfit for democratic rule, it was widely taken to be a problem of ignorance. And the point was not merely the obvious one, namely that most blacks were indeed illiterate (having suffered through a brutal slave system that prevented them from learning), it was said that they suffered from "a deeper ignorance of the world and its ways, of the thought and experience of men; an ignorance of self and the possibilities of human souls."[36] Let us suppose, for the moment, that this too is true.

Ignorance was not only a Negro problem. And their lack of knowledge was not the only challenge to satisfying the Enlightenment ideal of popular sovereignty. A more general obstacle to achieving rule by all through universal suffrage was the widespread ignorance of the people in general, including those who fancied themselves as smart. "The mass of men, even of the more intelligent men," writes Du Bois, "not only knew little about each other but less about the action of men in groups and the technique of industry in general."[37] This ignorance did not render them helpless, but it meant that they could only apply the political power they had with their ballot to the things that they knew or only knew partially. And this is precisely what we would expect of any group of persons who had to rule with limited knowledge.

So if ignorance is put forward as a reason for limiting political rule to exclude blacks, then white ignorance—both of the white masses and the white elite—was also a serious challenge to democracy. Yet this had not stopped the nation from forming and running a democratic society with white citizens who were far from omniscient. Indeed, as Du Bois claims, America taught the world that the "most unlikely classes and races" could govern themselves provided that they had education, economic opportunity, and protection of their basic civil, political, and social rights.[38]

Du Bois develops his thoughts in the chapter by showing how the shift from agricultural and small-scale economies to a larger industrial one not only compounded the problem of ignorance, as there was much that the great mass of people did not understand about commerce and trade under these new circumstances; it also allowed captains of industry to mock democracy and claim that they were best suited to rule (since they at least had the requisite knowledge of industry) and could be counted on to use their surplus wealth to help the unfortunate ignorant masses with philanthropy.

A widely used justification for excluding blacks from democratic rule—by denying them the ballot or making their exercise of it more burdensome—was the assumption, as Du Bois put it, "that only the intelligent should vote, or those who know how to rule men, or those who are not under benevolent guardianship, or those who ardently desire the right."[39] But this was merely a pretext for advancing the narrow self-interest of de facto industrial rulers, and—when used by white laborers and their unions—it was a pretext for advancing their white racial group interest in general. Thus, to paraphrase Du Bois, the pretextual argument for black disfranchisement went like this: Civilized democratic societies did not allow the ignorant to rule. America is a civilized democracy. American blacks are ignorant. Therefore, they should not be allowed to rule.

But this argument is of course too strong, as working-class whites quickly came to realize. Attributions of ignorance by those with industrial power, white power, or male power do not respect caste, race, or gender divisions. Just as blacks, Asians, or women could be denigrated with this label, so could whites considered to be of lower descent relative to whites of high birth. Indeed, as Du Bois points out, early twentieth-century America was being ruled by whites who a century earlier had been deemed unable to become a genuinely self-ruling people. They had proven the skeptics wrong, showing that ignorance and inexperience were not impediments to democratic rule. The American experiment with democracy, which extended political rule beyond a privileged few, who were believed to be better fitted to rule by "blood" or "divine right," turned out to be good for the development of civilization.

Rebutting the appeal to ignorance as a justification for less inclusive political rule suggests that Du Bois was a rationalist about political change. From this point of view, if we overcome ignorance (particularly white ignorance) we can then appeal to people's sense of reason to persuade them to extend the benefits of democracy to all. Du Bois understood, however, that this appeal to rational moral suasion would be ineffective against those moved by racial animus and who acted politically based on a narrow tribalism.

For instance, he knew that in the early twentieth-century South some people "must vote always and simply to keep Negroes

down."[40] And as he says, "such a denial of the fundamental principles of democracy is dangerous to the Nation." Part of the danger
is that wherever such a steadfast commitment to racial prejudice
prevails, this renders reason helpless. "It means," as he observes,
"that there are certain parts of the country where reason cannot
be applied to the settlement of great political questions."

Elsewhere in his work Du Bois illustrates with great effect the
irony that tribalism, or what he calls the "mob mind, the herd
instinct," stands to do the greatest damage not to black folks but
to whites. When they, particularly working-class whites, allow themselves to be co-opted in supporting the political disfranchisement
of blacks (and other groups), they unwittingly undermine their
own authority to raise grievances about their own plight and to
advance political reforms. He writes:

> Again and again we see the individual tragedy: a young white man,
> Southern by birth, tradition and belief, sees one matter he would
> reform, one point of disagreement. He is tolerated a while and then
> the herd turns and tramples him in fury. It is worse than lynching.
> The South lynches the bodies of black men, but the souls of white.[41]

I think that Du Bois overstates this point. However, the basic
idea, which is that political tribalism serves as much to control and
harm whites as it does to maintain the status of blacks as second-
class citizens, is clear and compelling enough.

The United States is arguably seeing this play out in real time
today, as working-class whites who signed up for Trump's plan
to make America great again—helping to vault him into power
despite his veiled and not so veiled appeals to a divisive white
racial tribalism—are now feeling the pain from many of his policies, from gutting the Affordable Care Act, to supporting anti-
union legal rulings, to starting a trade war with tariffs, and to cut-
ting taxes on corporations and the wealthy.

If Du Bois was a rationalist about political change, then, he was
certainly not a naïve one who underestimated the power of racial
tribalism and the racial prejudice that accompanied it to prevent
clear thinking about political matters. By the same token, he knew
that lack of knowledge is not the only thing that matters for political rule aiming for the universal good.[42] Selfishness, rooted either

in concern for one's narrow self-interest or for one's narrow group-based interest, can also be an obstacle to realizing the universal good. When this takes the latter form, the tribalism that results becomes a significant tool in the arsenal of antidemocratic forces which use racial politics to keep the working classes divided.[43]

At the same time, we must not overemphasize the role of race in Du Bois's account of democratic failure. In some of his earliest thinking about the repudiation of the democratic process in the South, in which blacks were denied the right to vote, Du Bois viewed this as primarily an economic problem that was strategically used by powerful factions to serve their selfish economic interests.

As blacks became more educated, especially due to industrial training in black schools, they competed increasingly with white laborers for jobs, creating an opportunity for some to stir up racial divisions to keep black and white laborers from joining forces to assert a claim to be equal partners in democracy with the de facto ruling class—the captains of industry. Southern politicians, who had their own fears about the formation of an industrial democracy, blamed the ills of the white working class on their black competitors and implored whites to use their ballots to keep blacks from power, which would only make matters worse. And "exploiting capitalists," as Du Bois describes them, threatened to replace white workers with black ones if they did not stop complaining about unfair treatment, low wages, and poor working conditions. Thus, according to Du Bois, attention to race prejudice, though a serious problem in its own right, was basically a way to put the spotlight on "a great labor problem."[44]

So establishing what Du Bois calls an "industrial democracy," in which the black and white working classes recognize their common oppression by plutocrats and politicians on their payroll seeking to save capitalism from democracy, and move to close ranks to demand a political voice in determining the rules of business and the distribution of its outputs, is vital for realizing a more inclusive ideal of democracy. More controversially, as I read him, achieving industrial democracy also means reassessing, and alas deemphasizing, the prominent preoccupation with white supremacy in understanding how we move twenty-first-century America toward a more ideal expression of genuine democracy.[45]

Largely because of ignorance about class exploitation and the workings of tribalism, Du Bois thought that the education of blacks as well as whites was crucial to counter divisive uses of race politics to prevent coalition building. Some sort of radical education would help develop a class consciousness to oppose the counterproductive use of racial politics by anti-democratic forces. If fearing loss of economic and physical well-being made the masses willing to entertain autocrats and others who supported the rule of the few, a radical education was necessary to help the masses resist and to see the wisdom of joining forces to combat a common oppression. Of course, if people were moved to do this not merely by reason or even by the perception of common interests but also by emotional appeals, then building the needed coalition would have to account for this.

However, with respect to reason, Du Bois argued that the labor movement had a vital role to play in imparting the knowledge needed to encourage the white and black working classes to close ranks, especially because schools and the press could not be counted on to do this. An educative labor movement, with a radical agenda, could dispel certain myths about workers, capitalists, and property to unmask the injustice of wealth inequality. One of these myths is that the poor envy the rich and want to deprive the rich of the just fruit of their efforts by law or force. Other myths are that property is gained solely by individual effort and is thus something that capitalists have the right to use as they see fit, and that industry is owned by one group—the capitalists—and that gives them the sole authority to set wages and working conditions, and that public interference with any of this is always unjust.[46]

So, in addition to tribalism and the selfishness that it breeds, as Du Bois appreciated, one problem among others for democratic rule based in universal suffrage certainly consists in "widespread ignorance." But this was not only about the masses lacking certain kinds of knowledge needed for political rule, e.g., policy knowledge or technocratic knowledge of social problems, it was also about the so-called smarter ruling elites lacking the knowledge necessary for democratic political rule built on a normative foundation of justice for all. Securing this knowledge required consulting directly with the masses about their pains, sufferings, and circumstances. According to Du Bois, the masses had first-person knowledge of their own souls and could be counted on to use this knowledge to pursue their self-defense. So, as far as Du Bois was concerned, both rule of the masses and rule of the few posed dangers in the absence of the right sort of knowledge.

Earlier I said that Du Bois did not resist epistocracy, *in the first instance*, by denying that the masses lacked certain knowledge. Thus far I have established that his first move was to show that ignorance was widespread, yet this was no obstacle to the white men who founded the United States—after being denigrated as too ignorant to rule—from launching their grand experiment in democratic government. Du Bois's second move was to argue that the masses did indeed possess certain knowledge. As is the case with all individuals, he claimed, the masses know their own "souls," and this knowledge is vital for securing democracy's normative aim to secure the broadest measure of justice for all. Du Bois's third and final move in "Of the Ruling of Men" is a response to a sound objection. If we suppose that the masses do indeed have knowledge needed for securing justice in society, one may object that they need not be given the ballot to secure it. Perhaps we only need to consult with them, say by conducting surveys of what they think, and then others can use this knowledge to secure justice. Du Bois answers this objection by arguing that the ballot is also necessary for self-defense: Women need to vote because they can be counted on, more than men, to secure the neglected rights of women and children, and blacks can be counted on, more than whites, to secure protection from lynching, discrimination, and other basic rights.

There are places in his writings where Du Bois shows that his defense of democracy is rooted not in blind, uncritical, devotion to it but in a pragmatic realism (democracy's not perfect but it's the best game in town) and an abiding faith in the masses to better their own conditions when give a real opportunity.[47] For example, in a conference paper published by the *American Historical Review* in 1910, he states: "The theory of democratic government is not that the will of the people is always right, but rather that normal human beings of average intelligence will, if given a chance, learn the right and best course by bitter experience."[48] Du Bois would be the first to admit, then, that democracy can make the wrong calls. Yet the answer was not to pursue less democracy. It was to have more. This was not only because he thought it was the best game in town, and he had faith in the masses. There was also an epistemic reason for this, which speaks to Du Bois's second move in the case against epistocracy. Here it is important to distinguish between a more exclusive form of epistocracy and a more inclusive one. If Du Bois could be described as an epistocrat, his ruminations on democracy support viewing him as the latter type. He thought that the masses had important knowledge that was needed to achieve justice for all—the normative goal of popular sovereignty.

Du Bois envisions a perfect democracy as one that is truly ruled by the people to secure justice for all. In such a society, "there shall be no man or woman so poor, ignorant or black as not to count."[49] We can fuss over whether to call this social democracy or something else, but whatever we call it, the point is that rule of all, including those labeled ignorant, can put us in a better position to realize justice or the universal good. Yet epistocrats ask: But what if this turns out to be false? What if preventing some people from wielding political power, say by disenfranchising them, discounting their votes, or double-counting the votes of the wise, proved to be a more reliable way to secure the universal good? Should we act accordingly? For Du Bois, the answer to this question is a resounding "no." And, ironically, the reason is that the challenge reflects a profound ignorance connected with overrating the knowledge of the "wise," and underrating the knowledge of the masses.

For Du Bois and some of his contemporaries, most notably Walter Lippmann and John Dewey, who grappled with American democracy's promises and perils during the second decade of the twentieth century, this question of whether to withhold political power from certain citizens did not arise on the heels of a fanciful philosophical thought experiment involving runaway trolleys. Rather, it was rooted in real doubts about whether the great masses of voters knew enough to deliver, collectively, benefits to secure the universal good. Du Bois did not deny that ignorance was a problem for democracy. However, he denied that black ignorance was its only epistemic problem. White ignorance—including ignorance of the ruling white (male) plutocracy about blacks, the white working class, and women—was also a serious epistemic barrier to attaining the universal good. The core of Du Bois's defense of democracy, in "Of the Ruling of Men," is to expose and eradicate this barrier.

The crucial premise of this defense is clearly stated in a speech entitled "Diuturni Silenti," which Du Bois gave at Fisk University—his alma mater—two years after *Darkwater*'s publication. He went to campus to address concerns raised by students (including his daughter) and alumni that the University president was lording over the campus like a dictator. His speech succinctly sums up the pivotal insight we find carefully developed in "Of the Ruling of Men." Du Bois says: "The theory of democracy is not that the people have all wisdom or all ability, but it is that the mass of people form a great reservoir of knowledge and information which the state will ignore at its peril."[50]

In *Darkwater*, Du Bois exposes how those who have wanted to hoard political power for themselves—making the franchise a special privilege for the few—have always found it convenient to justify excluding others by appealing to factors such as lack of ability, experience, or knowledge. They wrongly presume, however, that democracy requires participants to have complete knowledge. Thus, the excluders assume that they know what is best for those excluded, and know this better than the excluded know it. They also assume that they can be trusted to secure what is best for those excluded. But these assumptions must be flatly rejected.

History disproves the latter as well as the presumption that participants must be all-knowing. And as for the excluder-knows-best thesis, Du Bois accords persons epistemic deference regarding knowledge of one's own soul—particularly knowledge of one's hurts and suffering. As he puts it, while each person may not fully understand his unfortunate condition or how to fix it, "he knows when something hurts and he alone knows how the hurt feels."[51] And in response to men who presume to know what is best for women, Du Bois writes: "With the best will and knowledge, no man can know women's wants as well as women themselves."[52] Societies that do not consider this knowledge, whether they are effective aristocracies, benevolent dictatorships, or imperfect democracies, are bound to fail.

From here Du Bois's argument unfolds by attending to how imperfect democracies ignore the excluded wisdom of women, blacks, and in the case of industry, the wisdom of labor.[53] He sums up the case as follows:

> The real argument for democracy is, then, that in the people we have the source of that endless life and unbounded wisdom which the rulers of men must have . . . Democracy alone is the method of showing the whole experience of the race for the benefit of the future and if democracy tries to exclude women or Negroes or the poor or any class because of innate characteristics which do not interfere with intelligence, then that democracy cripples itself and belies its name.[54]

So, according to Du Bois, all persons, even the so-called ignorant masses, are what I call *sage souls*. His multifaceted argument for democracy, which highlights this fact and the necessity of including them in political rule to achieve democracy's possibilities, is an epistemic argument. The reason why *all* must rule, and not only those thought to have certain experience, ability, or knowledge which the masses lack, is because democracy is a way for society to secure the broadest measure of justice, and this can only be done if all souls have a hand in democratic rule. While the historically excluded souls are not omniscient because no mortals are, each person knows things that others do not, and this excluded wisdom is indispensable for our collective striving toward perfect democracy.[55]

Hence a society steadfastly and sincerely pursuing this ideal has a dual imperative: (a) to make the class of ignorant persons as small as possible, and (b) to make the class of mature voting-age persons as large as possible. Because when sage souls can speak for themselves politically, which they can do with the ballot, they can take steps to secure the full schedule of legal rights needed to undo the circumstances of democratic failure. And this is how they can contribute to democracy's survival.

How Democracy Survives

Democratic failure was a prominent theme in Du Bois's speeches and writings in the mid to late 1950s. After recounting his long history of voting for the lesser of two evils in US presidential elections—taking account of the prospective candidates' positions on Negroes to determine the lesser evil—Du Bois resolved not to vote in 1956 because, as he put it, "democracy has so far disappeared in the United States that no 'two evils' exist. There is but one evil party with two names, and it will be elected despite all I can do or say. There is no third party."[56]

Many people in America today, especially those who have been disproportionately harmed by democratic failure, e.g., black and brown people as well as working-class whites, undoubtedly share a similar view. Some of these folks hold out hope for a third-party movement, which is driven by the people rather than corporate power. Others are less hopeful about this prospect, maybe holding out hope that an existing party could be made a better champion of the pursuit of perfect democracy. Du Bois had his doubts about creating a viable third party in the United States.[57] He noted that efforts to create a viable third party, with a progressive social agenda calling for limits on corporate influence on the law, greater worker protections, nationalized healthcare, greater federal investment in education, and an expansion of social welfare, would be labeled "Communist" or "Socialist" to stifle the movement. And here, as in many other matters, Du Bois was prophetic.

After her stunning victory in June 2018 over longtime Democratic Party boss, Rep. Joseph Crowley of New York, Alexandria Ocasio-Cortez began making her media rounds to explain what it means to be a "democratic socialist," which television host Stephen Colbert said was "not an easy term for a lot of Americans." In what could be the stirrings of a viable movement toward a third party with a socialist bent (though for now it's being billed as a progressive reworking of the Democratic party), echoing Du Bois, Ocasio-Cortez explained to Colbert that in a society as wealthy and as moral as America professes to be, no one should be too poor to live. A democratic socialist believes this, and she also believes that healthcare, higher education, having a place to live, and having food are human rights necessary for living a dignified life in the United States.[58]

Du Bois would add to this that guaranteeing such rights is also essential for the preservation of democracy in America. The problems that Ocasio-Cortez raises—poverty, illness, and ignorance— are among the *circumstances of democratic failure*. Thus, the right to economic security, healthcare, and education are the normative safeguards of democracy. When these rights are secured for the masses and their needs are met, Du Bois presumes, plausibly in my view, that they will be less vulnerable to anti-democratic leaders promising to address their woes while working to undo the fundamentals of democracy and to advance their autocratic ambitions.[59]

To address any of the circumstances of democratic failure, and to gain the rights needed to undo them, the masses require the power of the ballot. And they must have it on the same terms as other citizens. The right to vote is not merely a privilege. It is, more important, a means of self-protection. Indeed, as Du Bois states it: "We believe that the right to vote is not for purposes of power primarily, but for the purpose of individual defence."[60]

Reinhold Niebuhr tells us that "Man's capacity for justice makes democracy possible; but man's inclination to injustice makes democracy necessary."[61] Echoing this thought one can say that our inclination to create and sustain injustice—by contributing to the circumstances of democratic failure—makes the right to vote a necessity for those who are most disadvantaged by ignorance, illness, poverty, and the like. Du Bois would agree. Having voting rights does more than simply allow particular groups to meet needs or satisfy individual wants and desires. It provides them with a means of self-defense. Furthermore, the right to vote allows them to help a democratic society secure the broadest measure of justice for all citizens.

Du Bois did not claim that democracy must guarantee certain rights and freedoms. Nor did he claim that its continued existence was necessary. The United States is certainly free to reject popular sovereignty and to opt for an alternative arrangement, which limits rule "by education, occupation, ability, birth, wealth, race, or some combination of these factors."[62] But if it does this, Du Bois says, "we must face the change frankly and adopt it logically."[63] To put it bluntly, his point was that if we are going to strip "ignorant" people of their voting rights, and ignorant people of all colors can be found in all classes—high and low—then let's make sure that all are equally excluded. Moreover, if state representation in Congress is constitutionally based on the proportion of voting citizens, then let us ensure that those states that choose to disfranchise voters see their representation reduced accordingly. These states should not be able to have it both ways.

In "Of the Ruling of Men," Du Bois limits his focus to just one circumstance of democratic failure—the problem of widespread ignorance and the need for a right to vote to remedy this situation. But in addition to ignorance he identified poverty and crime as the three principal problems Negroes face.[64] Although his argument applies to the other circumstances of democratic failure, I have limited my attention to the problem of ignorance.

Du Bois is well known for establishing the black contribution to these problems, and for outlining their duties to eradicate them. However, he devoted considerable attention to showing how these problems were largely the product of historical black subordination and oppression under slavery, then under Jim Crow segregation, which meant that white America had duties to address them as well.[65] One such obligation was to politically empower blacks to fix these problems by making them equal partners in the democracy. Thus, "a sincere desire among the American people to help the Negroes undertake their own social regeneration means," Du Bois says, "first, that the Negro be given the ballot on the same terms as other men, to protect him against injustice and to safeguard his interests in the administration of law."[66] And one of the most consequential things Negroes could do with the ballot was to advance their interests in black education, black colleges, and industrial schools so that ignorance could be overcome with knowledge. This would go a long way toward undoing this circumstance of democratic failure.

But Du Bois's argument was not only about establishing a moral responsibility to support black rights. It was also about taking proactive measures to reduce the risk of democratic failure by addressing a circumstance that was contributing to it in both the South and the North. If America truly considered itself a democracy and wanted the nation to flourish and survive as such, then Americans had a duty to use their political power to remedy the circumstances of the masses that threatened this. White America was certainly free to believe that blacks were primarily responsible for their own misfortunes and should therefore bear the greatest burden in fixing them. However, to do this, they needed the ballot—and not just on paper but in practice.

Thus, supporting more inclusive political rule by supporting blacks and women was, according to Du Bois, also about mitigating the risk of total democratic failure. This bad outcome would give plutocrats free reign to tyrannize not just blacks but also working-class white laborers and the great mass of Americans who were not wealthy and powerful. Some said that whites could be counted on to secure black interests, just as some said that men could be counted on to secure the interests of women. But Du Bois rejects this, contending that those who suffer most from the circumstances of democratic failure will have the most steadfast commitment to undoing these circumstances.

Yet this does not mean that one must have the same experiences as the sufferers to be inclined to help. And Du Bois certainly did not believe this. When women's suffrage was coming up for a vote in states across the United States in 1914, some blacks were rightly concerned that white women would use their ballots to support the continued exclusion of and domination of blacks. Du Bois's response was frank:

> [T]here is not the slightest reason for supposing that white American women under ordinary circumstances are going to be any more intelligent, liberal or humane toward the black, the poor and unfortunate than white men are. On the contrary, considering what the subjection of a race, a class or a sex must mean, there will undoubtedly manifest itself among women voters at first more prejudice and petty measures toward Negroes than we have now. It is the awful penalty of injustice and oppression to breed in the oppressed the desire to oppress others. The southern white women who form one of the most repressed and enslaved groups of modern civilized women will undoubtedly, at first, help willingly and zealously to disfranchize [sic] Negroes, cripple their schools and publicly insult them.[67]

Despite all of this, Du Bois insisted that white women should have the ballot and that blacks should support their efforts to attain it. Although white women did not share the same experience of anti-black animus and discrimination, or the unique experience of racial and gender oppression known to black women, white women had their own experience of oppression and injustice and thus could be counted on in the long run, or so Du Bois hoped, to use their voting rights to make democracy more inclusive, which was necessary for "the universal appeal for justice to win ultimate hearing and sympathy."[68]

Du Bois's case for how to save democracy from failure comes to this. There are circumstances such as widespread ignorance as well as illness and poverty that can lead to democratic failure. In addition to bearing responsibility for the existence of these circumstances, Americans who profess to enjoy a democratic society are obliged to use their political power to undo the circumstances that put democracy at risk of failure. They can do this by making democracy more inclusive, extending the right to vote even to those said to be ignorant, so that the disadvantaged can contribute not only to undoing these circumstances for their own self-defense but so that they can help realize the normative aim of a more perfect democracy, which is to secure the broadest measure of justice for all citizens. Others can certainly contribute to this, and those who are intimately familiar with other kinds of domination are likely to do so. However, because persons who suffer most directly can be most reliably counted on to secure justice for themselves, they must be empowered as equal partners in political rule. So all citizens—including those deemed ignorant—must vote. And with the vote they can work to secure the other rights they need to undo the circumstances of democratic failure.

Hence, Du Bois believed that extending political power to the excluded classes through the franchise was a path toward perfect democracy. He acknowledged the possibility that harm could come to the state and its citizens by putting the power to rule in the hands of persons suffering from ignorance, poverty, and disease. And he also conceded that this would be resisted and resented, especially by those who had the greatest investment in the status quo.[69]

Instead of depriving suffering citizens of the ballot, which renders democracy imperfect, we must remove the conditions that could result in harm. So, for instance, Du Bois reasoned that the enfranchisement of blacks should be accompanied by "education, a minimum of land and capital and a guardian Freedman's Bureau."[70] Education would guard against harms resulting from ignorance. Economic resources would guard against harms resulting from poverty. Empowering an administrative agency to protect newly acquired civil and political rights would guard against harms resulting from discrimination.[71]

Du Bois certainly did not think that the right to vote was the magic silver bullet that would vanquish all of the social troubles associated with anti-democratic rule. For instance, he did not believe that popular sovereignty would "immediately abolish color caste."[72] Nor did he think it would make "ignorant men intelligent or bad men good." After all, blacks were able to vote in the North, yet there was still color caste and discrimination, and there was some social progress in parts of the South despite blacks not having unfettered access to the ballot. Nevertheless, he thought that the only way to make real and sustainable progress toward perfect democracy would be to guarantee a right to vote—giving blacks and other excluded classes a permanent voice in shaping government policy and action. "[N]o permanent improvement in the economic and social condition of Negroes," Du Bois concluded, "is going to be made, so long as they are deprived of political power to support and defend it."

Moreover, as I have indicated, the right to vote was not merely an effective weapon of self-defense for the excluded classes, it was also necessary for securing the broadest measure of justice for all, or what Du Bois also calls the "real good of the world."[73] And to realize this good we must, he says, ultimately be guided by principles, not parties. He was not neutral regarding what these principles should be. They constituted a list of demands, which those fighting for a more perfect democracy should deliver to persons or parties seeking to represent them. Here are the demands:

1. Down with force and lawlessness.
2. Democracy unlimited by race, sex, religion, or color.
3. The abolition of poverty.
4. Health for all.
5. Education for all according to ability and regardless of wealth or birth.
6. Limitation of private wealth by public welfare.
7. Work for all at a decent wage.
8. Social equality of all human beings in accord with wish and without compulsion.
9. The right to all men to life, liberty and happiness, so far as this is possible under the Golden Rule.[74]

It is noteworthy that this list contains issues that we find today's most progressive political candidates running on. Du Bois maintains that the masses should use the weapon of voting to select representatives committed to seeking justice for all. He proposes these and other demands to add substance regarding what this entails. It is also worth noting that these are non–race specific remedies, and that Du Bois anticipates the pragmatic importance of seeking such remedies to address the profound inequalities that stem from imperfect democracy.[75] To achieve a more perfect democracy, in a country where our many differences have been used to divide us and distract us from all the ways in which the plutocrats have fleeced us, we must use political power to undo the circumstances that affect everyone excluded.

Identifying and addressing obstacles to achieving perfect democracy, such as the circumstances of democratic failure, makes Du Bois a forerunner of what philosophers now call *nonideal theory*. Because of the pioneering work of Charles Mills, nonideal theory is an established methodological approach in contemporary analytic political philosophy.[76] Drawing largely on history, sociology, and psychology, nonideal theory begins with a rich description of the social world as it is, rife with injustice, domination, and exploitation, and seeks principles for facilitating the transition to a more just society.[77] This involves accounting for and addressing the many barriers such as ignorance that stand in the way. Long before this method became a thing in contemporary philosophy, Du Bois was engaged in nonideal theorizing about democracy. And I have shown that he has much to teach us about societal duties and individual rights germane to the nonideal circumstances of imperfect democracy.

CONCLUSION

W. E. B. Du Bois is a fountain of wisdom for democratic struggles against the current wave of political leaders that have placed democracy at risk of failure. I have argued that in "Of the Ruling of Men" he illuminates one particular obstacle to achieving perfect democracy—citizen ignorance—and that he provides a philosophically useful perspective on how to respond. Instead of being tempted by epistocracy, or more specifically by an exclusive variety of it that limits rule to so-called wise men or wise white people, Du Bois urges that we address the circumstances that contribute to the discontent of the masses, and that we empower them through our ballots with the rights they need to be equal participants in political rule. This is a surer way to pursue the broadest measure of justice for all citizens.

NOTES

Thanks to Eduardo Martinez, Melissa Schwartzberg, and Daniel Vie-hoff for helpful written comments on this chapter. I also appreciate the constructive commentary provided by two contributors to this volume, Turkuler Isiksel and Mark Tushnet. And for spirited discussion I wish to thank participants at the 2018 NOMOS conference that convened at Boston University School of Law, as well as audiences at the University of Texas at Austin, the University of Toronto Centre for Ethics, Virginia Tech University, and Rutgers University.

1. W. E. B. Du Bois, "Democracy Fails in America, June 1954," 1. W. E. B. Du Bois Papers. Special Collections and University Archives, University of Massachusetts Amherst Libraries, http://credo.library.umass.edu.

2. W. E. B. Du Bois, "No Second-Class Citizens," in *Writings by W. E. B. Du Bois in Periodicals Edited by Others*, vol. 4: 1945–1961, ed. Herbert Ap-theker (Millwood, NY: Kraus-Thomson, 1982), 51.

3. Jedediah Purdy, "What Trump's Rise Means for Democracy," *Dissent*, May 4, 2016.

4. Other tactics such as gerrymandering, voter purges, and voter ID laws are being used today to strip blacks and other historically disadvan-taged groups of political power in the United States. Although Du Bois was particularly interested in vote denial, his views about how to save de-mocracy are still valuable despite certain disanalogies with the contempo-rary moment.

5. W. E. B. Du Bois, *Darkwater: Voices from Within the Veil* (New York: Do-ver, 1999).

6. Derrick Darby, "Democracy Born of Struggle," *Perspectives on Politics* 16 (2018): 449–54.

7. Michael G. Hanchard, *The Spectre of Race: How Discrimination Haunts Western Democracy* (Princeton, NJ: Princeton University Press, 2018).

8. Du Bois does not use the language of "perfect" and "imperfect" de-mocracy. This is my usage. On my reading, for Du Bois, a perfect democ-racy is defined, in part, by a certain end, namely, directing the actions

of many persons toward the greatest good of all. One worry is that this seems to imply that rule of a few, which is by some definitions aristocratic or oligarchic, could be an instance of democratic rule if it aimed at the common good. I do not think that this is a serious difficulty. In his autobiography, Du Bois reports on the kind of democracy that existed in his hometown of Great Barrington. It was democracy among the few whites—all men—who ran the town for what they took to be the common good. The influx of foreigners including the Irish Catholics disrupted this pattern. Du Bois might say that what is "democratic" in an imperfect democracy is both that some (though not all) people have a voice in political rule and that in ruling they aim to direct the actions of many persons to the greatest good. So a democracy becomes more perfect as more people, e.g., the Irish Catholics in Great Barrington, have a voice and as the ruling of many moves closer to the ideal of the greatest good. As I make clear in the text, Du Bois also believed that these two elements were related in that the more people who were given a voice, including women and blacks, the more likely the ruling of men would result in the greatest good of all.

9. For notable exceptions, see Manning Marable, *W. E. B. Du Bois: Black Radical Democrat* (Boulder, CO: Paradigm, 1986), Adolph L. Reed Jr., *W. E. B. Du Bois and American Political Thought* (New York: Oxford University Press, 1997), Cornel West, *Democracy Matters* (New York: Penguin Press, 2004), and Robert Gooding-Williams, *In the Shadow of Du Bois: Afro-Modern Political Thought in America* (Cambridge, MA: Harvard University Press, 2010).

10. Joseph Dana Miller, "The Difficulties of Democracy," *International Journal of Ethics* 25 (1914): 213–25, 214.

11. W. E. B. Du Bois, "Democracy in America, ca 1928," 9. W. E. B. Du Bois Papers. Special Collections and University Archives, University of Massachusetts Amherst Libraries, http://credo.library.umass.edu.

12. Jason Brennan, *Against Democracy* (Princeton, NJ: Princeton University Press, 2016).

13. Daniel A. Bell, *The China Model: Political Meritocracy and the Limits of Democracy* (Princeton, NJ: Princeton University Press, 2015), 30.

14. There are different versions of epistocracy in the contemporary literature. For present purposes I do not need to distinguish and track them. My reconstruction of Du Bois relies upon his general rebuttal of the idea that some citizens can be excluded from democratic rule on grounds that they are too ignorant to rule. His rejection of this view is complex, as I hope to show.

15. What explains my preference is that Du Bois himself concedes that despite the negative effect race has had on the American soul, when compared to older European forms of political rule, the nation managed to realize key elements of a democratic society, though it was limited by color

caste. See W. E. B. Du Bois, "Black America," in *Writings by W. E. B. Du Bois in Non-Periodical Literature Edited by Others*, ed. Herbert Aptheker (Millwood, NY: Kraus-Thomson, 1982), 170.

16. Admittedly, my reading of him as a champion of broadly inclusive democratic rule is somewhat surprising given Du Bois's elitist leanings associated with his doctrine of the Talented Tenth, his fascination with antidemocratic rulers (e.g., Chairman Mao) and nations (e.g., Russia), and his patriarchal practical dealings with black women leaders and intellectuals. For a useful summary of these criticisms, see Marable, *W. E. B. Du Bois: Black Radical Democrat*, Introduction. I will not pursue these tensions between Du Bois's anti-democratic affinities and his pro-democracy argument in *Darkwater*. The seriousness with which he defends democracy against an exclusive type of epistocracy is, in my view, all the more interesting given these tensions. I believe that Du Bois was indeed a "radical democrat," where this amounts to having a deep, thorough, and consistent commitment to pursuing the broadest measure of justice for all by removing obstacles to voting and political empowerment faced by the masses. So I agree with Bernard Boxill, who held that Du Bois was an "uncompromising democrat" by the time he wrote *Darkwater*. See Bernard R. Boxill, "Du Bois on Cultural Pluralism," in *W. E. B. Du Bois on Race and Culture: Philosophy, Politics, and Poetics*, ed. Bernard W. Bell, Emily Grosholz, and James B. Stewart (New York: Routledge, 1996), 85n74. And I disagree with Robert Gooding-Williams, who believes that Du Bois's vanguardist strains complicate this interpretation. See his book, *In the Shadow of Du Bois: Afro-Modern Political Thought*, 273n114, where Gooding-Williams writes: "Notwithstanding his democratic commitment, Du Bois persistently worried that the masses lacked the wherewithal (e.g., the intelligence, the knowledge, and the experience) for competent democratic citizenship." My interpretation of *Darkwater*, and supporting evidence from other works, concedes that this was a real worry for Du Bois. However, my argument is that he uses the problem of ignorance to double down on the importance of democratic rule on the broadest possible terms.

17. Although Du Bois placed great emphasis on voting, one should not think that participating in electoral politics through voting is the only way to have a voice that counts in politics. Indeed, looking at the political practices of black youth reveals the rich variety of ways that citizens can make their voices heard politically. For an insightful study, which examines politics beyond the voting booth, see Cathy J. Cohen, *Democracy Remixed: Black Youth and the Future of American Politics* (New York: Oxford University Press, 2010).

18. W. E. B. Du Bois, "Negro Ideals Described," in *Writings by W. E. B. Du Bois in Periodicals Edited by Others*, vol. 1: 1891–1909, ed. Herbert Aptheker (Millwood, NY: Kraus-Thomson, 1982), 361.

19. W. E. B. Du Bois, "Democracy, November 6, 1950," 1 and 6. W. E. B. Du Bois Papers. Special Collections and University Archives, University of Massachusetts Amherst Libraries, http://credo.library.umass.edu/.

20. Nancy MacLean, *Democracy in Chains: The Deep History of the Radical Right's Stealth Plan for America* (New York: Viking, 2017).

21. Du Bois, *Darkwater*, 84.

22. Ibid.

23. Ibid., 82.

24. Ibid., 84.

25. W. E. B. Du Bois, Letter to W. P. Robinson dated January 26, 1939, in *The Correspondence of W. E. B. Du Bois*, vol. II: 1934–1944, ed. Herbert (Amherst: University of Massachusetts Press, 1976), 184.

26. Du Bois, *Darkwater*, 78.

27. Ibid., 81.

28. Du Bois does not spend time theorizing about the distinction between instrumental and noninstrumental goods. My reading of what he has in mind by the latter category of goods, however, is that he believes that popular sovereignty allows us to partake of certain things that are arguably valuable for their own sake including individual self-development, self-knowledge, culture and civilization. He might say that these are valuable regardless of whether popular sovereignty leads to justice.

29. W. E. B. Du Bois, "The Possibility of Democracy in America," in *Writings in Periodicals Edited by W. E. B. Du Bois, Selections from The Crisis*, vol. 2: 1926–1934, ed. Herbert Aptheker (Amherst: University of Massachusetts Press, 1976), 521.

30. Although it would be interesting to distinguish different conceptions of ignorance in Du Bois's work, I will not pursue this task in the text. Nothing in my reconstruction of his defense of democracy turns on doing so. Some of what he says pertains to ignorance of what is taught in schools. Some of it has to do with ignorance of the workings of industry, social problems, policy matters, race privilege and, in the case of the white and black masses, ignorance of what is needed to build a larger coalition to confront plutocrats and political elites who benefit from exclusionary democracy.

31. W. E. B. Du Bois, "The Study of the Negro Problems," in *Writings by W. E. B. Du Bois in Periodicals Edited by Others*, vol. 1: 1891–1909, ed. Herbert Aptheker (Millwood, NY: Kraus-Thomson, 1982), 44. Historian John Rury and I argue that schooling in America was designed to produce black ignorance, stamping blacks with a stigmatizing badge of inferiority, which was then used to reinforce their separate and inferior schooling during and long after slavery's demise. See Derrick Darby and John L. Rury, *The Color of Mind: Why the Origins of the Achievement Gap Matter for Justice* (Chicago: University of Chicago Press, 2018).

32. In keeping with Du Bois's usage, I will use "Negroes" and "blacks," and "Negro" and "black" interchangeably throughout this chapter, though the former uses are no longer common in public discourse.

33. W. E. B. Du Bois, "The Present Outlook for the Dark Races of Mankind," in *Writings by W. E. B. Du Bois in Periodicals Edited by Others*, vol. 1: 1891–1909, ed. Herbert Aptheker (Millwood, NY: Kraus-Thomson, 1982), 79.

34. Du Bois, *Darkwater*, 79.

35. As Du Bois writes: "The laws of the Southern states for generations forbade us to learn and even today when it is assumed that the Negro is receiving too much education for his good, not one Negro child in three is attending regularly the public schools or having any reasonable chance to learn how to read and write. Not only are the Negro schools bad but save in some few cities they are worse today than they were ten years ago and there is no sign of their getting better." Du Bois, "Negro Ideals Described," 360.

36. W. E. B. Du Bois, "The Training of Negroes for Social Power," *Writings by W. E. B. Du Bois in Periodicals Edited by Others*, vol. 1: 1891–1909, ed. Herbert Aptheker (Millwood, NY: Kraus-Thomson, 1982), 180.

37. Du Bois, *Darkwater*, 78.

38. Du Bois, "No Second-Class Citizens," 47.

39. Du Bois, *Darkwater*, 81.

40. All the quotes in this paragraph are located here: W. E. B. Du Bois, "The Economic Aspects of Race Prejudice," in *Writings by W. E. B. Du Bois in Periodicals Edited by Others*, vol. 2: 1910–1934, ed. Herbert Aptheker (Millwood, NY: Kraus-Thomson, 1982), 1.

41. Du Bois, "The South and a Third Party," in *Writings by W. E. B. Du Bois in Periodicals Edited by Others*, vol. 2: 1910–1934, ed. Herbert Aptheker (Millwood, NY: Kraus-Thomson, 1982), 172.

42. Du Bois identifies tribalism, selfishness, and ignorance as individual factors that could undermine efforts at moral suasion. However, one could argue that they are related in ways that reinforce this effect. For example, tribalism might explain why white workers do not process information about how white elites exploit them, resulting in a certain kind of motivated ignorance that makes them impervious to arguments that joining with black workers is the right thing to do.

43. Recent evidence suggests that status threat to whites was a greater factor than economic hardship in explaining Trump's victory. See Diana C. Mutz, "Status Threat, Not Economic Hardship, Explains the 2016 Presidential Vote," *Proceedings of the National Academy of Sciences* 115 (2018): E4330–E4339. For criticism of this view, see Stephen L. Morgan, "Fake News: Status Threat Does Not Explain the 2016 Presidential Vote," https://osf.io.

44. W. E. B. Du Bois, "The Economic Aspects of Race Prejudice," in *Writings by W. E. B. Du Bois in Periodicals Edited by Others*, vol. 2: 1910–1934, ed. Herbert Aptheker (Millwood, NY: Kraus-Thomson, 1982), 2.

45. For more on this, see Darby, "Democracy Born of Struggle."

46. Labor movements, especially those that emerge from the grass-roots, constitute an insurgency seeking to realize a broader measure of justice. They play a vital role in working out the meaning of democracy in ways that counter the exclusive visions of it that have given us slavery, Jim Crow, and plutocracy. Part of this meaning-making involves counter-ing myths that support unjust social arrangements, thereby challenging these arrangements. It also involves giving us commonsense perspectives on the nature of more just arrangements and the constellation of rights and duties that they entail. Furthermore, it involves identifying the prob-lems, e.g., poor wages, working conditions, and worker safety and health protections, that contravene America's claim of being a just and demo-cratic nation. So, as Du Bois fully understood, labor movements and other social movements seeking broader justice help us better understand not only why democracies fail but how they flourish. For a recent analysis of how social movements like the one for a living wage have contributed to transformative meaning-making, see Deva R. Woodly, *The Politics of Com-mon Sense: How Social Movements Use Public Discourse to Change Politics and Win Acceptance* (New York: Oxford University Press, 2015).

47. This point puts Du Bois into conversation with contemporary polit-ical theorists thinking about epistemic democracy and its challenges. See, for example, Melissa Schwartzberg, "Epistemic Democracy and Its Chal-lenges," *Annual Review of Political Science* 18 (2015): 187–203. Du Bois's point was *not* that the masses will make the correct decisions; in fact, he believed they often would not. Nevertheless, he thought that they were an indispensable source of wisdom for securing the broadest measure of justice for all. And he relies on history as his primary evidence to support this claim. On my reading of Du Bois, this epistemic claim plays a pivotal role in his defense of democracy.

48. W. E. B. Du Bois, "Reconstruction and Its Benefits," in *Writings by W. E. B. Du Bois in Periodicals Edited by Others*, vol. 2: 1910–1934, ed. Her-bert Aptheker (Millwood, NY: Kraus-Thomson, 1982), 16.

49. Du Bois, "Socialism and the Negro Problem," in *Writings by W. E. B. Du Bois in Periodicals Edited by Others*, vol. 2: 1910–1934, ed. Herbert Ap-theker (Millwood, NY: Kraus-Thomson, 1982), 86.

50. W. E. B. Du Bois, "Diuturni Silenti," in *The Education of Black People, Ten Critiques, 1906–1960*, ed. Herbert Aptheker (New York: Monthly Re-view, 1973), 74.

51. Du Bois, *Darkwater*, 83.

52. Ibid., 84.

53. Ibid., 85. He also very briefly touches on excluding the wisdom of darker nations from international federations of democratic countries, which is of course a prominent theme in Du Bois's post–World War II book *Color and Democracy: Colonies and Peace* (New York: Harcourt, Brace and Co., 1945).

54. Du Bois, *Darkwater*, 84.

55. Many years after Du Bois made this point, John Dewey expressed a similar sentiment in a 1937 speech, arguing that no person was wise enough to rule others without their consent. Dewey argued that this form of coercion fails to account for important knowledge possessed by the masses. He writes: "The individuals of the submerged mass may not be very wise. But there is one thing they are wiser about than anybody else can be, and that is where the shoe pinches, the troubles they suffer from." See John Dewey, "Democracy and Educational Administration," in *The Later Works of John Dewey*, vol. II: 1935–1937, ed. Jo Ann Boydston (Carbondale: Southern Illinois University Press, 1987), 219. His use of this metaphor appears in an earlier writing, though still after Du Bois's observation. See John Dewey, *The Public and Its Problems* (Athens, OH: Swallow Press, 2016), 224, where he writes: "The man who wears the shoe knows best that it pinches and where it pinches, even if the expert shoemaker is the best judge of how the trouble is to be remedied."

56. W. E. B. Du Bois, "I Won't Vote," in *Writings by W. E. B. Du Bois in Periodicals Edited by Others*, vol. 4: 1945–1961, ed. Herbert Aptheker (Millwood, NY: Kraus-Thomson, 1982), 271.

57. W. E. B. Du Bois, "Third Party," in *Writings in Periodicals Edited by W. E. B. Du Bois, Selections from The Crisis*, vol. 2: 1926–1934, ed. Herbert Aptheker (Amherst: University of Massachusetts Press, 1976).

58. John Wagner, "'No person in America should be too poor to live': Ocasio-Cortez explains democratic socialism to Colbert," *Washington Post*, June 29, 2018.

59. Others have appreciated this point. For instance, see Sheri Berman, "Against the Technocrats," *Dissent*, Winter 2018, who sees a connection between voter dissatisfaction with elite rule and their willingness to elect politicians determined to bring down elites and democratic institutions. She writes: "That many Americans, in short, view democratic institutions and elites as fundamentally corrupt and unaccountable to them and are therefore willing to vote for politicians and parties who promise to blow them all up is not, unfortunately, all that hard to understand."

60. Du Bois, "Negro Ideals Described," 361.

61. Reinhold Niebuhr, *The Children of Light and the Children of Darkness: A Vindication of Democracy and a Critique of Its Traditional Defenders* (Chicago: University of Chicago Press, 1944).

62. Du Bois, "The Possibility of Democracy in America," 521.

63. Ibid.

64. Du Bois, "The Training of Negroes for Social Power," 182.

65. There is, of course, the philosophical question of how to think about the nature of this duty, particularly when we have white voters in mind. But remember that Du Bois was addressing an audience at the beginning of the 1900s. During that time one could more plausibly ground this duty to support black voting rights in the idea that whites were in some sense causally responsible for the legacy of black slavery and its aftermath and therefore had a backward-looking responsibility to act as saving democracy requires. And one could also say, somewhat weaker, that even if whites were not causally responsible for black disadvantage, they benefited from it and also suffered from it. Today, these arguments are still being made, but they are a much tougher sell. For more on why this is so, and how to proceed in light of this, see Derrick Darby and Nyla R. Branscombe, "Beyond the Sins of the Fathers: Responsibility for Inequality," *Midwest Studies in Philosophy* 38 (2014): 121–37.

66. Du Bois, "The Training of Negroes for Social Power," 183.

67. W. E. B. Du Bois, "Votes for Women," in *Writings in Periodicals Edited by W. E. B. Du Bois, Selections from the Crisis*, vol. 1: 1911–1925, ed. Herbert Aptheker (Millwood, NY: Kraus-Thomson, 1983), 79–80.

68. Ibid., 80.

69. For example, see Du Bois, *Darkwater*, 85, where he writes: "Every white Southerner, who wants peons beneath him, who believes in hereditary menials and a privileged aristocracy, or who hates certain races because of their characteristics, would resent this."

70. Du Bois, "Democracy Fails in America, June 1954," 1.

71. In her contribution to this volume, Turkuler Isiksel, raises concerns about whether Du Bois's support for administrative state agencies, which are run by technocratic experts with specialized knowledge, is in tension with his rejection of epistocracy.

72. All the quotes in this paragraph are located here: W. E. B. Du Bois, "The Negro Citizen," in *Writings by W. E. B. Du Bois in Non-Periodical Literature Edited by Others*, ed. Herbert Aptheker (Millwood, NY: Kraus-Thomson, 1982), 159.

73. W. E. B. Du Bois, "How Should Negroes Vote? Be Intelligently Selfish at Polls," in *Writings by W. E. B. Du Bois in Periodicals Edited by Others*, vol. 3: 1935–1944, ed. Herbert Aptheker (Millwood, NY: Kraus-Thomson, 1982), 212.

74. Ibid., 212–13.

75. My view is that the solution to racial inequality in contemporary America, given the profound impact of race and the myth that America is

"postracial," lies in remedies that are race-sensitive but not race-specific. I take Du Bois's insights about how democracy survives to support the kind of *principled pragmatic realism* that I defend elsewhere. See Derrick Darby and Richard E. Levy, "Postracial Remedies," *University of Michigan Journal of Law Reform* 50 (2016): 387–488. Furthermore, to the extent that there is a substantive difference between "democratic socialism" and "social democracy," the latter is more determined to operate *within* democracy to make it more inclusive by finding workable just solutions to social problems that cut across race, gender, class, and other intersecting identities. The latter is a more apt characterization of my perspective and, I believe, Du Bois's as well. For a perspective on this way of drawing the distinction, see Sheri Berman, "Democratic Socialists Are Conquering the Left. But Do They Believe in Democracy?" *Washington Post*, August 10, 2018.

76. See Charles W. Mills, *The Racial Contract* (Ithaca, NY: Cornell University Press, 1997). Other recent examples of nonideal theory include Tommie Shelby, *Dark Ghettos: Injustice, Dissent, and Reform* (Cambridge, MA: Belknap Press, 2016) as well as Darby and Rury, *The Color of Mind*.

77. Mills's most recent defense of nonideal theory as it applies to liberalism, along with a statement of his nonideal principles of rectificatory justice, appears in his *Black Rights/White Wrongs: The Critique of Racial Liberalism* (New York: Oxford University Press, 2017). For criticism from a fellow proponent of nonideal theory, see Derrick Darby, "Charles Mills's Liberal Redemption Song," *Ethics* 129 (2019): 370–97.

9

PRETEXTUAL POLITICS AND DEMOCRATIC INCLUSION

COMMENT ON DARBY

TURKULER ISIKSEL

Trump's triumph in the 2016 election prompted a wave of democratic disillusionment. Many chalked up his victory to his appeal to "white working-class voters," imagined as a demographic group whose members lack a college degree and one that trails the national average in terms of household income. Of course, the hypothesis that poverty and/or voter ignorance fueled Trump's rise is contested. In fact, there is compelling empirical evidence that middle-class white voters put Trump over the edge in the 2016 presidential election, and that Trump's share of the college-educated vote was comparable to any other Republican candidate.[1] It is equally controversial to attribute Trump's victory to socioeconomic anxiety on the part of the working class (rather than fears about cultural and racial predominance).[2] After all, despite being the least advantaged demographic group in America in socioeconomic terms, a resounding 94 percent of black women voted against him.[3]

Nevertheless, there certainly is a *perception* (primarily on the part of progressives) that Trump rose to power on the votes of white working-class voters who tend to be less affluent and less educated than his detractors. Whether or not that perception has a basis in reality, it deserves to be taken seriously, if only because it suggests that one segment of society (an *elite* segment) lacks what Melissa Schwartzberg calls "epistemic respect" for some of its

247

fellow citizens.[4] That is to say, elites have come to doubt the ability of their fellow citizens to judge political questions wisely, and the erosion of epistemic respect among citizens frays the fabric of democracy.

The concern with democratic failure due to voter ignorance motivates Derrick Darby's insightful and timely reconstruction of the democratic theory of W. E. B. Du Bois. According to Darby, "by rebutting [voter ignorance] and other justifications for less inclusive political rule," Du Bois offers an indirect defense of democracy, alongside other instrumental and non-instrumental reasons to prefer democracy.[5] Darby writes: "Instead of being tempted by epistocracy, or more specifically by an exclusive variety of it that limits rule to so-called wise men or wise white people, Du Bois urges that we address the circumstances that contribute to the discontent of the masses, and that we empower them through our ballots with the rights they need to be equal participants in political rule."

In and of itself, this is a compelling argument. However, framing it with reference to contemporary fears about the anti-democratic preferences of the white working class provokes some misunderstanding. For one thing, it creates the unfortunate impression that Darby's intervention is intended to vindicate the dignity and political wisdom of Trump voters (which is not, I think, its primary purpose). Second, there is a strong disanalogy between Du Bois's concerns and the situation of the white working class. The latter is not in any real danger of being deprived of the vote in the way that the protagonists of Du Bois's *Darkwater* essay (African Americans living under the thumb of Jim Crow and women living under domestic subjugation) were.

Third, it seems to me that, taken as an empirical case, the contemporary demographic group Darby flags, namely working-class whites, gives us reasons to *doubt* Du Bois's faith in the transformative potential of *merely having the vote* on two key outcomes (namely, education and affluence). Du Bois stakes a clear hypothesis on this front: "political control is the *cause* of popular education."[6] Exclusion perpetuates ignorance; democratic inclusion educates. But if the white working class in the United States has enjoyed one privilege (and enjoyed it longer than most other groups), it is surely the franchise. Having the vote, however, seems not to have alleviated the economic precariousness its members feel (nor strengthened their commitment to democratic institutions). *If* Trump's election was a cry for help motivated by economic insecurity, it is also an indication that democracy has failed to deliver on its promises of economic security and social mobility *even for the group that has long enjoyed racial dominance.*[7]

How Problematic Is Voter Ignorance?

Before we evaluate the purported remedy of tutelary rule by a narrow, enlightened segment of epistocrats, it is useful to ask whether and why so-called voter ignorance *matters*. Du Bois expresses a range of different concerns that enfranchising uneducated citizens might raise. First and foremost, the issue of voter ignorance functions in early twentieth-century American public debate as (what Darby calls) a "pretextual argument" a thin veil for racism that Du Bois, connoisseur of veils, tears right down. To expose this pretext, Du Bois points to the fact that while a good proportion of blacks clamoring for the franchise may have had no educational opportunities, many working-class whites (including newly arrived European immigrants) gained the franchise despite being no more educated than their African American counterparts.

I find the concept of *pretextual arguments* (or what I will more broadly call *pretextual politics*) that Darby derives from Du Bois's treatment of voter ignorance highly compelling and propose that we take it seriously as an indicator (if not a *cause*) of democratic failure today. Before I get there, however, I would like to explore Darby's proposition that beyond exposing the cynicism and underlying racism of the voter ignorance argument, Du Bois is also minded to dismantle it as a sincere, democratically motivated objection to extending the franchise.

A citizen's lack of a formal education, Du Bois insists, is no reason at all to exclude her from the political process. According to Du Bois, people have authoritative knowledge of their own life circumstances. An illiterate person or a manual laborer is no less competent to judge of his or her own needs, interests, and life plans than a college professor. In *Darkwater*, Du Bois writes: "in the last analysis only the man himself, however humble, knows his own condition."[8] Darby points out that although we tend to associate this insight with John Dewey, who famously used the metaphor of the shoe that pinches, Du Bois beat him to this point by a few decades. The oppressed masses are far more eloquent about the source of their sufferings than even well-intentioned elites, if only someone deigns to ask them, as Du Bois did.

While Du Bois clearly takes the issue of voter ignorance seriously, it is hard to tell how much that issue *worries* him. Perhaps it is just a pragmatic concession: Perhaps he only assumes *arguendo* that democracy presumes an educated citizenry, while making a strategic argument in favor of putting enfranchisement first (recall that in his view, "political control is the *cause* of popular education"). Alternatively (and this seems to find clear support in his work), Du Bois's concern about voter ignorance stems from his belief that education, as the key to a fulfilling life, is a fundamental right. To deny people the franchise on the basis of educational disadvantage is to shirk the democratic responsibility to empower citizens. But this is not an instrumental worry about the effects of voter ignorance on democratic judgment; it is a fundamental claim of justice. (I will come back to the role of deontological arguments in Du Bois's advocacy.)

A third possibility is that Du Bois cares about voter ignorance because he sees it as a prerequisite for avoiding the pathologies of collective self-rule. Darby is keen to unpack this reading, presumably because it has particular resonance in the context of Trump's rise. The classic fear is that voter ignorance may make democracy vulnerable to the "autophagy problem":[9] democracy's tendency to consume itself, most notably through voters inviting blustery populists and oily autocrats to power. Citizens may react to democracy's failure to correct injustice by resorting to counterproductive means of self-protection. I suggest that this is how we should read Du Bois's jarring claim that Jim Crow "lynches the bodies of black men, but the souls of white":[10] In societies where injustice and corruption (in the classical republican sense) have become endemic, people's perception of their own interests may become distorted and pathological. For instance, legitimate protests about fairness may find expression as racism, xenophobia, or tribalism. Democratic failure is a response to democracy's failure to meet people's needs, most importantly their need to live dignified lives.

But if we interpret Du Bois as sincere in the view that voter ignorance poses a risk to democracy, this creates a tension with his commitment that lack of education is no barrier to wisdom. Du Bois seems to be both troubled by voter ignorance *and* confident that the people are wise enough. How should we square this circle? The question is not only important for understanding the priorities of Du Bois's democratic theory; it also confronts us in real time. How do we retain the anti-vanguardist intuition built into democracy while remaining clear-eyed about the lure of populists peddling hate, fear, and prejudice (and obstructing possibilities for true emancipation)?[11] Du Bois emphasized that the latter are mere strategies for manipulating the masses and preventing real class-based alliances from forming, but this does not make them any less effective or any less dangerous.[12]

THE TRAP OF PRETEXTUAL POLITICS

Darby emphasizes that although Du Bois took the voter ignorance objection seriously and addressed it sincerely, he was also well aware that purported concerns about voter ignorance functioned as an acceptable pretext for unacceptable political aims.[13] The fact that concerns about voter ignorance flared up at the prospect of the enfranchisement of African Americans, but were rarely applied to the waves of (if anything) equally under-educated white immigrants, revealed that the real agenda was to reserve political power for whites at the expense of black citizens. Today, we are all too familiar with the kind of pretextual politics that voter ignorance represented in Du Bois's day. Since the 2016 election, wholly unsubstantiated accusations of massive voter fraud have functioned in much the same way. Elected officials from the Republican party have invoked voter fraud to justify massive voter suppression campaigns directed against citizens of color, cloaking racial disenfranchisement in legitimate-sounding concerns about the integrity of the democratic process. To take another example, when the US Commerce Department decided to include a question about US citizenship in the 2020 census (a break with recent precedent), it claimed that doing so would improve the enforcement of minority voting rights as per the Voting Rights Act. As observers quickly noted, however, the citizenship question would also serve a handy partisan function at direct odds with principles of democratic representation. Most notably, it was expected to under-count communities with a high proportion of immigrant residents, which would in turn diminish the congressional seats and federal funding allocated to districts that tend to vote for Democratic candidates.[14] The federal court that reviewed the Commerce Department's decision concluded that its purported democratic rationale was "pretextual," that is to say, a bad faith misrepresentation of underlying motives.[15] This finding was affirmed by the US Supreme Court.[16]

As these examples suggest, the genius of pretextual arguments is to sanction practices that are blatantly at odds with liberal democratic principles while claiming the mantle of liberal democracy. They also shield their proponents from having to acknowledge these contradictions, much less to repudiate liberal democratic principles themselves. Du Bois's ambivalence toward the purported problem of voter ignorance illustrates how pretextual arguments in politics ensnare democrats in a dilemma. On the one hand, taking such legitimate-sounding excuses for disenfranchisement as voter ignorance or voter fraud at face value forces democrats to play along with the charade staged by their opponents and to pretend that their underlying political agenda does not exist. On the other hand, trying to unmask these arguments to expose the underlying power grab subjects democrats to charges of hysteria and overreaction, and allows the champions of anti-democratic practices to portray themselves as the champions of reasonable democratic principles. In short, pretextual arguments are difficult to counter, because they abuse the presumption of sincerity—however rebuttable—built into public discourse. In taking the voter ignorance objection seriously (even *arguendo*), Du Bois ends up shadow-boxing with a claim that has little persuasive hold on anyone engaged in the debate (racists and anti-racists alike), even though he knows (as do the racists) that the voter ignorance argument is merely a pretext for excluding people of color from power. The important takeaway, I submit, is less Du Bois's reflection on voter ignorance as a substantive issue, and more the persistent menace that pretextual arguments pose in democratic politics.

Debating Epistocracy's Rightful Place

Darby's thesis that "Du Bois resisted epistocracy" contradicts some received wisdom. Countering the easy identification of Du Bois with the "talented tenth" thesis, Darby maintains that Du Bois sought to widen and deepen democracy. But this should not lead us to overlook the role that Du Bois carves out for robust administrative (one might say tutelary) remedies to the failures of democracy. He devotes part of the essay "Of the Ruling of Men" to the problem of "majority tyranny": a classic refrain in democratic thought that traditionally refers to the poor majority expropriating the rich minority. In Du Bois's telling, the most immediate instance of majority tyranny in America is that of whites claiming black bodies and black labor as their property, and later, excluding African Americans from the franchise and from the enjoyment of most public goods. "[I]n this land" where "black folk . . . are but a tenth," Du Bois observes, a majoritarian system is bound to produce forms of oppression that even full democratic inclusion may be powerless to dispel.[17]

Du Bois responds to this particular type of democratic failure (namely, the problem of the tyrannical white majority) by calling for proportional representation and, more relevant for us, emphasizing administrative safeguards. In *The Souls of Black Folk*, he extols the hopeful mission of the Freedmen's Bureau, established by Congress in the aftermath of the Civil War to integrate formerly enslaved and oppressed people into society as full members. Here is a situation where a powerful epistocratic body was needed to empower people newly emancipated from centuries of bondage to lead future lives as free and independent citizens. In order to succeed at its immense task of social reengineering, Du Bois notes, the Freedmen's Bureau would have had to be a powerful government unto itself, with comprehensive, long-term authority and resources. He laments that this, alas, did not happen.[18] In Du Bois's telling, then, Reconstruction was (among other things) an *administrative* failure, one that allowed the white majority to recover its tyrannical position.

Nor are the lessons of the Freedmen's Bureau confined to that highly exceptional time. As Darby writes, Du Bois's democratic creed "requires securing for the masses a set of universal legal rights including to education, economic security, and protection against discrimination." If anything, the formidable institutional infrastructure required to reach these goals has grown more complex and contested. Take protection against discrimination. Discrimination on the basis of race (as well as ethnicity, gender, sexual orientation, and disability) continues to pervade all spheres of American society. Combatting it requires a complex web of oversight agencies (not to mention courts) to monitor domains such as housing, lending, education, elections, employment, public transportation, and all kinds of "public accommodations."

We might take an Elyan tack[19] and argue that this is not the kind of epistocracy that should worry democrats, because it merely ensures the preconditions of democratic freedom rather than narrowing its scope.[20] But there are other domains of public power that are more fraught in democratic terms. Ensuring economic security, for instance, requires an immense institutional infrastructure. The economic crisis precipitated by the collapse of Lehman Brothers revealed the extent to which our economic security as citizens is dependent on zealous and fleet-footed regulators vigilantly overseeing powerful private actors. If anything, it showed that their scope of authority needs to be more comprehensive and more intrusive. We depend on institutions like the SEC, the Federal Trade Commission, the Federal Reserve System, or the Consumer Financial Protection Bureau to (variously) keep powerful economic actors in check, contain financial risk, allow for long-term financial planning, and cushion global shocks. Furthermore, regulatory institutions need to be at least partially shut off from democratic control by a number of factors, including technical expertise, attenuation from partisan struggle, and long-term policy planning.[21]

This is a modern democratic dilemma to which Du Bois is well attuned. He acknowledges, for instance, that making the system of industrial production fairer is likely to require commandeering an even *greater* amount of power. Yet he worries that running a massive enterprise (or an entire economy) through popular vote is a risky proposition.[22] This leaves his two commitments—as a democrat and as a believer in economic fairness—in tension. The contemporary implications of this tension are clear. Democracies attempting to navigate the choppy waters of advanced capitalism are compelled to delegate a significant measure of power to agencies that cannot themselves be democratic. As Jane Mansbridge observes in her contribution to this volume, the puzzle of how to open up the vast apparatus of the regulatory state to citizen participation is one of the most pressing for today's democratic theorists.

Du Bois is also too seasoned a political observer to put all of his faith in administrative impartiality. Those who possess the requisite expertise and power to steer the workings of the modern economy are likely to have motives of their own. In "Of the Ruling of Men," Du Bois rejects the depoliticizing gambit of laissez-faire as so much self-serving pap. He argues that insulating the economy from popular control in the name of the omniscient self-regulating market has only allowed the industrialists to rig the system in their favor. In other words, Du Bois sees that there is always someone manning the levers, and the temptation to use them to one's own advantage, or in accordance with one's ideological commitments and political biases, may prove too great. As Aziz Huq argues in this volume, epistocratic authority can reinforce rather than alleviate existing patterns of domination.[23]

Perhaps it is a consolation that—with due respect to holdouts—the principle of one person, one vote is no longer seriously vulnerable to a sincere epistemic objection about voter ignorance. Of course, as I have already noted, America's long-standing tradition of excluding poor people and racial minorities from the electoral process is still with us. Numerous Republican-controlled state governments are busy purging the voter rolls and gerrymandering millions of voters of color into civic oblivion. But epistocratic wisdom is no longer the preferred pretext for such practices. The rub of the epistocratic agenda today is not so much to bar certain people's access to the ballot box (that is done on other facetious grounds), but to limit what the electorate can do *through* the ballot box. And this is a much trickier question to answer.

SEARCHING FOR THE FOUNDATIONS OF DU BOIS'S DEMOCRATIC THEORY

Darby treats Du Bois's views on epistocracy as a conduit toward reconstructing the foundations of the latter's democratic theory. As I noted earlier, Darby interprets Du Bois's rebuttal of

"justifications for less inclusive political rule," including the claim
that "the excluded are too ignorant to rule," as an indirect defense
of democracy. This interpretation differs sharply from the conventional view of Du Bois as a champion of epistocracy who ardently
defends full equality for the "talented tenth" but proves a rather
less enthusiastic champion of the remaining nine-tenths. Darby (I
think rightly) dismisses this as a caricature of views that Du Bois in
any case seems clearly to have superseded in his later writings. In
addition, Darby maps several instrumental and non-instrumental
routes by which Du Bois defends democracy, some of which, in
my view, prove more circuitous than others, and one or two are
culs-de-sac.

One such route resembles contemporary epistemic arguments
for democracy. Du Bois's assertion that "the mass of people form a
great reservoir of knowledge and information"[24] recalls Aristotle's
metaphor for popular rule as a feast that is more lavish for being
sourced from many kitchens, even though none of the contributors is an expert chef. This reading is bolstered by the pluralism
Du Bois espouses in *The Souls of Black Folk*, where he contends that
all cultures and peoples have essential contributions to make to
the enlightenment and progress of humankind. I have already
pointed to some tensions that I think are inherent to this reading of Du Bois. The fact that he takes the voter ignorance objection seriously militates against any epistemic interpretation of his
democratic theory.

This contrasts with a more demanding, quasi-Rousseauian democratic theory that Darby teases out of Du Bois. In Darby's reconstruction, "The reason why *all* must rule . . . is because democracy
is a way for society to secure *the broadest measure of justice* and this
can only be done if all souls have a hand in democratic rule." This
is also why Du Bois mistrusts tutelary or vanguardist arguments:
There is no single person or group benevolent enough, or *knowledgeable enough*, to bring about the greatest measure of justice for
all. I find this skeptical point compelling, and Darby establishes
that mistrust toward tutelage is a keystone of Du Bois's democratic
theory. But I want to express some doubt about Du Bois's assertion
that the end of political rule should be "the greatest good of all,"[25]
which strikes me as flirting with a metaphysical idea of the common good. Defending democracy as the mechanism that is most

likely to "achieve the universal good" or realize universal justice either outsources the definition of justice to some other process (the original position, divine inspiration, mathematical aggregation) or gets caught in a tautology (because justice *is* what the democratic procedure yields). Further, it cuts into Du Bois's critique of epistocracy insofar as it implies the existence of an epistemic standard that is distinct from and altogether independent of the outputs of procedural democracy. Finally, the expectation that it will "realiz[e] the universal good" seems to me to place democracy under an impossible burden.

Fortunately, Darby gives us an alternative, negative rendering of this argument that is more compelling. On this reading, Du Bois sees in democracy not the route to some collective *summum bonum*, but a safeguard against the *summum malum*. Democratic inclusion may be the best way to stave off mass injustice such as slavery, apartheid, economic exploitation, or imperialism. To have the vote is to have a measure of security against suffering grave wrong, since nobody wills subjugation for themselves. (Or, as Frederick Douglass memorably puts it, "There is not a man beneath the canopy of heaven, that does not know that slavery is wrong for him.")[26] Nonetheless, as his critique of majority tyranny indicates, Du Bois is too much of a realist to trust in the efficacy of democratic inclusion to prevent such catastrophic wrongs.

Last but not least, we find in Du Bois what Darby terms the "deontological view" of democracy. On this view, democratic inclusion is a sign of respect and equal standing, even if it fails to remedy grave injustices. Democratic inclusion is simply what members of a political community owe one another. Exclusion is a moral wrong. I believe it is this view (more than any other argument in favor of democratic inclusion, however clever) that ought to energize the struggle against democratic exclusion today. Let me sharpen this point. Felon disenfranchisement, mass incarceration, voter suppression tactics, and the denial of a path to citizenship for millions of migrants who have made this country their home are *not* objectionable *primarily* because:

- They detract from the epistemic quality of collective decision-making.
- They deny people the opportunity to better their condition.

- They may increase the likelihood of grave injustice (such as systematic state violence against black and brown people).

They are objectionable because they *are* forms of grave injustice, full stop. To condemn them because they make democratic practice suboptimal by some epistemic or consequentialist criterion is to miss the point. They are moral wrongs because they betray the principle of equal freedom. Furthermore, they are specifically *democratic* wrongs because they contradict the very principle (again, the principle of equal freedom) that makes the practice of democracy non-instrumentally valuable. If our reason for turning to Du Bois is the need for a democratic theory that picks out contemporary forms of democratic failure for what they are, *this* seems to me to be the most resonant aspect of his democratic theory today.

A MORE RADICAL CRITIQUE OF DEMOCRACY

Clearly, his theory of democracy is just one facet of Du Bois's prolific and wide-ranging political, philosophical, and artistic oeuvre. To conclude, I would like to suggest that treating Du Bois as a democratic theorist might occlude the global concerns that structure his political thought (particularly his mature works). Democracy presupposes a bounded political community; and the two forms of injustice (namely, racial domination and economic exploitation) that most trouble Du Bois are, in his view, inherently global problems. After all, "the color line" is "the problem of the twentieth century," not just of the American Republic. The capacity of a single, self-contained democratic community (even one as mighty as the United States) to resolve injustice is constrained by the fact that democracy's scope of concern is necessarily limited. By contrast, the categories of Du Bois's analysis (such as "the color line" or the "Dark world") are global. White supremacy is a global injustice that can only be overcome by subaltern solidarities across cultures and continents.[27] Even a maximally inclusive democracy fails to attain the morally appropriate degree of inclusion because it comes up against the bounds of territorial sovereignty. Du Bois the democratic theorist appears conservative by the lights of Du Bois the anti-imperialist, because the latter forces the former to admit that democracy cannot effectively resolve the very problems of exclusion (exploitation, racial hierarchy) that hobble its ability to make good on its own promises of equal freedom.

NOTES

1. Pew Research finds that Trump carried white voters with a college degree by 49% to Clinton's 45%. Analysis by Nicholas Carnes and Noam Lupu suggests that at the primary stage, two-thirds of all Trump supporters had household incomes of $50,000 more, putting them in the top half of the American income distribution. They furthermore argue that Trump attracted about as many college graduates as a percentage of the vote as any successful Republican candidate. Nicholas Carnes and Noam Lupu, "It's Time to Bust the Myth: Most Trump Voters Were Not Working Class," *Washington Post*, June 5, 2017. www.washingtonpost.com. Nate Silver has argued that "only 12 percent" of Trump supporters had incomes below $30,000, meaning that "about twice as many low-income voters have cast a ballot for Clinton than for Trump" in 2016. Nate Silver, "The Mythology of Trump's 'Working Class' Support," Fivethirtyeight blog, May 3, 2016. https://fivethirtyeight.com. He contends that the level of education better explains voters' preference in the 2016 presidential election, marshaling county-level data to show that many Trump voters have incomes above the national average although they do not have a college degree. Nate Silver, "Education Not Income Predicted Who Would Vote for Trump," Fivethirtyeight blog, November 22, 2016. https://fivethirtyeight.com. For a critique of these analyses, see Stephen L. Morgan and Jiwon Lee, "Trump Voters and the White Working Class," *Sociological Science* (2018) 5: 234–45. www.sociologicalscience.com.

2. Pippa Norris and Ronald Inglehart, *Cultural Backlash. Trump, Brexit, and Authoritarian Populism* (New York: Cambridge University Press, 2019).

3. Matthew Yglesias, "What Really Happened in 2016, in 7 Charts," September 18, 2017. www.vox.com.

4. Melissa Schwartzberg, "Relating as Equals in the Trump Era," working paper presented at the American Political Science Association 2017 Annual Meeting, on file with the author.

5. All references to Darby refer to the chapter in this volume.

6. W. E. B. Du Bois, *Darkwater: Voices from Within the Veil* (New York: Dover, 1999), 139, emphasis added.

7. As Darby points out, Du Bois sees white supremacy as an attempt by the "Captains of Industry" to conceal economic exploitation and ward off proletarian solidarities across the "color line" by "distract[ing]" working-class whites with "race hatred." Du Bois, *Darkwater*, 137. In *Black Reconstruction in America* (1935, reprinted by Oxford University Press, 2007), Du Bois

construes whiteness as a form of compensation that may hold particular value for whites who have been ground down by capitalism.

8. "Of the Ruling of Men," 143, in W. E. B. Du Bois, *Darkwater: Voices from Within the Veil* (New York: Dover, 1999). Tellingly, the laissez-faire ideologues who insist that the market aggregates the situated wisdom of economic actors (and that this wisdom surpasses that of any centralized regulator, however benevolent) are unwilling to apply the same lesson of collective wisdom in the political realm.

9. Melissa Schwartzberg, *Democracy and Legal Change* (New York: Cambridge University Press, 2007).

10. As quoted in Darby's chapter in this volume.

11. On the anti-vanguardist thrust of democracy, see Ian Shapiro, "Elements of Democratic Justice," *Political Theory* 24, 4 (1996): 579–619.

12. As Darby notes, Du Bois viewed trade unions as capable of forging these solidarities (like a Tocqueville for the industrial era, Du Bois treated unions as schools of democracy). In Du Bois's era as now, unions are under attack from the very institutions of democracy that they are supposed to help citizens control: aided by the Supreme Court, Republican-controlled state governments have been waging a relentless campaign to eradicate them in the form of "right to work" laws (a masterful stroke of Orwellian rhetoric).

13. There are plenty of arguments in democratic theory that emphasize the rational ignorance and epistemic poverty of voters. Some critique democracy based on these assumptions. Although I find these arguments faulty on other grounds, I do not mean to portray their proponents as engaging in pretextual politics, as their claims do not necessarily track racial, gendered, or other unjust hierarchies.

14. Diana Elliott, Rob Santos, Steven Martin, and Charmaine Runes, *Assessing Miscounts in the 2020 Census* (Washington, DC: Urban Institute, 2019). Available at www.urban.org.

15. *New York v. Dept. of Commerce*, No. 1:18-cv-02921, 2019 (S.D.N.Y. Jan. 15, 2019) at 245.

16. *Department of Commerce v. New York*, No. 18–966, 588 U.S. ___ (2019).

17. W. E. B. Du Bois, *Darkwater*, 151.

18. On this point, see Lawrie Balfour, *Democracy's Reconstruction. Thinking Politically with W.E.B. Du Bois* (New York: Oxford University Press, 2011), ch. 2.

19. In his celebrated defense of the Warren Court, John Hart Ely argued that what others objected to as the activism and interventionism of the Court's desegregation decisions should be understood as an attempt "to ensure that the political process—which is where [particular substantive] values *are* properly identified, weighed, and accommodated—was

open to those of all viewpoints on something approaching an equal basis." In other words, these instances of judicial review were not impermissible intrusions into the process of popular self-rule but so many attempts to enhance its qualities as a democratic process. John Hart Ely, *Democracy and Distrust. A Theory of Judicial Review* (Cambridge, MA: Harvard University Press, 1980), 74.

20. In its current form, the US Supreme Court appears to disagree. One of the reasons the Supreme Court gave for striking down section 4(b) of the Voting Rights Act in its 2013 *Shelby County v. Holder* decision was that it encroached on democratic sovereignty at the state level.

21. On this point, see Giandomenico Majone, "From the Positive to the Regulatory State: Causes and Consequences of Changes in the Mode of Governance," *Journal of Public Policy* 17, no. 2 (1997): 139–67; Bruce Ackerman, "The New Separation of Powers," *Harvard Law Review* 113, no. 3 (2000): 633–729.

22. W. E. B. Du Bois, *Darkwater*, 158–59.

23. For a defense of the regulatory state as the prerequisite for effective citizen participation and a healthy modern democracy, see Blake Emerson, *The Public's Law. Origins and Architecture of Progressive Democracy* (New York: Oxford University Press, 2018).

24. As quoted in Darby's chapter in this volume.

25. W. E. B. Du Bois, *Darkwater*, 134.

26. Frederick Douglass, "What to the Slave Is the Fourth of July?" in *The Oxford Frederick Douglass Reader*, William L. Andrews (ed.) (New York: Oxford University Press, 1996).

27. Du Bois, "The Souls of White Folk," in David Levering Lewis, ed., *W. E. B. Du Bois: A Reader* (New York: H. Holt and Co., 1995). A new wave of literature explores the global scope of Du Bois's critique of race including Adom Getachew, *Worldmaking after Empire: The Rise and Fall of National Self-Determination* (Princeton, NJ: Princeton University Press, 2019); Ella Myers, "Beyond the Psychological Wage: Du Bois on White Dominion," *Political Theory* 47 no.1 (2019): 6–31; Inés Valdez, *Transnational Cosmopolitanism. Kant, Du Bois, and Justice as a Political Craft* (New York: Cambridge University Press, 2019).

10

DEMOCRATIC REMEDIES IF IGNORANCE THREATENS DEMOCRACY

MARK TUSHNET

Derrick Darby's interesting defense of democracy against epistocracy has, I believe, two elements. Identifying these two elements suggests that epistocracy properly understood is democratic—and so democracy need not be defended against epistocracy.

Initially we need a definition of epistocracy. I will take it to mean rule by the knowledgeable rather than rule by the wise. We can readily imagine people who are wise—who, for example, exhibit sound judgment whenever they act based upon the information they have available—but who lack knowledge with respect to some matters. We have no assurance that their decisions will be wise when they lack relevant information.

Sometimes we take knowledgeability as a proxy for general intelligence or wisdom. To some extent literacy tests as a qualification for voting and tests of knowledge about public affairs as a condition for naturalization rest on the thought that there is some association between the knowledge being tested and the ability to carry out one's civic duties. The examples, though, show why the "proxy" assumption is problematic: The history of literacy and civic-knowledge tests is not a happy one. As Darby emphasizes, sometimes the assertion that knowledge is a proxy for judgment and the like has been a pretext for discrimination on questionable grounds, and sometimes the proxies have been far too loosely connected to the asserted goal to be rationally justified.

As a general matter knowledgeability is not systematically related to general intelligence. We can readily imagine people who are knowledgeable about some matters, and who make sound judgments with respect to those matters, but who lack knowledge about others and do not make sound judgments about them.[1] Sometimes, indeed, the accumulation of knowledge about a specific matter will interfere with a person's ability to make good judgments about other matters: The image here is of a scientist who has learned everything there is to know about some arcane but important chemical process associated with how human memories are created and stored in the brain, but who has nothing valuable to say about the extent to which humans contribute to climate change.

These considerations already suggest that epistocracy as defined as rule by the knowledgeable might run into trouble. Perhaps, though, there is something to be said for democratic epistocracy. The key, I suggest, lies in developing appropriate criteria for determining what counts as knowledgeability—or for determining what we think citizens should be knowledgeable about.

First, epistocrats might be wrong in imputing politically relevant sorts of ignorance to ordinary people. In addition, ordinary people might at the moment be ignorant of some matters relevant to governance, but that ignorance should be ignored as true democrats pursue programs that would eliminate this kind of ignorance. After developing the distinction between these two points, I conclude with some comments on the political valence of Darby's discussion.

The first point is that ordinary people are in fact not ignorant about politically relevant matters in any interesting sense. Politically relevant knowledge covers a vast range of things, and in particular is not confined to knowledge about, for example, the effects of free trade on domestic economic well-being.[2] Because not everyone can know everything relevant to politics, knowledge of matters across the range is distributed differentially among people. In particular, the elites who epistocrats favor as governors know a great deal about some things but very little about others. As Darby puts it, epistocrats "overrat[e] the knowledge of the 'wise,' and understat[e] the knowledge of the masses."

Further, what counts as knowledge is itself sometimes contestable. For example, most economists seem to "know" that free trade benefits people around the world: It lowers prices to consumers and increases wages to workers. To say that ordinary voters are ignorant about that fact when they oppose free trade is, however, a mistake, because the economists' conclusions ignore voters' concerns about the distribution of domestic costs and, in particular, their concerns that the costs free trade imposes on workers in the domestic economy will not be offset, as they could be in principle, by compensatory payments ("trade adjustment assistance," in the policy jargon). More generally, many discussions of voter ignorance take as "knowledge" beliefs widely shared by elites. Almost by definition, doing so will favor epistocracy.

In contrast, Darby properly emphasizes, ordinary people are "sage souls" who know a great deal about *other* politically relevant things—and, importantly, more than the elites do about those things. He quotes W. E. B. Du Bois: "The theory of democracy . . . is that the mass of people form a great reservoir of knowledge and information which the state will ignore at its peril." Put another way, elites knowledgeable about some politically relevant matters are themselves ignorant of other such matters. An epistocracy in which everyone with politically relevant knowledge rules is democratic—and, even more, likely to produce better public policies than a system in which the rulers know only a skewed subset of politically relevant knowledge.

An interesting literature in industrial relations makes a similar point. In contrast to managers who bring explicit technical expertise to designing production processes, workers on the shop floor have "local" knowledge that, when coupled with the managers' technical expertise, can improve output. These workers, with shopfloor knowledge, are the equivalent of Darby's sage souls in politics, and for convenience I will use the term "shopfloor knowledge" to refer to politically relevant knowledge (differentially) held by ordinary people as against elites.

How can this political shopfloor knowledge be deployed in structuring a well-functioning political system? In principle of course it could be deployed at every level of political decision-making, and in particular could be deployed in elections and similar processes at the national level. But, as the term itself suggests, and as the associated idea of "local" knowledge also suggests, it might be easier to deploy shopfloor knowledge, at least initially, at more local levels.

In the first instance, that is, sage souls might have greater effect in shaping good public policy in decentralized settings. This is, I think, a Deweyan thought, compatible with the underpinnings of Darby's argument.[3] Modern Deweyans associated with Charles Sabel's work on democratic experimentalism describe ways of giving shopfloor knowledge effect on a large scale.[4] Here is a crude sketch of the argument: A polity finds itself confronted with a problem that elites have been unable to solve. Rather than allow the elites to continue to thrash about seeking a solution, the polity initially delegates the problem downward, to decentralized elements within it. It describes the problem and asks these localized decision-makers to come up with their own ideas about how to solve the problem. The political equivalent of shopfloor knowledge—again, available to and brought into play by ordinary people—shapes the localized proposals (not all of which will be the same). The larger polity observes the results of the local policies and—through a complex iterative process that involves identification and dissemination of "best practices" ideas and sometimes the redefinition of the problem to be solved—ultimately takes advantage of the accumulated results of the deployment of shopfloor knowledge to adopt national policies that, it is important to observe, neither were nor could have been developed by elites.

I want to stress that I have described a democratic epistocracy, because policy rests firmly on a basis of knowledge (the epistocratic component) while recognizing that ordinary people have access to knowledge less readily available to elites (the democratic component).

I turn now to the second element in Darby's argument. Here ordinary people are indeed ignorant—at the moment—of some things relevant to governance.[5] I think it worth identifying, if only to put to one side, a specific form of this ignorance—what the literature describes as rational ignorance. A person is rationally ignorant if she knows that there is relevant knowledge to be had but calculates that it is not worth the time and effort she would have to expend to acquire the knowledge. Consider for example the question of whether turning on the large hadron supercollider posed a substantial risk that it would generate a black hole that would consume the entire earth.[6] An ordinary person is rationally ignorant on that question: Learning about the topic would consume far too much time relative to the person's ability to affect the decision. Much better, from the rationally ignorant person's point of view, to leave the decision to experts.

In the present context we can describe rational ignorance as a revocable delegation of decision-making authority to people who already have the relevant knowledge. The delegation makes sense as long as the choices made by those with delegated authority generate policies that are "good enough" from the point of view of the rationally ignorant person. A policy fails the "good enough" requirement when that person calculates that the policy chosen by the delegated authority has costs to her greater than the cost of acquiring the knowledge. As I suggested, I believe that we can put the rationally ignorant person to one side. The reason is that the polity I have described is, once again, a democratic epistocracy. The rationally ignorant person is not excluded from the decision-making process because of her ignorance; she chooses to delegate her decision-making power and can revoke that delegation at will.

What of the person who is indeed ignorant, but not rationally so?[7] Darby suggests that a democrat would first ask, Why does this person lack politically relevant knowledge? That inquiry might identify sources or reasons for that ignorance. If those sources and reasons can be removed, the democrat says, they should be—certainly in preference to creating an epistocracy of those who happen to know things that are in principle available to the ignorant person whose access to them is blocked.

Given the possibility of rational ignorance, material impoverishment (defined appropriately) is a primary candidate as a source of this sort of ignorance. In Darby's words, "poverty, illness, and ignorance are among the *circumstances of democratic failure.*" The thought, put rather informally, is that people have to have sufficient resources available to them so that they can have a real choice between rational ignorance and informing themselves about some politically relevant matter. Even more informally, if a person is struggling to get enough to eat or to live in minimally decent housing, she is unlikely to be in a position to spend even an hour or two finding out about something politically relevant to the point where she can rationally choose between learning more and delegating the policy choice to someone else.

Eliminating knowledge-obstructing material impoverishment might not be enough, though, for reasons hinted at in the preceding paragraph. People can learn about some things for themselves, but—as the history of education shows—we often need help from people who already know things. Here too Dewey, in his role as the philosopher of progressive education, is instructive. Epistocratic education (if there is such a thing) would be indoctrination: The epistocrat knows that the world is round and simply tells those who have no settled views what the answer is. Democratic education takes the form of assisted discovery. Students do experiments that lead them to conclude for themselves that the world is round, for example.

Progressive education on political matters is sometimes parodied, with reference for example to the inmates running the asylum or to pathologies associated with experiments like Summerhill.[8] But, again, there are decent examples of democratic learning through self-governance, associated for example with techniques like participatory budgeting, a process that takes advantage of local knowledge but also expands the participants' horizons.[9] There are models of participatory civic education as well.[10]

My comments so far have taken the critique of epistocracy to support something like a social democratic political program. I conclude, though, with another possibility, suggested to me by some aspects of what is nothing more than a tone in Derrick Darby's chapter. That tone, I think, is best heard as critical of contemporary liberals who are insufficiently committed to social democracy.

Such a criticism might move in a different political direction, though, while preserving Darby's argument that ordinary people are sage souls with what I have called local or shopfloor knowledge. The direction is that taken by what I believe to be the most prominent recent discussion of voter ignorance, by Bryan Caplan. Caplan is a libertarian who wants to shrink the government's size.[11] That might take the form of quite substantial decentralization. And, the argument goes, decentralizing allows people to take advantage of what they already know: They will run their schools better, keep their roads in better repair, and the like, than will governments far removed from them.

The degree of decentralization necessary to make truly local knowledge the only basis for policy is quite substantial—utopian, in my view. And the institutions of the libertarian utopia—including the treaties among communities that Robert Nozick envisioned in his libertarian phase—are even more utopian. Social democracy, in contrast, seems to me closer at hand, and for that reason a more realistic political platform.

So, to conclude: Sage souls already know a great deal that makes democracy an appropriate form of governance despite epistocrats' claims. Where knowledge is lacking, programs of eliminating the features of social life that obstruct rational ignorance and programs of progressive education are available, again making epistocracy inferior to democracy. Du Bois, Dewey, and Darby are right.

Notes

1. My favorite examples involve winners of Nobel Prizes in the sciences when they move outside their areas of expertise. They do not always demonstrate bad judgment outside those areas, but their knowledgeability in itself does not carry with it assurances about the quality of their judgment regarding other matters.

2. I use this example because it plays an important role in a prominent recent work on political ignorance, Bryan Caplan, *The Myth of the Rational Voter: Why Democracies Choose Bad Policies*, rev. ed. (Princeton, NJ: Princeton University Press, 2011).

3 Darby refers to Deweyan thought in note 55 of his chapter.

4. For representative studies, see Charles Sabel, "Dewey, Democracy, and Democratic Experimentalism," *Contemporary Pragmatism* 9 (December 2012): 35–55; Michael C. Dorf and Charles F. Sabel, "A Constitution of Democratic Experimentalism," *Columbia Law Review* 98 (March 1998): 267–473.

5. This element is consistent with the first if we recognize that knowledge is differentially distributed, with elites knowing some things better than ordinary people, and ordinary people knowing some things better than elites. I note the implication here is that elites as well as ordinary people should be the targets of the kinds of policies I discuss in the text.

6. For a law-related discussion of this issue, see Eric E. Johnson, "The Black Hole Case: The Injunction Against the End of the World," *Tennessee Law Review* 76 (Summer 2009): 829–908.

7. In the context of what I have described as the second element in Darby's argument, the fact that the person has *other* political relevant knowledge—shopfloor knowledge—is irrelevant.

8. For its founders' description, see A. S. Neill, *Summerhill: A Radical Approach to Child Rearing* (New York: Hart, 1960). For assessments, see *Summerhill: For and Against*, A. S. Neill, ed. (New York: Hart, 1970).

9. See Archon Fung and Eric Olin Wright, "Deepening Democracy: Innovations in Empowered Democratic Governance," *Politics & Society* 29 (March 2001): 5–41.

10. See Meira Levinson, *No Citizen Left Behind* (Cambridge, MA: Harvard University Press, 2012).

11. Caplan, *Myth*. See also Ilya Somin, *Democracy and Political Ignorance: Why Smaller Government Is Smarter* (Stanford, CA: Stanford University Press, 2013).

INDEX